When Communication
Became a Discipline

When Communication Became a Discipline

William F. Eadie

LEXINGTON BOOKS

Lanham • Boulder • New York • London

Published by Lexington Books
An imprint of The Rowman & Littlefield Publishing Group, Inc.
4501 Forbes Boulevard, Suite 200, Lanham, Maryland 20706
www.rowman.com

86-90 Paul Street, London EC2A 4NE

British Library Cataloguing in Publication Information Available

Library of Congress Cataloging-in-Publication Data

Names: Eadie, William F., author.
Title: When communication became a discipline / William F. Eadie.
Description: Lanham : Lexington Books, [2022] I Includes bibliographical
    references and index.
Identifiers: LCCN 2021041057 (print) I LCCN 2021041058 (ebook) I
    ISBN 9781498572156 (cloth) I ISBN 9781498572163 (epub)
Subjects: LCSH: Communication—Study and teaching.
Classification: LCC P91.3 E13 2022 (print) I LCC P91.3 (ebook) I DDC 302.2—dc23
LC record available at https://lccn.loc.gov/2021041057
LC ebook record available at https://lccn.loc.gov/2021041058

Contents

Acknowledgments   vii

1   The Discipline of Communication   1

2   Histories of Communication Study   13

3   Becoming an Academic Discipline of Communication,
    1964–1982   27

4   Communication as the Formation and Change of Individual
    and Public Opinion   51

5   Communication as Language Use   69

6   Communication as Information Transmission   93

7   Communication as Developer of Relationships   107

8   Communication as Definer, Interpreter, and Critic of Culture   125

9   After 1982: Communication's Development as a Discipline   139

Bibliography   161

Index of Names   175

Index of Topics   179

About the Author   183

Acknowledgments

For a project that has been in process for years, both as an idea and as an idea realized, there are far too many people to thank and far too great a chance of leaving someone out. My interest in communication began in high school and was stirred by the speech and the debate coach there, who managed to dispel me of any interest to play on the tennis team, which he also coached. My professors, both at UCLA and Purdue, pushed me to learn and learn more, including tolerating my dogged determination not to be labeled as a specialist. The same was true of colleagues, both faculty and staff, at Ohio University, California State University, Northridge, and San Diego State University, where I held tenured faculty positions. (Truth be told, I was always conflicted about declaring myself to be a specialist, but I reckon that identifying as a student of the academic study of communication has become a good fit.)

My eight years at what is currently known as the National Communication Association crystalized my interest in what, at the time, I called "the sociology of the communication discipline" and provided access to "insider information" from which arose the idea that the political history of an academic discipline is as, if not more, important than its biographical and intellectual history. I am grateful to NCA colleagues for making that realization come to life. I am also grateful to the leadership and staffs of the International Communication Association and the Association for Education in Journalism and Mass Communication for their help in gathering materials for this project.

My ability to serve as temporary faculty at the University of Minnesota, Minneapolis, and the University of Maryland, College Park, exposed me to new perspectives and supportive colleagues who would continue as friends. Likewise, the friendships developed from my long involvement with the Western States Communication Association came from people who modeled effective teaching, research, and service.

My nonacademic friends have demonstrated remarkable patience with hearing me babble on about "the book." Unfortunately, they will probably have to continue to tolerate my enthusiasm for some time yet, so I thank them in advance for their indulgence.

Finally, thanks to readers for spending time with my "argument with historical evidence." You are to whom this book is dedicated.

Chapter 1

The Discipline of Communication

It comes down to this: communication is an academic discipline, because we made it so.

Defining terms can be tricky. We don't have an agreed-upon definition for "communication," though several individuals and groups have tried. The 1968 New Orleans Conference on Research and Instructional Development [in communication] offered "spoken symbolic interaction" as a definition (Kibler & Barker, 1968). The U.S. Department of Education's Classification of Instructional Programs (CIP) has defined its category that includes "Communication, Journalism and Related Programs" in higher education as "focusing on how messages in various media are produced, used, and interpreted within and across different contexts, channels, and cultures" (National Center for Educational Statistics, 2010). A working group of more than 100 administrators in communication programs crafted this definition in 1995: "The field of communication focuses on how people use messages to generate meanings within and across various contexts, cultures, channels, and media. The field promotes the effective and ethical practice of human communication" (Korn, Morreale, & Boileau, 2000). Peters (1999) identified two principal components of communication study: dissemination and dialogue. Craig (1999), while contending that communication is a conglomeration of research traditions that only showed promise to form what he termed a "practical discipline", nevertheless offered a definition of communication as "a constituent process that produces and reproduces shared meaning" (p. 125). O'Hair (2006) offered three components of communication as an ideal: "Voice," or freedom and ability to express oneself; "Community," or patterns of interaction that serve to define both small and large groups; and "Responsibility," or the obligation to use communication knowledge and ability to improve both the human condition and societal conditions.

All these definitions share common assumptions that communication is a process that is used for expression, interaction, dissemination, creation, and reproduction and is rooted in commitments to both self and others and doing so "authentically" (Peters, 1999). Communication may be judged to have varying degrees of "success" based on its ability to fulfill one or more of these functions.

Defining the idea of an "academic discipline" is almost as tricky as defining "communication." Traditionally, "discipline" was defined in scientific terms, through theory-testing via standard methods of hypotheses that had the potential to be falsified. But there were holes in such a definition, and, in particular, it did not fit well with academic study in nonscience fields. Anthropology, for example, has been traditionally divided into physical and cultural sub-disciplines. Each has its questions for study and its methods, and while the two areas were once considered linked only by a common interest in the development and maintenance of culture, the lines between the two have blurred over time. By traditional terms, sociology had difficulty establishing itself as a discipline, because its scholars were interested in a wide variety of topics, used different methods to investigate questions, and often those questions could not be falsified.

Thomas Kuhn (1962) set this sort of science on its ear in his book, *The Structure of Scientific Revolutions*. Kuhn, a historian of science, examined the patterns of the development of knowledge in science and concluded that the idea of using mathematics or formal logic to derive hypotheses from theory and build on that theory bit by bit in a smooth fashion did not fit the historical pattern. Rather, Kuhn argued, communities of scientists developed patterns of "normal science" from studying similar questions. Research results that proved to be contrary to the norm, rather than used to falsify hypotheses, would remain unpublished and would be discarded. Eventually, though, new ideas would burst forth, often the product of some "big thinker," causing upset and consternation. These new ideas would, however, account for some of the discarded research results, and eventually what Kuhn called a new "paradigm" would supplant the old and normal science would resume.

So, a discipline, according to Kuhn, is really characterized by the set of problems it decides to consider, as well as the intellectual history it develops around those problems. Clearly, decisions about which problems to study and when to move on are made by those identified with the discipline, though not always in concert with others, and perhaps not always deliberately.

Louis Menand (1997) contextualized the formation of disciplines in terms of the evolution of the contemporary idea of a research university. Between 1870 and 1915, Menand wrote, American institutions of higher education transformed themselves from liberal arts colleges that focused on a general curriculum designed to produce well-rounded individuals who were prepared to become leaders in society to a focus on a more particularized curriculum designed to allow students to specialize and prepare for careers, in addition to studying the liberal arts. Graduate programs proliferated as means of both credentialing professionals in a variety of highly skilled occupations and training individuals to conduct the sort of specialized research that would support the credentialing process. Just as universities turned out medical doctors and lawyers, they also replicated themselves through an apprenticeship model where graduate students worked hand-in-hand with professors as a means of becoming professors themselves. The Morrill Act of 1862 provided land grants for individual states to develop universities, and as states did so, there was an ever-increasing demand for professors as trained specialists.

Menand contended that this era of professionalization was demarcated by the formation of scholarly societies that corresponded to academic disciplines as they developed. Thus, the Modern Language Association was founded in 1883, the American Historical Association in 1884, the American Mathematical Society in 1888, and the American Physical Society in 1889. Coming later to the table were the American Political Science Association (1903) and the American Sociological Society (1905). The era of discipline formation came to a close in 1915, Menand wrote, with the formation of the American Association of University Professors (AAUP), an organization devoted to the development and maintenance of the concept of academic freedom.

The advent of AAUP was significant, in that it signaled that professors were to be treated as professionals. They were not "merely" teachers who minded classrooms, but they were scholars who generated specialized knowledge. As professionals, they governed themselves and set, through their scholarly societies and their peer-reviewed journals, standards for what "counts" as adequate contribution to specialized knowledge. They also internally set standards for the process by which one becomes credentialed (e.g., earns a Doctor of Philosophy degree) in a particular area of specialized knowledge, as well as the level of achievement that is expected to work as a professor in a university. As scholars, professors were trained to competency in methods appropriate to their discipline and maintained a substantial amount of disinterest in their results so that their findings could be trusted. The fact that Americans were enamored with "pure" science and the principle that "unfettered inquiry is the best path to truth" (p. 206) became the basis for academic departments in research universities to become synonymous with "academic disciplines."

According to Becher and Trowler (2001), the idea that disciplines create "a particular 'way of being', a personal and professional identity, set of values, attitudes, taken-for-granted knowledge and recurrent practices" (p. 48) went mostly unchallenged until the rise of postmodernism which provided the insight that newcomers to a discipline continually reconstruct it rather than simply conform themselves to it. Communication seems to be a particular example of this kind of discipline, as its professors, while clinging to some basic tenants, have consistently found new forms of communication to study. Probably, the days are gone where professors hung pictures of revered disciplinary scholars in their offices (a physicist might display Einstein, or a psychologist Freud), but most communication scholars would consider such a practice to be gauche (or would have a difficult time deciding whose picture to hang, perhaps favoring a picture of a group of beloved colleagues over a single individual).

Disciplines, therefore, are communities of inquiry organized around a particular topic. They are most easily distinguished as academic departments in research universities, where their scholars generate specialized knowledge at a level of quality to be consistently judged as worthy of publication in the discipline's journals and where new scholars are apprenticed. These communities of inquiry generate knowledge that "makes enough sense" that it can be developed into a curriculum which undergraduate students (and faculty colleagues from other disciplines) find to be coherent.

Returning, then, to my opening formulation, "communication is an academic discipline because we made it so," the only undefined term remaining is "we."

Given the previous discussion, however, "we" can only be the scholars whose work created academic departments with "communication" in their titles, became members of scholarly societies whose names included or were changed to include "communication" as a prominent element, created and published in scholarly journals whose content focused on "communication" of various sorts, and mentored students in becoming communication scholars. "We" created sets of communication courses that eventually gelled into full-fledged undergraduate curricula. "Our" students went from saying, "I don't know what I'm studying, but I do enjoy what I'm studying," to achieving an ability to explain "communication" study to outsiders in a reasonably coherent fashion.

"We" are, for the most part, former speech and journalism professors. Some of us still prefer those old designators, and many of us appreciate and want to celebrate our heritage in those fields of study as well as our identity as scholars of communication. Some of us have been historic rivals, and we've competed to be the group on our campus to associate ourselves with "communication." We've even debated whether the appropriate term was "communication" or "communications" (and, for the record, "communication" seems to have won as the academic identifier for "us," but outsiders often add the "s" to the end when referring to our academic departments or what we study).

We are scholars who understood that speech and journalism professors suffered from an inferiority complex: we were perceived as teachers but not scholars or researchers, and we severed a relationship with the discipline of English over what to teach and how to teach it, not over some clear paradigmatic difference. We made ourselves visible on our campuses in order to be appreciated, personally, as valued colleagues, because some of the same individuals did not think much of our scholarly work. We had trouble deciding on important questions on which to focus our scholarship, but, as I will argue, we did find broad topics to study. Somehow, we sensed that shifting our focus to "communication" provided us with an opportunity to advance ourselves in the academic world, though in doing so we were bound to create internal strife. We kept working on our identity as a discipline that studied communication, even when that work plodded instead of soared.

When Communication Became a Discipline proposes to tell the story of how journalism and speech professors succeeded in becoming communication professors. I have put the somewhat arbitrary time boundary of 1964 through 1982 around this story, though clearly much happened before 1964 (and, also, after 1982). I argue that by 1982 communication was only poised to become a discipline—it would take several years more before its disciplinary status would be recognized.

Yet, there were events in each of the boundary years that provided markers in the story. Both markers involved the journalism scholarly society, the Association for Education in Journalism (AEJ). In 1964, after several years of discussion, AEJ members voted a major revision in the association's constitution, including allowing for the first time an interest group titled "Theory and Methodology" to become a formal part of the association's structure. At the same time, the members rejected a proposal, advanced by a public relations professor and an advertising professor, to change the association's name from "Association for Education in Journalism" to "Association for Education in Communications."

My story takes more the form of an argument than it does a history, though I do support that argument with historical evidence. There will be points (perhaps too many for those trained as historians) where I will essentially speculate "what if," particularly in describing the motivations of decision-makers and other actors. In many cases, there are either no records about these motivations, or if there are, I have not found them.

This story is also to a small degree autobiographical. In the fall of 1964, shortly after AEJ conducted its constitutional deliberations in what may well have been sweltering summer heat and humidity in Houston, I began my undergraduate education as an "undeclared" major. I would soon switch to Speech, however, after a session with a career counselor suggested to me that I should major in something I enjoyed, something in which I could excel. I had participated in high-school forensics and thought that speech would be an enjoyable major for me (and it was). By 1982, I had completed a PhD degree in communication and had established myself as a faculty member in a department titled, "Speech Communication." I was unaware of AEJ's 1964 constitutional revision and was probably only vaguely aware of that same organization's decision, in 1982, to add the words, "and Mass Communication" to its title, making it the last of the major disciplinary societies to include the word, "communication," in its name.

I was certainly aware to some degree as an undergraduate that speech was changing its disciplinary focus. The major requirements in effect when I began my major changed before I finished four years later. While I studied speech-making and rhetorical criticism, oral interpretation of literature, and the structure of language, the department had to waive a required course in voice and diction, because it was no longer being offered. I even took a course in journalism, one focused on writing arts reviews, an interest I returned to as I was approaching retirement. Toward the end of my undergraduate career, there were new courses in communication to take, and those courses had proliferated by the time I enrolled as a master's student at the same institution. When I entered a communication doctoral program, in 1971, the national disciplinary societies with which I identified were titled the Speech Communication Association and the International Communication Association. My doctoral curriculum was focused on organizational communication, though my advisers tolerated my ongoing interest in what was by then termed, "literature in performance." During my doctoral study, rhetorical scholars, such as Ernest Bormann (fantasy themes) and Roderick Hart and Don Burks (rhetorical sensitivity), were writing about what were by then deemed to be "communication" topics.

It was clear to me as a young scholar that speech was rapidly moving away from a discipline that had been defined by Charles Woolbert (1923) as including (1) *speaking* (e.g., talk, conference, conversation, public speaking and eloquence, and rhetoric in theory, history, and practice); (2) *reading* (the study of reading or reciting from the printed page, including involving the whole body to portray the meaning of what is being read); (3) *speech sounds* (the study of speech sounds as sounds); and (4) *speech science* (the body of knowledge and insight gleaned from the study of speaking, reading, and speech sounds). What replaced Woolbert's definition was the idea that speech (communication) could be conceived as "spoken symbolic interaction" (Kibler & Barker, 1968) and that infinite amounts of scholarship could emanate from this font.

While the basics of "spoken symbolic interaction" remain true to Woolbert's formulation, the shift to communication as a central tenet of the study of speech was actually a radical one. Where Woolbert envisioned the study of all sorts of oral communication, in practice speech scholars of the time were most interested in public performances: speaking, debate, reading aloud—as well as the ideas about the rhetoric that underlay such study. The formulation that participants at the 1968 New Orleans Conference on Research and Instructional Development, that was co-sponsored by the

Speech Association of America and the U.S. Office of Education, shifted the emphasis away from public speaking and toward what became known as interpersonal communication. Implied by this shift was less concentration on understanding rhetoric as the basis for communication and more understanding of social psychological and sociological theories of language use and social interaction. The definition also re-oriented communication study away from communicators as people and toward the process of producing messages. And it made hash of Lasswell's (1948) journalistic formulation of communication: "Who? Says What? To Whom? With What Effect?"

Speech professors became communication scholars almost overnight. Of course, the roots of this transformation had been seeded and tended for many years before their sprouts burst forth. But, burst forth they did. A 1968 summer conference sponsored by the Speech Association of America was ablaze with discussion of the New Orleans Conference recommendations, particularly the ones about using knowledge of communication to promote social change. Held in Chicago prior to the Democratic Convention, the atmosphere was charged with the possibilities for a social revolution in American politics.

Later that year, the speech association returned to Chicago for its annual meeting. The riots at the Democratic Convention and the subsequent splintering of the Democratic Party, leading to the election of Richard Nixon as president, provided a backdrop for the disciplinary turmoil that roiled the meeting. The split, mirroring many such disputes in the 1960s, occurred along generational lines. Two groups emerged: The Old Guard and The Young Turks. The Old Guard was perceived as defending speech over communication, while The Young Turks was perceived as leading the discipline toward necessary change.

At the center of this controversy was Marie Hochmuth Nichols, the first woman to be elected president of the association by popular vote (according to Blankenship, 2004, four previous women presidents had been selected by committees). Nichols was a seasoned and highly respected scholar, as well as an eloquent speaker. But, to the membership, she clearly represented The Old Guard.

The Young Turks continued to push an agenda to refocus its scholarly organization on communication. This agenda enjoyed support from even some in The Old Guard. A proposal was put forth to change the society's name to Speech Communication Association, but a change of name can never be done quickly, particularly in academe.

This time proved an exception. There was already in place a structure committee charged with examining the association's constitution and bylaws. By the 1969 meeting, in New York, this committee had done its work, including putting forth the proposed name change as part of a sweeping revision of how the organization operated.

Nichols was president during that time, and she devoted her presidential address to cautioning about moving too quickly. Unfortunately, she titled her speech, "The Tyranny of Relevance" (Nichols, 1970), and the title alone drew, according to Blankenship, a substantial crowd, including several who came so that they could walk out in disgust.

But, the constitution and bylaws revision passed, and the Speech Association of America became the Speech Communication Association in July 1970. There would be several attempts to drop "speech" from the name, but these attempts would not succeed until 1996, when the membership approved The National Communication Association as the society's name.

The period immediately following the SCA name change was one of intellectual ferment. Rhetorical scholars, who had been challenged by Robert L. Scott's (1967) "On Viewing Rhetoric as Epistemic" and Lloyd F. Bitzer's (1968) "The Rhetorical Situation," as well as the relatively rapid popularity of communication study, decided to hold a two-part conference to plan new directions for the study of rhetoric. Called the "Wingspread Conference," the volume produced from it, titled *The Prospect of Rhetoric* (Bitzer & Black, 1971), set the agenda for rhetorical scholarship for many years to come.

The 1970s also saw new dynamism emerge in existing journals, as well as the start of new journals. This dynamism was especially evident in *The Quarterly Journal of Speech* under the editorship of Robert L. Scott (1972–1974) and Edwin Black (1975–1977), which saw the publication of several landmark studies that would help to set the tone for scholarship that would follow. *Speech Monographs* renamed itself *Communication Monographs* in 1976, during the editorship of Roger E. Nebergall. At that same time, during the editorship of Kenneth L. Brown, *The Speech Teacher* became *Communication Education* and began to feature scholarship in classroom communication and learning, while moving away from documenting teaching practices (another journal devoted to those practices, titled *Communication Teacher*, would be created in 1986).

The International Communication Association began to upgrade the quality of *The Journal of Communication* by transferring it to the University of Pennsylvania in 1974. George Gerbner, long-serving Dean of the Annenberg School for Communication, edited the journal through 1991, when ICA reclaimed control of it and selected editors for terms of more traditional lengths. ICA also began a second journal, *Human Communication Research*, in 1974, with Gerald R. Miller as its initial editor. This journal focused on publishing quantitative scholarship, at least initially focusing on face-to-face communication.

Mass communication scholars were also making significant strides in building on media effects scholarship that already had a history, particularly in sociology. Two important new theories came into being during this period.

George Gerbner's Cultivation Theory emerged from research on the effects of violence in media, particularly in television (Gerbner, 1969; Gerbner & Gross, 1976). Agenda-setting Theory (McCombs & Shaw, 1972) challenged the conventional wisdom of the "two-step flow" proposed by sociologist Paul Lazarsfeld and his associates (Lazarsfeld, Berelson, & Gaudet, 1944) that assumed that media news coverage had minimal direct effects on public opinion. McCombs and Shaw's research indicated that media coverage set an agenda for public discussion instead of telling people what to think.

Besides these two theories, there emerged a significant body of research on media effects carried out under the theme of media "uses and gratifications" (Katz, Blumler, & Gurevitch, 1973). Again, drawing on media effects scholarship originated by sociologists, "uses and gratifications" served as a set of organizing concepts for, at least initially, relatively atheoretical quantitative studies by mass communication scholars, who were usually housed with journalism in U.S. universities, but whose scholarship became an important counterpoint to the professional orientation of journalism education. Speech communication scholars would copy journalism's professional orientation in revising their curricula to focus less on speech and more on communication. Though they might have been unaware of the connection, this focus of drawing scholarship out of practical concerns had its roots in the bringing together of an interdisciplinary collection of scholars at the University of Chicago to work on a single topic, which, in this case was "communication" (Wahl-Jorgensen, 2004). In recounting this history, Wahl-Jorgensen noted that the work of the interdisciplinary committees was not intended to lead to the establishment of communication as a discipline at Chicago. But the work might have served as a model for the initial group of scholars who established the National Society for the Study of Communication, which founded *The Journal of Communication* and which later renamed itself as the International Communication Association.

While the 1970s saw the dominance of quantitative methods and theory-building based on hypothesis testing, other methodological approaches were being tried and, in some cases, found to be useful. Gerry Philipsen (1975) published the first ethnography in a communication journal, an event that set off considerable interest in the value of this method as a means of understanding the richness of communication. Robert Nofsinger (1977) alerted communication scholars to the usefulness of various strategies for studying conversation specifically and discourse more generally.

In media studies, a large body of work began to be produced in the 1970s based on the seminal ideas of scholars from Germany (the Frankfurt School) and Britain (the Birmingham School). This work carried the general title, "cultural studies," and it focused on the interactions between media and society, particularly regarding perspectives from feminist theory and critical race theory. These perspectives, while new in the late 1970s, would eventually come to rival hypothesis testing as a means for explaining media effects.

Interpersonal communication, which was the genesis of communication study by speech scholars, also evolved as different theoretical perspectives emerged. Charles Berger's theory of uncertainty reduction in the evolution of relationships (Berger & Calabrese, 1975) provided a set of axioms and theorems that guided scholarship for years to come. The emergence of communication scholarship based on the work of the Palo Alto group (Watzlawick, Beavin, & Jackson, 1967) provided a means of studying relationships from a systems perspective. Karl Weick's (1979) work on patterns of interaction in organizations expanded the systems approach to demonstrate how evolutionary cycles could explain the process by which organizational cultures were established and changed.

Journalism and speech were established as disciplines in the same era, though journalism preceded speech by several years. Zelizer (2011) noted that journalism often set a tone for discipline development, which speech followed, even though there was generally little direct contact between the two groups. As communication became established as an academic discipline, journalism's influence receded, and, according to Zelizer, "in some places, it disappeared altogether from the discipline" (p. 7). Nevertheless, my narrative of the establishment of a discipline of communication could not proceed without the participation of journalism and its sometimes-reluctant embrace of mass communication scholarship. The "strands" of scholarship I discuss as the central part of this narrative occurred to some degree or another in both journalism and speech as a discipline of communication emerged.

I found five "strands" of communication scholarship that crystalized during the 1964–1982 period. These strands don't by any means account for all the scholarship that existed, but I believe that they are broad enough to encompass a good deal of it. I also contend that each of these strands continues to be prominent in the communication discipline, generating significant contemporary scholarship.

1. *Communication as Shaper of Individual and Public Opinion*, including work on persuasion and attitude change, credibility, strategic message and campaign construction, and media influences in shaping public opinion and individual perceptions of political and social issues.
2. *Communication as Language Use*, including rhetorical theory, analysis and criticism, discourse and conversation analysis, scholarship on the impact of language in message construction, and analysis of language use, by linguistic and ethnographic means.
3. *Communication as Information Transmission*, including analyses of cognitive and affective changes related to messages presented via face-to-face

and mediated means, as well as the relationship between information and uncertainty in communication systems.

4. *Communication as Developer of Relationships*, including processes by which relationships are formed, maintained, and decayed in face-to-face and mediated environments.

5. *Communication as Definer, Interpreter, and Critic of Culture*, including analysis of media representations, cultural influences on language use and individual interactions, and critical perspectives of underrepresented groups.

The plan for the remainder of the book is as follows: in chapter 2, I will present three types of disciplinary history and use those types to provide a gloss of communication's development as a topic of academic study prior to 1964. In chapter 3, I'll review the key events of the development of communication as an academic discipline between 1964 and 1982. In chapters 4–8, I will provide examples of how the five strands of scholarship in communication were manifested in the discipline's scholarly books and journals. Finally, in chapter 9, I will examine the development of communication as a discipline after 1982 and speculate about the discipline's continuing development.

REFERENCES

Becher, T. & Trowler, P. (2001). *Academic Tribes and Territories: Intellectual Enquiry and the Cultures of Disciplines* (2nd edition). Buckingham, UK: Open University Press/SRHE.

Berger, C. R. & Calabrese, R. J. (1975). Some explorations in initial interaction and beyond: Toward a theory of interpersonal communication. *Human Communication Research, 1*, 199–112. doi:0.1111/j.1468-2958.1975.tb00258.x

Bitzer, L. F. (1968). The rhetorical situation. *Philosophy & Rhetoric, 1*, 1–14.

Bitzer, L. F. & Black, E. (eds.) (1971). *The Prospect of Rhetoric: Report of the National Developmental Project, Sponsored by Speech Communication Association*. Englewood Cliffs, NJ: Prentice-Hall.

Blankenship, J. (2004). Marie Hochmuth Nichols (1908-1978): A retrospective. *Review of Communication, 4*(1/2), 75–85. doi:10.1080/1535859042000250295

Craig, R. T. (1999). Communication theory as a field. *Communication Theory, 9*, 119–161.

Gerbner, G. (1969). Toward 'Cultural Indicators': The analysis of mass mediated message systems. *AV Communication Review, 17*(2), 137–148.

Gerbner, G. & Gross, L. (1976). Living with television: The violence profile. *Journal of Communication, 26*(2), 172–199. doi:10.1111/j.1460-2466.1976.tb01397.x

Katz, E., Blumler, J. G. & Gurevitch, M. (1973). Uses and gratifications research. *Public Opinion Quarterly, 37*, 509–523. doi:10.1086/268109

Kibler, R. J. & Barker, L. L. (1968). *Conceptual frontiers in Speech Communication: Report on the New Orleans Conference on Research and Instructional Development.* Annandale, VA: Speech Association of America.

Korn, C. J., Morreale, S. P. & Boileau, D. M. (2000). Defining the field: Revisiting the ACA 1995 definition of communication studies. *Journal of the Association for Communication Administration, 29,* 40–52.

Kuhn, T. S. (1962). *The Structure of Scientific Revolutions.* Chicago, IL: University of Chicago Press.

Lasswell, H. D. (1948). The structure and function of communication in society. In Bryson, L. (ed.), *The Communication of Ideas: A Series of Addresses* (pp. 203–243). New York: Institute for Religious and Social Studies.

Lazarsfeld, P., Berelson, B. & Gaudet, H. (1944). *The People's Choice: How the Voter Makes Up His Mind in a Presidential Campaign.* New York: Columbia University Press.

McCombs, M. & Shaw, D. (1972). The agenda-setting function of mass media. *Public Opinion Quarterly 36,* 176–187. doi:10.1086/267990

Menand, L. (1997). The demise of disciplinary authority. In A. Kernan (ed.), *What's Happened to the Humanities?* (pp. 201–219). Princeton, NJ: Princeton University Press.

National Center for Education Statistics. (2010). Detail for CIP Code 09. Retrieved from http://nces.ed.gov/ipeds/cipcode/cipdetail.aspx?y=55&cipid=88043.

Nichols, M. H. (1970). The tyranny of relevance. *Spectra, 6*(1), 1, 10.

Nofsinger Jr., R. E. (1977). A peek at conversational analysis. *Communication Quarterly, 25*(3), 12–20. doi:10.1080/01463377709369259

O'Hair, H. D. (2006). *The Promise of Communication.* Presidential address delivered at the annual convention of the National Communication Association, San Antonio, Texas.

Peters, J. D. (1999). *Speaking into the Air: A History of the Idea of Communication.* Chicago, IL: University of Chicago Press.

Philipsen, G. (1975). Speaking 'like a man' in Teamsterville: Culture patterns of role enactment in an urban neighborhood. *Quarterly Journal of Speech, 61,* 13–22. doi:10.1080/00335637509383264

Scott, R. L. (1967). On viewing rhetoric as epistemic. *Central States Speech Journal, 18,* 9–16. doi:10.1080/10510976709362856

Wahl-Jorgensen, K. (2004). How not to found a field: New evidence on the origins of mass communication research. *Journal of Communication, 54,* 547–564. doi:10.1111/j.1460-2466.2004.tb02644.x

Watzlawick, P., Beavin, J. & Jackson, D. (1967). *Pragmatics of Human Communication: A Study of Interactional Patterns, Pathologies, and Paradoxes.* New York: Norton.

Weick, K. E. (1979). *The Social Psychology of Organizing* (2nd edition). Reading, MA: Addison-Wesley.

Woolbert, C. H. (1923). The teaching of speech as an academic discipline. *Quarterly Journal of Speech Education, 9,* 1–18. doi:10.1080/00335632309379407

Zelizer, B. (2011). Journalism in the service of Communication. *Journal of Communication, 61,* 1–21. doi:10.1111/j.1460-2466.2010.01524.x

Chapter 2

Histories of Communication Study

History can be written from many different perspectives, and disciplinary history is no exception. One of the most common forms of disciplinary history is biographical, which essentially summarizes the acts of particular individuals in creating ideas, establishing structures to study and perpetuate those ideas, and becoming well enough known to allow the ideas and their supporting scholarship to become known, both inside the discipline and outside of it.

The advantages to biographical history are that key individuals are often easy to identify, and once identified their contributions can also be discussed by those knowledgeable of the discipline itself. It would seem sacrilegious, for example, to discuss the discipline of psychology without alluding to the contributions of Freud and Skinner. And the more established the discipline, the longer the list of names that knowledgeable historians would ignore at their peril.

In communication, several biographical histories have been written. In particular, the Association for Education in Journalism and Mass Communication commissioned a history in conjunction with its seventy-fifth anniversary (Emery and McKerns, 1987) that focused heavily on profiling the individuals who had served the association over the years. Rogers (1994) also provided a biographically oriented history of the communication discipline, though most of the scholars he profiled were ones that Rogers believed had provided overarching theories that intellectually undergirded the communication discipline. He did, however, make a central claim that the discipline of communication was founded by Wilbur Schramm, who formed the first university-sponsored communication research center, at the University of Iowa's journalism school.

A second kind of history is intellectual history. This sort of history is based on ideas. Typically, an intellectual history will take one or more concepts and will trace the development of the concepts over time. Oftentimes, these histories will review the scholarship associated with the concept and will offer some conclusions about how the concept has evolved and what further development is needed.

Herman Cohen's (1994) volume provided an intellectual history of various topics related to the study of speech communication, including heavy emphasis on rhetorical theory and criticism. Cohen also incorporated material on aspects of communication that became associated with the study of public speaking, such as oral interpretation of literature, speech correction, and other manifestations of orality. Those manifestations included theatre and other forms of performance, psychological and sociological dimensions of persuasion and group discussion, and philosophical concerns such as ethics, freedom, and democracy. Cohen's volume was organized both topically and chronologically and covered the period from 1914 to 1945. Unfortunately, a projected second volume was never completed. Additional examples of intellectual history may be found in Delia (1987) and Park and Pooley (2008).

Communication as a concept itself was the subject of intensive consideration between 1964 and 1982. There was debate regarding how to define communication, and there was lament regarding how many definitions of communication were extant, as well as about the difficulty in reconciling the many definitions with each other. As I will describe in the next chapter, there was a concerted effort to lay aside the speech tradition and to replace it with a focus on communication. There were also efforts to integrate previous research traditions with a new communication paradigm.

These debates were often held under the aegis of disciplinary societies, and the debates are interesting in themselves as records of how thinking about the study of communication both evolved and shifted over time. I would assign the label, "political history," to this sort of study, and I'd contend that the study of the actions taken by the three principal societies, known currently as the National Communication Association (NCA), the International Communication Association (ICA), and the Association for Education in Journalism and Mass Communication (AEJMC), did as much to shape the character of the communication discipline as did the contributions of individual scholars and the intellectual development of major topics of study (e.g., Association for Education in Journalism and Mass Communication, 2010). While there can be some dispute over the inclusion of other, related, disciplinary societies, I chose these three as being the most influential in forming a discipline of communication.

In this chapter, I will outline three history-based stories: two of the disciplines of speech and journalism, and also the multi-disciplinary story of the concept of "communication" that ultimately intersected with both journalism and speech to pave the way for an academic discipline of communication. In so doing, I will draw primarily on my interpretation of the work of others. This section is intended as background, since I am not proposing to write an exhaustive history of either "communication" as a topic of study nor of the three scholarly societies that arose to sponsor its study via forums, such as conferences and journals. As all three of these histories begin within a few years of each other, I will begin with the speech history.

THE SPEECH STORY

Speech as an academic discipline initially was defined by what it was not rather than what it was. First, it was not literature or writing, which were considered the province of the established discipline of English. Speech was also not elocution, the study of speaking in a stylish and "proper" manner, according to the standards of the day. Elocution was often not taught by academics (it was satirized by George Bernard Shaw in his 1913 play, *Pygmalion*).

And, its proponents were not English teachers, even though many of them had joined the National Council of Teachers of English (NCTE) when it was established in 1911. There had been controversy about this point since the very beginning of NCTE's speech section. This point of view was often espoused by university professors who wished to establish themselves apart from English departments. On the other hand, high-school teachers were often proud to be known primarily as English teachers, while also teaching public speaking to their students.

In 1913, NCTE's speech section agreed to poll its membership regarding whether to continue as a unit of NCTE or establish its own organization. Results of the poll were announced at the 1914 meeting of the section: those results showed that the membership was evenly split on remaining in NCTE and forming a separate organization. At that point, a group of seventeen university professors held a meeting and determined to start a separate scholarly society, allowing those who wished to remain in NCTE to do so.

The seventeen were primarily from public universities in the U.S. Midwest, though one was from Harvard, and another, who would rise to prominence, was from Cornell. Prior experience probably influenced the membership of the group: an Eastern Public Speaking Conference had begun in 1910 as a meeting primarily attended by faculty from elite private liberal arts colleges in the region. As word of the conference spread, professors from public universities began to attend and present their perspectives. Public universities were often products of the Morrill Act of 1862, which established "land grants" to states to establish universities that would focus on both liberal and practical education, including study in engineering, technology, and agriculture. In contrast to private liberal arts colleges, which educated the children of elites, public universities deliberately reached out to children of farmers and the middle and working classes. While private universities focused on classical education in traditional disciplines, such as languages and literature, history, and the sciences, public universities often offered majors in career-oriented fields of study.

Public universities often saw themselves as promoters of democracy, meaning that they saw higher education's goals to include providing a means for students to become effective citizens. As technology advanced and industry developed, graduates of public universities didn't so much become corporate owners as managers or technicians: those who had developed sufficient skill to oversee the work of others.

The study of speech differed in public and private universities, to a degree. In private universities, speech was looked upon as an activity where students would learn how to present ideas to audiences in a manner that would engage those audiences, both intellectually and emotionally. Speech may have been taught as one or more courses, but more likely it was developed through participation in debating societies that existed outside of the classroom. In classical terms, debating society students focused their attention on developing into what Quintilian called "a good man [sic] speaking well."

In public universities, speech was perceived as an essential part of developing into an effective citizen of a democratic society. A course in public speaking was often required of most or all students, and that course taught students about different types of speaking, as well as how arguments are developed and supported. Students learned different types of speaking (informative, persuasive, and ceremonial—which was commonly referred to by the word, "epideictic"). Debating societies often existed in public universities, but they weren't looked on as the primary method of instruction in argumentation and speech.

Several of the founders of what eventually became known as the National Communication Association were interested in doctoral education in speech. They realized that they were carving out new academic territory and that this new territory would not be accepted easily by colleagues. In particular, English professors saw significant scholarly overlap between themselves and Speech professors. Even though the primary interest of those who initially joined the National Association of Teachers of Speech was how to teach speech courses better, several of the founders realized that they needed to develop a body of scholarly knowledge in order to succeed. A journal, the *Quarterly Journal of Speech Education*, was quickly begun, and James Winans, the professor from Cornell, wrote an essay titled, "The Need for Research," in the first issue. Winans (1915) chided his colleagues by saying, "We have lacked scientific foundation for our special work" (p. 17).

Winans continued his argument by writing, "I am talking to my own kind now. I have no great humility before teachers in other lines. Toward them we bristle with defiance. But that is just the trouble—we do bristle. We are not able yet to take ourselves for granted. We shall feel better and do better when we can" (pp. 17–18).

Winans recommended that speech scholars establish multiple perspectives on their work, essentially laying the groundwork for a "big tent" approach to creating an academic discipline. And the big tent functioned to hold disparate elements of speech together, from the study of speech disorders and their correction, anchored by a knowledge of speech science, including the structure of language, to the psychological basis for persuasion, to the study and criticism of rhetoric, and to the performance of literature. In 1923, Charles Woolbert, another of the founders, published a summary of speech as an academic discipline, one that he described as being of the most basic type, because it studied behavior that humans engaged in daily.

Woolbert (1923) outlined four broad components of the speech discipline. The first was "speaking," which included what he called public talk of all kinds, conference or problem-solving communication within groups, and conversation, or interpersonal interaction. The second was "reading" aloud, or reciting the written word from memory, in a manner that serves to interpret the text. The third was "speech sounds," or the study of how speech is produced, leading to identifying disordered speech and methods for its correction. Woolbert saw this process as primarily an educational one, as most speech problems were identified and treated in schools—a medical model of disordered speech would come later and would lead to the separation of this area of study from speech. The fourth was "speech science," which Woolbert defined as the building of knowledge about various aspects of speech through systematic study. Woolbert had trained in social psychology, and he had contributed to understanding of means by which speakers would be persuasive with audiences.

The work on speech discipline had progressed sufficiently that what was then called the National Association of Teachers of Speech could celebrate itself at its 13th annual convention, in 1927. James O'Neill (1928), who had served as the first president in 1914, wrote to the founders and a number of others asking them to reflect on the goals of forming this association and indicated whether they had been realized.

Frank Rarig, of the University of Minnesota, responded most succinctly. He wrote that the purposes were: "(1). The separation of Speech as a profession and as an academic subject from English; (2). The establishment of Speech in colleges and universities as a separate and worthy academic subject; (3). The development of a body of knowledge worthy of such an academic subject through the encouragement of research in the scientific phases of the field; and (4). The establishment and publishing of a journal which would circulate among the members of the profession, and furnish them with means of communication as to the results of research work, and of teaching methods and teaching problems." Rarig allowed that these objectives had all either been met or were well in process of being met (1928, pp. 245–246).

It would be left to James Winans to provide an excellent measure of the success of the speech discipline, one that would still resonate with those who continue to attend the association's conferences. Winans wrote:

> I think we have succeeded beyond any dreams I had at the time, almost too well. I often regret the passing of the days of small things, when the meetings were to me a delight and a joy that lasted till I could begin to look to the next. That is no longer true. Too big and confused; but I know it is for the best. And still I would not miss going if I could help it in any reasonable way. (1928, p. 248)

Like a good deal of academia, speech settled into its role within colleges and universities, especially during the years of the Great Depression and World War II. The "big tent" idea continued, but as some areas grew, they split off into their own specialized societies. The American Speech and Hearing Association formed in 1925, and the Educational Theatre Association formed in 1936. Interestingly enough, the Speech Association maintained an interest group in "speech science," and one in "theatre." It is likely that these groups remained because academic departments with "speech" in their titles sometimes also contained speech and hearing faculty and/or theatre faculty.

Scholarship in speech continued to grow, and the association recognized that social science approaches were becoming more significant. In 1934, that recognition resulted in the start of a second journal, titled *Speech Monographs*. It would not be until 1952 that the association started a third journal, titled *Speech Teacher*. By this time, its name had become the Speech Association of America (SAA), and a major scholarly book had appeared. Titled *Speech Criticism: The Development of Standards for Rhetorical Appraisal* (Thonssen & Baird, 1948), the work laid out a method that would become standard for years.

Speech also negotiated the formation of a separate organization that would serve its social-science scholars. Titled the National Society for the Study of Communication (NSSC), it was formed in 1950 after being planned at the 1948 SAA convention and recognized as an affiliate organization of SAA at the 1949 convention. NSSC would eventually become the International Communication Association, a development I will address in chapter 3. Scholars using the Thonssen and Baird method and social science scholars in speech grew consistently further and further apart in the 1950s and 1960s, united only by the fact that they were all speech teachers.

THE JOURNALISM STORY

Journalism as a profession in the United States was established by printers, who published newspapers and who needed writers to provide content for those newspapers. Oftentimes, budding journalists would apprentice themselves to a professional printer and would learn journalism as part of learning the printing trade.

Like speech, journalism as an area of academic study was helped enormously by the establishment of Land Grant universities across the United States. While speech was established as primarily a co-curricular activity at elite colleges, journalism was a trade in search of academic legitimacy. Land Grant universities, especially those in farming states, had a great need for accurate and timely information, particularly about agricultural matters, such as weather, pricing of crops, and information on increasing yields. As Daniel Czitrom (1982) has noted, the development of the telegraph made timely news possible.

Clearly, there was a need to make journalism a profession, as opposed to a trade. And public universities in the Midwest were quick to see that academic courses of study could be developed. While coursework in journalism was created at several colleges and universities following the Civil War (Folkerts, 2014), The University of Missouri established the first degree-offering School of Journalism in 1908. Other such schools quickly followed.

Of course, journalists who had learned their craft through apprenticeship were not about to let the academics take over. Debates over who should be journalists and what journalists should know would continue even after academic programs were established. Folkerts reported that some college graduates hid their degrees while applying for journalism positions (p. 229).

The cause of professionalism may have been helped along by the late nineteenth-century trend toward "yellow journalism," or the sensationalizing of the news. This trend was particularly noticeable in newspapers published by William Randolph Hearst and Joseph Pulitzer. Pulitzer may have seen the error of his ways, though, as he provided funds to Columbia University for awards recognizing the year's distinguished work in journalism. The funds also went toward the establishment of a Journalism School at Columbia, the first such school at an Ivy League University.

Academics also rushed to promote their cause to each other. In 1912, they formed the American Association of Teachers of Journalism (AATJ). The conference to form the association was spearheaded by Willard G. Bleyer, who also organized the School of Journalism at the University of Wisconsin–Madison. Bleyer was elected the first president of the new organization, whose membership reached 107 by 1915 (Emery & McKerns, 1987).

Bleyer, whose nickname was "Daddy," became known as the leading voice in curriculum construction in journalism. Bleyer held that journalists should know how to write various kinds of news stories but more importantly, they should be able to understand and interpret what they were reporting. He advocated that a good deal of the undergraduate journalism major should be taken up by studying the liberal arts, particularly social sciences, such as politics, history, and sociology. Much of news reporting meant looking at the politics underlying a controversy or understanding the issues underlying persistent societal problems. Bleyer was persuasive, and his ideas have persisted and become taken-for-granted in journalism education. Bleyer also started the first doctoral program in journalism, and there he focused on journalism as a social science and emphasized analysis of empirical data as a means of scholarly discovery.

Despite Bleyer's influence, there were significant discussions in academic journalism regarding how to ensure that students earning degrees received an appropriate, high-quality, education. An alternative curricular philosophy existed at the University of Missouri, which included several elements of the apprenticeship model: for example, Missouri's School of Journalism operated its own newspaper and eventually presented news in broadcast form as well. Students were required to participate in practicum courses as an integral part of their education, and through this participation students learned how to interpret what they were reporting.

Some of this discussion was influenced by rivalries among journalism programs. Alliances among "top" Schools of Journalism were formed, and competing alliances were started by those who were unhappy about not being included. Eventually, these rivalries led to agreements on standards for the undergraduate curriculum, which, in large measure, conformed to what Bleyer had advocated. An accrediting body, eventually known as the Accrediting Council for Education in Journalism and Mass Communication (ACEJMC), administered the standards and approved programs for accreditation based on rigorous self-studies and site visits by a team of accreditors.

Individual students did not receive accreditation, though. Licensure of journalists was discussed, but it never came to pass. And, indeed, many journalists were hired by press organizations without degrees in journalism. Rather, English, history, and politics seemed to be the most common majors for many years. Over time, though, Schools of Journalism partnered with news organizations not only to provide experience for their students but also to show editors and publishers the value of undergraduate journalism education.

Journalism faculty often came from the ranks of working or retired journalists. And even after doctoral programs in journalism began to produce sufficient graduates to work as faculty in the various programs around the United

States, there was a bias in hiring in favor of individuals who had significant press experience. Journalists dominated the AATJ meetings (AATJ changed its name to the Association for Education in Journalism in 1950), and they resisted the steady encroachment of faculty in public relations and advertising, as journalism schools expanded their curricular offerings.

Like the speech scholars, journalism scholars focused mostly on teaching at their annual gatherings. Despite Bleyer's influence, AATJ members did not form a Committee on Research until 1924 (Association for Education in Journalism and Mass Communication, 2010). A journal quickly followed, and space on the program for the annual meeting was set aside for presentation of research findings.

Journalism scholars tended to analyze press content, and scholars became sophisticated at content analysis as a method. Scholarship also focused on journalism's role in U.S. society, especially on the U.S. Constitution's guarantee of Freedom of the Press and other First Amendment issues. It would be some time before theories started to be built and research would become more systematic.

Following World War II, journalism, as speech, experienced a wave of intellectual ferment. Some of this ferment came from cross-fertilization of work on communication, brought by scholars such as Wilbur Schramm. This ferment eventually led to a greater recognition of the role of scholarly research, whose specifics I will describe in chapter 3.

THE COMMUNICATION STORY

While there is evidence of scholarly interest in aspects of communication dating to ancient civilizations (Asante, 2006, 655–656), the most comprehensive extant treatments of communication topics came from philosophers in Ancient Greece. Plato and Aristotle disagreed over the nature of "rhetoric," with Plato contending that logical disputation was the sole path to truth and Aristotle contending that rhetorical reasoning would yield approximate truth that would serve to unite societies until new consensus could be reached on a different form of the same truth. Plato and Aristotle also outlined elements of language use to achieve beauty.

It is not my intent to summarize here the development of the study of rhetoric. Suffice it to say, both Plato and Aristotle's tenets waxed and waned in scholarly popularity, and the study of rhetoric remained a cornerstone of what might be considered an "educated" person.

Still, there were technological developments that brought focus to the term, "communication," as a topic of study. Developments, such as the telegraph, the telephone, film, and radio, pointed to significant changes in societies, as the speed of electronic transmission revised societal expectations of how "news" would be spread.

Such developments held significance when the academic discipline of sociology was established at the University of Chicago soon after the university itself was founded, in 1892. It was some time before a focus on communication developed, but the theorizing of Robert E. Park is credited as being the earliest scholarship that linked rapidly developing mass media with its societal impacts.

Much of the story of the early development of interest in communication is the story of prominent thinkers and writers who applied their unique perspectives to some aspect of the communication experience. Chicago housed several of those scholars in its early years, including John Dewey, whose ideas about the interaction between individual thought and problem solving in groups became broadly taught by speech scholars. Others included Charles Cooley, who wrote about how self was influenced by the experience of living in and interacting with society. George Herbert Mead, another Chicagoan, would expand Cooley's ideas and connect them to the social nature of language. Chicago's scholars with an interest in communication met to discuss the topic (Wahl-Jorgensen, 2004), but the university never developed an academic department devoted to the study of communication.

It would fall to a journalist named Walter Lippmann (1922), however, to pioneer the topic that would consume a good deal of communication scholarship for years to come. Lippman's book, *Public Opinion*, was a comprehensive description of how societies made decisions, particularly with the assistance of news media. It fueled a good deal of interest in the effects of media on society, particularly on democratic society.

Scholars from other disciplines began to study communication as well. Political Scientist Harold Lasswell was a student at the University of Chicago, and the book based on his dissertation (1927) became a major resource for the burgeoning study of propaganda. Lasswell's work was influenced by his interaction with the Chicago scholars studying communication, and his scholarship included a focus on the symbolic aspects of propaganda. Lasswell was an empiricist, and he was a leader in creating what has become known as "the received view" in communication. Lasswell (1948) summarized that view in a simple but not simplistic model: "Who? Says What? To Whom? With What Effect?"

Other prominent communication scholars were immigrants who escaped from Nazism in Europe. One was Paul Lazarsfeld, who had been prominent in the Vienna Circle. Trained as a mathematician, Lazarsfeld had learned to apply his quantitative knowledge to the study of social institutions. Once in the United States, Larzarsfeld became a research entrepreneur as a means of being accepted as an émigré. He moved from one position to another, eventually establishing an institute for social research. The research he conducted led to his appointment as head of the Princeton office of the Radio Research Project, which was aimed at understanding mass communication. Lazarsfeld's research on the 1940 election led to the development of landmark theory in mass communication, as documented by his books, *The People's Choice* (Lazarsfeld, Berelson, & Gaudet 1944) and *Personal Influence* (Katz, Lazarsfeld, & Roper, 1955). Trained as a scientist, Lazarsfeld was also a collaborator, and his sphere included academics who would establish independent reputations in communication scholarship.

Kurt Lewin was a second scholar who emigrated to the United States and became prominent. Lewin's path was similar to that of Lazarsfeld. He arrived in 1933, having previously been affiliated with Germany's Institute for Social Research and the Frankfurt School, which had been established there. A visiting appointment at Stanford University in 1930 led to a series of academic appointments at a number of major universities, including MIT, where he established the Center for Group Dynamics. Lewin's work was wide-ranging, but his interest in how groups formed and operated led to his work on understanding communication in groups. Lewin was also a collaborator, and he mentored a number of scholars who would become prominent in the emerging area of social psychology.

A third scholar from this period was an American professor of English at the University of Iowa named Wilbur Schramm. Despite having formed the famed Iowa Writers' Workshop, Schramm was an interdisciplinarian whose curious mind was always seeking new ideas. Schramm participated in research discussions at Iowa that included Kurt Lewin, and Schramm was impressed with Lewin's ideas. As World War II broke out, Schramm a patriotic man, contacted Archibald MacLeish, the U.S. Librarian of Congress, whom he had met through the Iowa Writers' Workshop, and volunteered to work with the Office of Facts and Figures, the Federal government's central propaganda agency (Chaffee & Rogers, 1997). He was soon in Washington, and his skill at networking put him in touch with many of the leading social scientists, including Laswell, Lazarsfeld, survey researcher Rensis Likert, experimental social psychologist Carl Hovland, and anthropologist Margaret Mead, with whom Schramm shared a carpool. Soon, Schramm was organizing and chairing a monthly dinner group to discuss interdisciplinary collaboration in wartime social science. Mead, in her role as program director for nutrition research at the National Research Council, had funded one of Kurt Lewin's most famous field experiments, which concentrated on changing American housewives' attitudes toward "inferior" cuts of meat, such as liver and heart, so that the more desirable cuts could be fed to troops fighting World War II.

A Congressionally mandated change of focus for the Office of Facts and Figures led Schramm to return to the University of Iowa in 1943. His former position at Iowa had been capably filled, but he was offered a position as director of the School of Journalism. Schramm agreed to take the position, and he used his Washington experience to establish a doctoral program in mass communication, as well as to begin a research institute. His Iowa colleagues, many of them journalists who left the profession to teach, were generally not pleased with this course of action, even though Schramm's work set the stage for Iowa to become prominent in communication scholarship. When the Iowa administration refused Schramm's request for a significant source of ongoing funding for his vision, Schramm moved on to the University of Illinois, where he created the Institute for Communications Research, as well as a doctoral program in mass communication. Chaffee and Rogers (1997) reckoned that Schramm was the first person to hold the title, Professor of Communication. Schramm would later establish similar institutes at Stanford University and at the East-West Center of the University of Hawaii. He was, if nothing else, ever the evangelist for an emerging discipline of communication.

Following the end of World War II, the United States quickly shifted from a wartime to a peacetime economy. It became clear that the inadequate technical infrastructure for communication was hampering this effort. Bell Labs, the research arm of the legislatively sanctioned telephone monopoly, began an ambitious program to find ways to correct this problem. From this effort emerged Claude Shannon's (1949) mathematical theory of information transmission, a theory that focused on how channels for telephone service could be constructed to minimize interference, or "noise." An elaborated version of Shannon's theory (Shannon & Weaver, 1963) became the basis for a more general transmission-based approach to understanding communication. At the same time, Norbert Wiener (1948) published a volume on "cybernetics," which applied General Systems Theory to the processing of information and set the stage for several scientific breakthroughs, including high-speed computing.

Social psychologist Carl Hovland returned to Yale following his wartime stint in Washington, DC. There, he formed and led the Yale Group, a program of research focused on communication and attitude change. Hovland's associates, many of whom became leading social psychologists, also continued Lewin's work on group dynamics. Publications from this group influenced theory and research that was developing in the 1950s among speech and journalism scholars in both interpersonal and mass communication phenomena. They were aided by an influx of college and university students, who were encouraged to complete degrees because of the availability of funding through the G.I. Bill, a program designed to assist war veterans to return to civilian life.

In essence, communication, as a field of study, was the product of an interdisciplinary commitment to the development of social science research, spurred by entrepreneurial academics, some of whom were motivated to settle in the United States because of religious persecution, others of whom were motivated by patriotic duty to the country during wartime. As higher education grew and prospered in no small measure due to government assistance, so did interest in communication, at a technical level, a societal level, and an interpersonal level.

REFERENCES

Asante, M. K. (2006). A discourse on black studies: Liberating the study of African people in the western academy. *Journal of Black Studies, 36*, 646–662. doi:10.1177/0021934705285937

Association for Education in Journalism and Mass Communication (2010, June 25). AEJMC history. Retrieved from https://www.aejmc.org/home/about/aejmc-history

Chaffee, S. H. & Rogers, E. M. (eds.) (1997). *The Beginnings of Communication Study in America: A Personal Memoir*, by Wilbur Schramm. Thousand Oaks, CA: Sage Publications.

Cohen, H. (1994). *The History of Speech Communication: The Emergence of a Discipline, 1914-1945.* Annandale, VA: Speech Communication Association.

Czitrom, D. (1982). *Media and the American Mind: From Morse to McLuhan.* Chapel Hill, NC: University of North Carolina Press.

Delia J. G. (1987). Communication research: A history. In Berger, C. R., and Chaffee, S. H. (eds.), *Handbook of Communication Science* (pp. 20–98). Newbury Park, CA: Sage Publications.

Emery, E. & McKerns, J. P. (1987, November). AEJMC: 75 years in the making: A history of organizing for journalism and mass communication education in the United States. *Journalism Monographs, 104.*

Folkerts, J. (2014). History of journalism education. *Journalism and Communication Monographs, 16*, 227–299. doi:10.1 177/1522637914541379

Katz, E., Lazarsfeld, P. F. & Roper, E. (1955). *Personal Influence: The Part Played by People in the Flow of Mass Communications.* New York: Routledge.

Lasswell, H. D. (1927). *Propaganda Technique in the World War.* New York: A. A. Knopf.

Lasswell, H. D. (1948). *Power and Personality.* New York: Norton.

Lazarsfeld, P. F., Berleson, B. & Gaude, H. (1944). *The People's Choice: How the Voter Makes Up His Mind in a Presidential Campaign.* New York: Columbia University Press.

Lippmann, W. (1922). *Public Opinion.* New York: Macmillan.

O'Neill, J. M. (1928). After thirteen years. *Quarterly Journal of Speech, 13*, 242–253.

Park, D. & Pooley, J. (2008). *The History of Media and Communication Research: Contested Memories.* New York: Peter Lang.

Rogers, E. M. (1994). *A History of Communication Study: A Biographical Approach.* New York: The Free Press.

Shannon, C. E. (1949). *The Mathematical Theory of Communication.* Urbana, IL: University of Illinois Press.

Shannon, C.E. & Weaver, W. (1963). *The Mathematical Theory of Communication.* Chicago, IL: University of Illinois Press.

Thonssen, L. & Baird, A. C. (1948). *Speech Criticism: The Development of Standards for Rhetorical Appraisal.* New York: Ronald Press Company.

Wahl-Jorgensen, K. (2004). How not to found a field: New evidence on the origins of mass communication research. *Journal of Communication, 54,* 547–564. doi:10.1111/j.1460-2466.2004.tb02644.x

Wiener, N. (1948). *Cybernetics, or, Control and Communication in the Animal and the Machine.* New York: John Wiley and Sons.

Winans, J. A. (1915). The need for research. *Quarterly Journal of Speech Education, 1,* 17–23. doi:10.1080/00335631509360453

Woolbert, C. H. (1923). The teaching of Speech as an academic discipline. *Quarterly Journal of Speech Education, 9,* 1–18. doi:10.1080/00335632309379407

Chapter 3

Becoming an Academic Discipline of Communication, 1964–1982

The previous chapter explained that academic disciplines in speech and journalism were established at similar times in the early part of the twentieth century. Both speech and journalism professors were focused primarily on teaching at the start, and teaching remained important to both disciplines as they matured. Speech scholars recognized that their discipline would most likely succeed if they had as large a "tent" as possible, and so for a number of years the study of speech included performance of various kinds, including theater, as well as what was known as speech correction, techniques for managing or eliminating common physical speech problems, such as stuttering. The core of speech scholarship focused on the analysis and criticism of speeches, from a rhetorical perspective. There were professors who trained as social scientists and who studied topics more related to communication, but they were slow to develop until the end of World War II.

Journalism, on the other hand, retained a focus on journalism as a press activity and as part of a First Amendment guarantee of press independence in both reporting on, and expressing opinions about, government. Journalism as a discipline was slow to recognize the importance of the study of advertising and public relations, both of which were important to the viability of the press. Journalism was also slow to recognize the importance of broadcast media, such as radio and television, as its professoriate was often required to have press experience in addition to academic training. While there were adherents to Bleyer's emphasis on scholarship and doctoral education, there were others who valued experience over academic credentials.

Meanwhile, a number of individual scholars had become interested in communication phenomena, particularly as media technologies burgeoned and developed a clear means of influencing both individuals and the public. Particularly after the end of World War II, some speech and journalism scholars became aware of the communication scholarship that had developed around them and began to extend that work. More speech and journalism scholars trained as social scientists than had been the case previously.

While the focus of this chapter is on events occurring between 1964 and 1982, primarily events where the scholarly societies in speech and journalism were involved, some context is necessary. Below, I will describe how interest in communication developed in the 1950s and early 1960s before arriving at the Association for Education in Journalism (AEJ) annual meeting in 1964.

THE NATIONAL SOCIETY FOR THE STUDY OF COMMUNICATION AND *THE JOURNAL OF COMMUNICATION*

The formation of The National Society for the Study of Communication (NSSC) provided a palpable sign that communication was becoming an increasing topic for scholarship by members of the speech and, to some degree, journalism, disciplines. NSSC was founded by a group of speech professors, and it was affiliated with the Speech Association of America (SAA) in 1949, prior to its formal establishment in 1950. NSSC members decided to be deliberately interdisciplinary so members could study communication from a number of perspectives. The group also wanted to reach out to practitioners in business, governmental, and military organizations and it succeeded in attracting a few of those individuals, particularly some academics who were affiliated with the U.S. Air Force.

Weaver (1977) published a history of this scholarly society, and a longer version of that history (Weaver, 1973) is held by the International Communication Association (ICA), which was the name the NSSC took when it reorganized itself in 1968. My purpose here is to focus on NSSC as an organization that was formed by SAA members and remained affiliated with SAA but would not compete with SAA. As Weaver wrote:

> Of major concern during the 1949 SAA convention was the relationship the new group would have with SAA. Sentiment was strong that it should remain loyal. This sentiment even affected the naming of the new society. The name finally decided upon was the National Society for the Study of Communication. "Study" was the key word. It was felt that a study group would not be a competing group with the SAA. (1977, p. 609)

The NSSC quickly established a series of study committees based on the interests of its members. These study committees focused as much on a transition to a focus on communication within speech as they did on developing theory or conducting research. For the first three years, NSSC held its annual convention in conjunction with SAA. After that time, NSSC held a separate meeting.

NSSC also quickly established a journal, *The Journal of Communication*. Apparently, having a journal devoted to the topic of communication was perceived as a key element of the NSSC's identity, as it began publication in 1951, only a year after the organization was formed.

Early on, much of the journal's content was aimed at the membership, including reports from the various study sections and announcements about the annual meeting's program. "Think pieces" were also being published, but very little in the way of theoretical or empirical research was in the journal. Articles were brief, only a few pages in length. The journal came out semi-annually. In only a few years, the number of issues had increased to four per year. Toward the end of the first decade, the journal was regularly publishing reports of research and articles that outlined theoretical positions. Interestingly, many of the individuals publishing theoretical essays or reports of experiments were not speech professors. Nevertheless, the study of communication was finding traction among speech professors and scholars in related disciplines, while those who had conducted much of the scholarship in the 1930s, 1940s, and through the mid-1950s were losing interest or finding themselves plateauing in terms of generating significant findings.

BERELSON'S "THE STATE OF COMMUNICATION RESEARCH"

As the 1950s progressed, the group of scholars that had pioneered communication scholarship began to move on to other projects, or, in some cases, died. By 1959, when Lazarsfeld associate Bernard Berelson published an essay titled "The State of Communication Research," in *Public Opinion Quarterly*, he could accurately state that Laswell, and Lazarsfeld had, at the time, developed other interests, Lewin had died in 1947, and his students had not continued to build directly on his scholarship, and Hovland's Yale group had broken apart. Hovland himself would die in 1961 after having developed cancer.

Berleson used this evidence, as well as how diffuse other work on communication phenomena had become, to contend that, while communication itself was an important topic for research, advances in communication scholarship had become moribund following some early successes.

The journal published three responses to the Berelson essay, one from Wilbur Schramm, who, at the time, was at Stanford University, one from sociologist David Riesman, author of the landmark book, *The Lonely Crowd*, and one from Raymond Bauer, a Harvard Business professor who had published on social indicators, mass communication, and advertising, among other topics. Each of the responses suggested that communication study was still finding its bearings. For example, Schramm commented:

> We sometimes forget that communication research is a field, not a discipline. In the study of man, it is one of the great crossroads where many pass but few tarry. Scholars come into it from their own disciplines, bringing valuable tools and insights, and later go back, like Lasswell, to the more central concerns of their disciplines. (Berelson, 1959, p. 8)

Riesman wrote:

> Work in the field of communications is inviting, at the moment, because of its very ambiguity and lack of structure. It is a somewhat transient waystation where people can meet who don't quite want to commit themselves to the field of literature (as monopolized by English departments) or to the social sciences (as monopolized by departments of sociology or political science)—and, as Mr. Berelson indicates, there is also room for people with an interest in economics and aesthetics. Some of the very best students, and some of the very worst, are attracted by the ability to delay a commitment to one of the established powers of academia. Some institutional rubric is necessary to protect them from those powers and, correspondingly, from the definitions of success or productivity emanating from them. (Berelson, 1959, pp. 10–11)

Bauer summarized his point of view in this way:

> Basically, then, my argument is that the early approaches carried with them necessary oversimplifications which have become clear only because the approaches were pushed to the point where they exposed their own limitations. The result has been not only a recognition of the complexity of the communications process but a shift to primary concern with the substance of the problems with less commitment to a particular device of investigation. (Berelson, 1959, p. 16)

BERLO'S *THE PROCESS OF COMMUNICATION*

David Berlo (1960) may or may not have read Berleson's 1959 declaration before he finished the text for *The Process of Communication* in February 1960. If he did, it probably didn't matter to him. His purpose in publishing was, as he noted in the Preface, "not intended as an abstract or review of what is known about communication, or as an attempt to construct a comprehensive theory" (1960, p. v). Rather, he intended his work to be a text for those beginning to study communication. And, in fact, Berlo included elements of a traditional college textbook, including questions for discussion at the end of each chapter and a list of suggested additional readings at the end of the book.

Berlo's audience seemed to be more than graduate students or advanced undergraduate students (the level of writing and conceptualization, while nontechnical, did not call itself out as suitable for first-year college students). He also seemed to be providing a primer for colleagues who may have been curious about the idea of communication and wanted to know more.

The book also did not try to break new ground, though it did so by gathering the information it presented in a single place. Berlo's perspective was rooted in behavioral social science, and he defined communication in terms of moving a message from a sender to a receiver. Communication could be observed, and its behavior studied.

Even the concept of "process" was not new to Berlo's work: *Journal of Communication* authors had been using the term in scholarly articles. Berlo defined it as dynamic and fluid, while at the same time language-based and thus requiring structure. Because of the structure, scholars can examine the ingredients of communication, as well as how those ingredients interrelate. Berlo listed who is communicating, why that person is communicating, what is being communicated and in what style, how the communication is occurring, and what response was given to the communication. Berlo drew upon the Shannon and Weaver (1949) model of communication, ultimately simplifying it to four elements: source, message, channel, and receiver, which he labeled SMCR.

Elaborating on these elements, Berlo identified four source-based elements that affect fidelity of communication: communication skills, attitudes, knowledge level, and position within a social–cultural system. He specified that these same elements would affect the receiver, who, in a conversation, would also serve as a source. He identified code, or a meaningful structure of symbols, content, and treatment, or style. He identified channel as the means by which the message was transmitted, as well as the decisions that went into selecting the appropriate channel. Each of these decisions is made to affect the receiver's understanding of, and responses to, the sender's communication behavior.

Berlo's remaining chapters explored key concepts affecting communication: (a) learning and development of habits; (b) interaction, leading to relational interdependence and the development of empathy; (c) social systems, such as groups, organizations, and cultures and the bases they bring for making predictions about interaction; (d) meaning, in its various forms, as well as how meaning is derived from language use, (e) perception, and how observations and judgments combine to understand similarities and differences, (f) inference, and the role logic plays in understanding structure, and (g) the role of definition in specifying meaning.

While Berlo did not attempt to set an agenda for communication scholarship in *The Process of Communication*, others adapted the SMCR model, primarily as a rubric for designating programs of research as fitting into a theory-building framework. In fact, Berlo seemed to believe that the SMCR model was useful for synthesizing research into what would become a "process" explanation for communication phenomena. In fact, speech and journalism scholars who relied on Berlo typically ignored the process aspects of his model, a point on which Smith (1972) would eventually challenge the emerging discipline.

THE DEATH OF CARL HOVLAND

Hovland, the founder and bright light of the Yale Program in Communication and Attitude Change, died on April 16, 1961. When he learned he had cancer, he worked until he could work no more. The Yale Program by this time had mostly run its course, and Hovland's most well-known colleagues, Irving Janis, Harold Kelley, Herbert Kelman, and Muzafer Sherif, had either moved on or developed other interests. Nevertheless, the work of the Yale group lived on in a great number of published books and papers. But work specifically on communication languished among social psychologists after Hovland's death.

THE PROFESSIONALIZATION OF THE SAA

The SAA led the way among the three major scholarly societies in speech and journalism in professionalizing its operation. The other two major societies were the AEJ and the NSSC. Until 1963, all three of these scholarly societies were administered by volunteer Executive Secretaries with support from their home universities. SAA broke this mold by establishing a national headquarters in New York City and by hiring William Work as executive secretary (Work & Jeffrey, 1989).

The stated reason for settling in New York was that it was the home of major foundations that SAA hoped to tap to advance its agenda. At first, the professional staff with degrees in speech were William Work and Fergus Currie, who served as Work's assistant director. Currie was replaced in 1966 by Robert N. Hall, who, like Work, would hold lengthy tenure with the association.

Clearly, interest into incorporating communication into the speech discipline was a priority for the newly professionalized organization. The national office staff began publishing *Spectra*, a quarterly newsletter about its activities and featuring news of members' activities. Hall began a directory of graduate programs, and convention abstracts were compiled into a volume. Summer conferences were established. The early ones sought to educate members on professionalizing scholarship via grantmaking, governmental affairs, and tying research and development.

The earliest major project, however, was a conference devoted to the role of communication in the speech discipline. This conference was supported by a grant from the U.S. Office of Education, and it was held in two phases. In the first phase, SAA gathered an interdisciplinary group of scholars to discuss the current state of communication scholarship. In the second phase, SAA gathered speech scholars to present position papers and discuss the role of communication in speech. I will return to a more detailed discussion of this conference and its impact later in the chapter.

1964: AEJ REVISES ITS CONSTITUTION

While research in communication had developed in both journalism and speech, it was the speech scholarly society that moved communication scholarship forward most aggressively. Journalism, on the other hand, had been wary of communication-related scholarship, perhaps because it didn't seem particularly germane to the journalist members who dominated the AEJ. So, communication scholars found other ways of presenting and discussing their work. Bowers (1977), who chronicled the eventual acceptance of theory and methodology in AEJ, traced the official start of the recognition of research to two groups. One was the Council on Communications Research, which came into being in 1950, when the American Association of Teachers of Journalism remade itself as the AEJ. This council had begun as an activity of the Association of Accredited Schools and Departments of Journalism, one of several attempts to designate a group of "top" journalism programs in the United States.

A separate group, which Bowers (1977, p. 1) called "the more important and more influential of the progenitors," was formed in 1955. It was called the Quantitative Research Group, and it held what were called "rump" sessions in conjunction with the annual AEJ meeting. The Council on Communications Research had official status in AEJ and was able to present generally one program, often a general session, on research. It also organized a number of publications of use to AEJ members. The rump sessions allowed individual scholars to present their work for colleagues. Bowers reported that scholars from four programs, at Illinois, Wisconsin, Minnesota, and Stanford, provided the basis for these sessions.

It would not be until 1964, however, before AEJ would consider making room for theory and research. The AEJ membership considered the first constitutional revision that had been proposed since the 1950 reorganization. According to the extensive minutes of the meeting (Beth, 1965), two alternative proposals for reorganization were brought by members of a task force that had been deliberating for several years. The task force members had settled on what was called Plan 2 and moved its adoption. There were adherents of Plan 1, however, but an attempt to substitute Plan 1 for Plan 2 failed.

Interestingly, Plan 2 still focused on the supremacy of journalism in AEJ going forward. John Marston, a leading public relations professor, introduced a motion to call the new organization the Association for Education in Communications. This motion was defeated. Marston then moved to amend the organization's purpose statement to read, "The purpose of the association shall be the improvement of education in the fields of mass communication such as Journalism, Advertising, Broadcasting, Public Relations, and Communications Research." This motion also lost, but by only six votes of 118 cast.

What did survive was a subsection of the purpose statement, which read "To foster research and inquiry in the field of mass communications."

Perhaps the most major change provided a process for the development of new divisions of AEJ. Bowers reported that this provision was the hallmark of Plan 2 and was not in Plan 1, so the failure of the motion to substitute Plan 1 for Plan 2 was a significant endorsement of an organizational structure that allowed for the establishment of member-driven divisions that would be formally represented in the program-planning process. The inclusion of "mass communications" as a specific goal of the association also paved the way for the establishment of a division devoted to mass communication scholarship.

That division would be called Theory and Methodology, and it would be proposed for the 1965 annual meeting. The last rump session of the Quantitative Research Group was also held in 1965.

Bowers reported that the division proposal provided for three goals: (1) development of significant communications theory; (2) production and dissemination of research of both a substantive and methodological base; and (3) application of research and theory to salient social and scholarly issues. The division, which was one of nine approved in 1965, also adopted a constitution that elaborated on the general goals: (1) improvement of education and scholarship in those areas commonly labeled journalism research, communication research, research methodology; (2) foster the development of communication theory; (3) foster the production and distribution of pertinent theoretical and methodological knowledge; and (4) foster the application of research findings and theory to teaching, to journalism practice, and to significant social and theoretical issues. (1977, p. 17)

According to Bowers, the Theory and Methodology Division quickly grew into one of the largest units within AEJ. It established a practice of presenting a "state of theory and methodology" address by the division head, and titles of the address included "On Being Comfortable in Communication Research: The Case for Taking a Fresh Look at the Process of Communication" (Jack McCleod, 1968); "Toward a Communications Discipline" (Bruce Westley, 1971); "How Much of Communication Research is Worth Knowing About?" (Peter Clarke, 1973); "Applying Social Science Methodology to News Reporting" (Maxwell McCombs, 1975); and "An Information Processing Approach to Mass Communication Research" (Dan Wackman, 1976).

1968: SAA HOSTS A CONFERENCE ON COMMUNICATION

Once William Work and Robert Hall had been hired, the SAA's national office began to plan conferences aimed at developing the membership, both in numbers and on topics that would advance the study of speech. The first was held in July 1965 and focused on how federal legislation might impact the scholarly study of speech. Conferences on the mechanics of applying for grants and on governmental relations followed (Work & Jeffrey, 1989).

A breakthrough in the conference-planning process came in 1967, when SAA was successful in obtaining a $58,000 grant from the U.S. Office of Education to support a two-event project called The Conference on Research and Instructional Development in Speech-Communication. The principal investigator for the grant was John E. Dietrich, Michigan State University, who had served as SAA president in 1959.

Dietrich got to work quickly and, with the help of an advisory commit-tee, organized an interdisciplinary colloquium that met at the Wingspread Conference Center in Racine, Wisconsin, on October 10 and 11, 1967. The advisory committee, which had been formed as part of the grant application process, deliberately represented the breadth of the membership of SAA. It consisted of J. Jeffery Auer, a rhetoric and public address specialist from Indiana University, who was also immediate past president of SAA; Samuel L. Becker, University of Iowa, a communication researcher; Theodore Clevenger, Florida State University, a communication researcher; F. Craig Johnson, Michigan State University, and former chair of SAA's Research Board; along with Executive Secretary William Work and U.S. Office of Education liaison Irving M. Brown. (Dietrich, 1968).

By the time the interdisciplinary colloquium occurred, there had already been discussions of how to account for communication in the study of speech. Apparently, the SAA Research Board had proposed using "speech-communication" as the new designator of the area of study, knowing that this formulation was somewhat controversial. The Research Board had also decided that a similar conference should be held on the status of rhetoric in speech. I shall return to the rhetoric conference later in the chapter.

The interdisciplinary colloquium featured scholars from what were considered to be cognate fields of study. The scholars presenting were: Harold B. Allen, University of Minnesota, Linguistics; Basil B. Bernstein, University of London Institute of Education, Sociolinguistics; Morton Deutsch, Columbia University, Social Psychology; Malcolm S. MacLean, University of Iowa, Journalism and Mass Communication; Herbert Menzel, New York University, Sociology; Richard S. Rudner, Washington University, Philosophy; George G. Thompson, Ohio State University, Developmental Psychology; and Wilcomb E. Washburn, Smithsonian Institution, American Studies. Members of the advisory committee received the papers about a week before the conference began and members shared responsibility for leading discussion on the papers.

The discussions were synthesized by the advisory committee, and the synthesis was used to finalize the planning for the second conference. In particular, the advisory committee used its experience with the scholars from other fields to decide on the final format for the second conference as well as which scholars to invite to that conference. In the end, twenty-four speech-communication scholars were invited as participants; a number of others were invited as observers. Four were invited to submit main papers, and eight others were asked to respond to those papers.

The advisory committee had scheduled a general session for the December 1967 SAA convention. Committee members reported on the interdisciplinary colloquium, presented preliminary plans for the conference, and took questions and comments from those in attendance. Formats for the conference sessions were finalized after processing the comments from the December session and other comments received by the advisory committee. Those attending received the four invited papers plus material on the interdisciplinary colloquium ahead of the start of the conference.

The advisory committee wished for the conference to be interactive, so little time was spent on presenting only summaries of the four papers and the brief responses. Rather, participants rotated through small discussion groups focusing on the topics of the papers, which were drawn from the presentations at the interdisciplinary colloquium: (1) language acquisition and behavior, (2) human information processing, (3) decision-making and conflict resolution, and (4) research methodologies. Time was set aside for participants to suggest other substantive areas for discussion. Discussion groups focused on (1) issues and responsibilities of the field, (2) research priorities, and (3) implications for graduate training. The participants rotated through these committees, and then selected one to join for the formal drafting process of recommendations.

The three groups produced a total of forty-six recommendations, mostly addressed to their colleagues and to the leadership of SAA. Of the recommendations, the first was undoubtedly the most significant: "Spoken symbolic interaction is the central focus of study in the speech-communication area." Essentially, this formulation was proposed to replace Woolbert's (1923) formulation of the discipline as including speaking, reading (primarily reading aloud), speech sounds, and research on the first three, what Woolbert called "speech science." In reality, the New Orleans conferees took away a focus on types of communication and refocused their colleagues on the behavior of spoken symbolic interaction. While a significant departure in terms of emphasis, it still left open the traditional forms of study that Woolbert saw as ideal.

The conferees also made two significant recommendations (and one corollary recommendation) that became crucial to my argument: they recommended (#4) that "academic units" seriously consider changing their names to include the word, "communication," and (#8) that academic units currently called "speech" reorganize themselves to implement a focus on communication scholarship. They also recommended (#3) "that the SAA consider changing its name to include the word, 'communication.'" (p. 21) The SAA membership took these recommendations, and many of the others, to heart. As I argue, changes of names of scholarly societies to include the word, "communication," became a significant marker that an academic discipline of communication was forming.

Early in the deliberations, conferees took up the research board's proposal to hyphenate "speech" and "communication" to indicate that speech was creating a hybrid form of itself that would focus on the study of spoken symbolic interaction. Some argued that "communication" was the appropriate master term, while others were adamant that "speech" should not be lost in the process. Some thought that the hyphen created more confusion than clarification. In the end, a majority agreed that "speech-communication" was the appropriate term to use, though comments were made to the effect that a broader discussion would undoubtedly resolve the hyphen issue (and did: the compound noun "speech communication" emerged as the preferred usage). One of the conference participants, Frank E. X. Dance, continued to advocate for the inclusion of "speech" with "communication" throughout his career (Dance, 2006).

The rest of the forty-six total recommendations focused on how the academic discipline of speech should remake itself to accommodate the formal addition of communication. There were suggestions about how undergraduate and graduate curricula should be structured; how research efforts in speech-communication should be mounted and with what agenda, particularly with regard to addressing social issues; and the role of SAA in developing and promoting research in speech-communication.

The 1968 New Orleans conference (and the book that reported on it: Kibler and Barker, 1968) had nearly immediate impact on speech professors. The conference findings were discussed at the 1968 SAA Summer Conference, particularly those recommendations relating to the pursuit of what became to be called "social relevance," as well as the first of many calls to diversify speech-communication. At the Summer Conference, an *ad hoc* Committee on Social Relevance was formed (Daniel, 1995). A young assistant professor at the University of Pittsburgh named Jack Daniel was asked to chair the committee.

The 1968 SAA convention was held in Chicago. At the time, SAA alternated meeting in Chicago on the last week of December with the Modern Language Association. SAA had the even years. December 1968 was a time of national turmoil, especially in Chicago, where riots had erupted at the Democratic Nominating Convention that past summer. Richard Nixon had been elected president over Hubert Humphrey but hadn't been inaugurated yet. The turmoil and uncertainty had extended to the SAA convention. A panel advertising a discussion between what was called "The Old Guard" vs. "The Young Turks" was in such demand that people crowded around the door straining to hear.

The ad hoc Committee on Social Relevance (which, according to Daniel, would later become known as the Committee on the Profession and Social Problems) had a session at the convention to present its work, and there it presented "A Manifesto to the Speech Profession" that took to task existing curricula, textbooks, graduate education, and the structure of SAA itself. Daniel described the open meeting where the committee reported as "a true 1960s 'happening'." The room was packed to capacity, and before Daniel could get far, he was interrupted first by Charles Hurst, the chair of the Speech Department at Howard University, and then by Arthur Smith, later to be known as Molefi Kete Asante. Between the two of them, the terms of the meeting became focused exclusively on Black issues, ignoring the other issues planned for discussion. Daniel called that episode the moment of conception for what would become the association's Black Caucus.

Daniel would also report (pp. 9–10) on being invited to speak at the spring 1969 convention of the Speech Association of the Eastern States, which was meeting in New York City. Daniel reported being racially harassed while with his wife in their hotel room. The next day, Daniel reported saying the following as part of the introduction to the address he had been invited to give:

Friends and enemies, I must acknowledge my enemies because anytime that I speak to an audience this large, there must be some enemies present. And given what happened while my wife and I were attempting to sleep last night, I know for certain that I have some enemies in this room. (p. 10)

The planner of the 1968 convention was Marie Hochmuth Nichols, of the University of Illinois. Nichols was the first woman elected to the SAA presidential cycle by a vote of the entire membership. She was clearly an intellectual leader, with a substantial publication record, an admired teaching record, and a recent term as the first woman Editor of *The Quarterly Journal of Speech*, the flagship journal of SAA. She managed the conference theme, "Cultural Re-Orientation," by skillfully balancing interests. One of her innovations was to restore the presidential address, which was delivered by Douglas Ehninger with the title, "Of Relevance, Relatedness, and Reorientation" (Blankenship, 2004).

Despite these successes, which were especially significant because of the turmoil in the United States, as well as within SAA, in 1968, Nichols faced anger and rejection when she delivered her 1969 presidential address. Titled, "The Tyranny of Relevance," Nichols attacked the careless use of the word, "relevance," as a bullying tactic, and she questioned the use of ideology to determine what is "relevant" and what is not.

Nichols' title was clearly incendiary, and it had that affect. Blankenship reported that

Some people came to walk out of her speech. One past president made a public point by leaving during the speech. People left the room sharply divided over what they had just heard. The name-calling was harsh and left little middle ground. People were either for or against the message. (p. 79)

Nevertheless, SAA moved forward with recommendations from the New Orleans conference. It organized a Committee on Structure in 1968, which was charged with drafting a new constitution. The committee was small: it consisted of Douglas Ehninger, the SAA president, John Dietrich, the organizer of the New Orleans Conference, and J. Jeffrey Auer, an SAA past president, along with William Work, the executive secretary. The committee had a new constitution to propose to the 1969 Legislative Assembly, and the new constitution included a new name: Speech Communication Association (no hyphen). The new constitution passed the legislative body in December 1969 and the membership by mail ballot in spring 1970. The new name became effective on July 1, 1970 (Work & Jeffrey, 1989, p. 39). The quick move by the speech association to include "communication" in its title undoubtedly sent a message to its membership that the project of convincing university colleagues to accept a redefinition of "speech" and an academic unit title that included the word, "communication," was the proper course of action.

1969: NSSC BECOMES ICA

The NSSC had, over time, struggled with its presumed identity as a subgroup of the SAA. For a while, NSSC had met at the same time as SAA, and even after NSSC developed to the point where it hosted its own meetings, the membership remained heavily overlapped with SAA. An association that was supposed to welcome in scholars from a variety of disciplines who were interested in communication consisted mostly of speech professors, according to Weaver's (1977) history, which was published as an Appendix to the first volume of *Communication Yearbook*.

Weaver indicated that an initial solution to the "speech professor" problem was to recruit industry professionals who worked in communication. There was some early success with this strategy because some of these professionals held doctorates in aspects of communication and had taken jobs other than at U.S. colleges and universities. Several of these individuals worked for the U.S. Air Force, and a series of them served as president of the NSSC. They were Kenneth Clark, in 1954; Kenneth H. Harwood, in 1956; Francis A. Cartier, in 1959; and John B. Haney, in 1962. In 1965, an internal management consultant at General Electric named Clarence J. "Mickey" Dover assumed the presidency. In 1968, Lee Thayer, another management consultant, became president. In 1969, Darrell T. Piersol, an internal consultant at IBM, became president. In the full, unpublished, version of his history, Weaver (1973) noted that it was difficult to attract non-academics to NSSC, primarily because its "study group" structure didn't fit with both the fast pace of their jobs, nor were they particularly rewarded for developing and publishing research results.

In 1967, Frank E. X. Dance became president of NSSC and oversaw a revision of the constitution and bylaws that had been going on under the leadership of second vice president George A. Sanborn. Some urgency to revise the study group structure arose from a financial crisis precipitated by a large overrun of expenses in printing a proceedings of the 1967 convention, according to Weaver's (1973) version of the history. It was clear that NSSC could no longer operate as it had been doing. Sanborn's committee was stalled on how to deal with the study groups, most of which were nonfunctional. Committee member Robert Goyer drafted a version that departed radically from the former structure. Goyer's version established four divisions in place of the study groups. Dance led the NSSC board to approve the documents, and the four divisions were established in 1968.

They met for the first time at the April 1968 convention in New York City. They were: Division 1: information systems; Division 2: interpersonal communication; Division 3: mass communication, and Division 4: organizational communication.

The new set of bylaws negated the need to include the word, "study" in the association's name. Apparently, new names had been proposed without success, but suddenly, NSSC President Goyer was announcing that the board had, at its April 1969 meeting, decided unanimously to propose a bylaws amendment to change the name to ICA (Weaver, 1973, pp. 238–241). Goyer's letter to the membership specified that several names were considered, the criteria that were used to evaluate the suggested names, and that the board had decided that the proposed name best fit the criteria. The membership needed to vote on the amendment by mail ballot, and a two-thirds vote of ballots returned was sufficient to ratify the change. The Tellers' Committee reported that the vote was 371 to 145, and NSSC became ICA.

1970: SCA SPONSORS THE NATIONAL DEVELOPMENTAL PROJECT ON RHETORIC

When the SAA Research Board began to plan what would become the New Orleans Conference, it decided that there would be a similar conference on rhetoric. Rhetorical theory served as the basis for speech instruction and speech criticism, and what were referred to as "the traditionalists" in speech tended to feel under attack as communication scholars, known, sometimes positively, sometimes negatively, as "the behaviorists," encroached further into the heart of the emerging discipline. Many swipes, jabs, and sometimes, outright hatred emerged between the two groups.

Truth be told, the study of rhetoric was undergoing its own change, at least partially in response to advances in the study of rhetoric in other disciplines. Thonssen and Baird's (1946) method of speech criticism was still being taught at the undergraduate level (I wrote one of those, in 1966, on Adlai Stevenson's 1952 presidential election campaign rhetoric), but breakthrough essays in rhetoric were published between the Research Board's promise and its actual delivery. Among those were Robert L. Scott's (1967) "On Viewing Rhetoric as Epistemic" and Lloyd Bitzer's (1968) "The Rhetorical Situation." Bitzer's article had the distinction of being the lead article in the first issue of *Philosophy and Rhetoric*, a journal begun by Henry W. Johnstone, Jr., a philosopher at Pennsylvania State University. In addition, a Canadian literary theorist named Marshall McLuhan (1964) had shaken up both scholarly and public understanding of the emerging realm of entertainment television in his book, *Understanding Media: The Extensions of Man*.

The format of The National Developmental Project on Rhetoric was simi-
lar to The Conference on Research and Instructional Development in Speech-
Communication, otherwise known as the New Orleans Conference. In both
cases, a Project Planning Committee was created. For the rhetoric conference,
the planners were Carroll C. Arnold, Pennsylvania State University, James
J. Murphy, University of California, Davis, and Gerald R. Miller, Michigan
State University, along with William Work, the SCA executive secretary, and
James Roever, the SCA director of research. There were two events in each
of 1967 and 1970, both held at the Wingspread Conference Center, in Racine,
Wisconsin. At both Wingspread events, an interdisciplinary panel of experts
presented papers and heard responses. The second event for the rhetoric
conference was held at the Pheasant Run Conference Center, in St. Charles,
Illinois. Like the New Orleans conference, the second conference participants
were speech communication scholars. These twenty-three scholars received
a report of the proceedings of the Wingspread conference and then were
charged with seeking to "refine, amplify, and translate Wingspread ideas
into recommendations meeting specific needs and potentialities related to the
humanistic study of rhetorical communication" (Bitzer & Black, 1971, p. vi).

The participants at Pheasant Run were divided into three committees: (1)
Committee on the Advancement and Refinement of Rhetorical Criticism,
(2) Committee on the Scope of Rhetoric and the Place of Rhetorical Studies
in Higher Education, and (3) Committee on the Nature of Rhetorical
Invention. The committee members met for three days and formulated
recommendations, which were then debated and voted upon by the entire
group.

The committee recommendations were many and overlapping, so Bitzer
and Black wrote a conclusion that summarized the deliberation via four
themes. The first acknowledged the rapid development of electronic media
and contended, "it is imperative that rhetorical studies be broadened to
explore communicative procedures and practices not traditionally covered"
(p. 238). In practice, this theme was taken to mean that rhetorical criticism
should be expanded to a variety of additional texts, most of them media based.

The second theme contended that "our recognition of the scope of rhetorical theory and practice should be greatly widened" (p. 238). That is, rhetorical
ideas and methods should be applied to deliberations regarding how technological advances themselves should be developed and implemented.

The third theme proposed that "a clarified and expanded concept of reason
and rational decision must be worked out" (pp. 238–239). Conferees took to
heart Professor Johnstone's Wingspread paper on how the nature of reason
had changed through the public use of shouts, obscenities, and non-negotiable
demands. Understanding reason, the conferees concluded, was a key to pre-
serve the values of a democratic society.

Fourth, the conferees strongly believed that "rhetorical invention should be restored to a position of centrality in theory and practice" (p. 239). The conferees professed to be happy about the addition of communication, and thus, the so-called "scientific method" to speech, but they worried that the world does not live by facts alone. Indeed, they thought that rhetorical invention would help "to determine relevant criteria, to form new definitions, to critique values and hierarchies of values, to bring sentiments and feelings into relation with thoughts" (pp. 239–240).

The *Prospect of Rhetoric* did not have the kind of immediate impact on SCA as did *Conceptual Frontiers in Speech-Communication*, but it did succeed in broadening scholars' awareness of what rhetoric could do beyond the Thonssen and Baird approach to speech criticism. This broadening was reflected in what was published in the 1970s going forward by rhetorical scholars and those employing other "non-scientific" methods.

Reflecting on both New Orleans and Pheasant Run, former SCA Director of Research James Roever (1974) wrote:

> I think we are at the stage where both science and humanism have been properly sanctified, at least for the moment. Those whose methodologies best serve science and the study of statements of fact and those whose methodologies best serve the humanities and statements of value—I presume that each serves equally the social sciences—have symbolically come together. Let us not continue to go over old ground and examine the recommendations of the two projects. Let us not be concerned with recommendations to guide the field for the next four or five years. Let us be guided by the next ten or the next twenty or the next thirty years for now we have acknowledged the potential blend of scientific and rhetorical approaches that should better enable us to attack those problems common to all of us. (p.10)

Looking back on Pheasant Run some fifty years later, Thomas W. Benson, *emeritus*, Pennsylvania State University, wrote:

> I believe that all the Pheasant Run participants, rhetoricians of many ages and flavors (but all men) were secure in the view that they could work happily in departments that made full accommodation to the development of social scientific approaches to the domain. Another whole generation went by before I began to hear serious talk about the need for speech-rhetoric to create alliances with English-rhetoric for the sake of survival. Trust in the alliance of rhetoric (speech) and communication had frayed somewhat—not everywhere but in enough places to create organizational strains. That perhaps is another story.
>
> In any case, as I recall it, the Pheasant Run conferees were confident about their happy relationship with the emergence of social science approaches, and

some were part of it (Herb Simons, Sam Becker). The themes of scope that most seemed to concern the Pheasant Run rhetoric conferees were broadening (1) to acknowledge and nurture and understanding of rhetorical behavior, as multi-modal, thus requiring new theories and modes of studies of a wide diversity of symbolic forms; (2) to meet the urgent demands of social unrest created as part of the Civil Rights movement, the Vietnam War, and related movements—taking rhetoric into new forms; not to do so would be to fail to meet the needs of our students and the needs of the broader society, which was under enormous strain, including attacks on First Amendment exercise of the right to protest, as especially emphasized by the killings at Kent State the week before the conference (which kept one of the conferees, Phil Tompkins, at Kent State trying to support his students and colleagues).

So these developments were not especially about the New Orleans "Speech Communication" charter, but were entirely consistent with it, as opening the discipline to new realities and understandings, and I believe were understood as such. (personal communication, March 23, 2020)

1960S AND 1970S: JOURNALS CHANGE NAMES, NEW JOURNALS BEGIN

The 1964 revision of the AEJ structure brought with it new divisions and interest groups. Some of those new units started peer-reviewed journals. Eventually, many of AEJ's divisions and interest groups would publish journals, but some moved very quickly to do so. *Journalism History* began in 1965, and the *International Communication Research Journal* began in 1966. The Newspaper Division began the *Newspaper Research Journal* in 1979. That same year, the Cultural and Critical Studies Division started the *Journal of Critical Inquiry*. Interestingly, *Journalism Quarterly*, the association's flagship journal, did not change its name until 1995, when it became *Journalism and Mass Communication Quarterly*. And, *Journalism Monographs*, another journal sponsored by the entire association, became *Journalism and Communication Monographs* in 1999. By 1982, only the International Communication Division's journal had "communication" in its title. The other AEJ journals did not.

SCA members debated how to rename their association-wide journals, *The Quarterly Journal of Speech*, *Speech Monographs*, and *Speech Teacher*. The debate resulted in two name changes. *Speech Monographs* became *Communication Monographs* and *Speech Teacher* became *Communication Education*, both in 1976. *The Quarterly Journal of Speech* retained its name and continues to be published under that name, even after the Speech Communication Association dropped "speech" from its name. SCA would start a new association-wide journal, *Text and Performance Quarterly*, in 1980. It had previously been a divisional journal, and SCA banned divisional journals after TPQ was inaugurated.

The four regional speech associations also changed the names of the journals they published. The southern association changed its journal's name from *Southern Speech Journal* to *Southern Speech Communication Journal* in 1971. It would drop "speech" from the journal name in 1988. The western association would rename its journal from *Western Speech* to *Western Speech Communication* in 1975 and would rename the journal again to *Western Journal of Speech Communication* in 1977. It would drop "speech" from the journal name in 1992. The eastern association changed its journal's name from *Today's Speech* to *Communication Quarterly* in 1976. The central association kept its journal title, *Central States Speech Journal*, until 1989, when it would be renamed as *Communication Studies*.

ICA "sold" *Journal of Communication* to the Annenberg School of Communication, University of Pennsylvania, in 1973 (Weaver, 1977). Annenberg's George Gerbner became the journal editor, and the editorial board was selected jointly by ICA and the Annenberg School. ICA members received the journal at reduced cost, and ICA received some portion of the institutional subscriptions. ICA would "buy" the journal back in 1992 and would retain full control over the journal from that point forward.

ICA would also begin two new publications in the 1970s. The first was *Human Communication Research*, which was first published in 1974. This journal initially published (1) reports of original research, (2) descriptions of methodological approaches, (3) critical synthesis of research literature, and approaches, and (4) theoretical papers (Weaver, 1977, p. 614). The second was *Communication Yearbook*, which began publication in 1977. This publication took the form of an annual volume and was designed to include: "(1) generic reviews and commentaries on theoretical and research developments of the field, (2) theory and research overviews in each of the Divisions of ICA, and (3) selected studies from each division and the Association as a whole" (Weaver, 1977, p. 614).

There were two other communication journals that were begun during this period. The first was the *Journal of Applied Communications Research*, which was started by Mark Hickson and Don Stacks when both were working at the Pentagon during the 1970s (Cissna, Eadie & Hickson, 2009). Both Hickson and Stacks had interests in communication, and both joined the Metropolitan Washington Speech Communication Association, where they were inspired by the idea of social relevance that was exciting that group's members. Both started attending ICA conventions in 1972, and in their conversations with each other, they realized that there was no journal devoted to ethnographic and participant-observation research in communication, particularly organizational communication. They used the equipment they had access to at the Pentagon to produce the initial copies of the journal, and they had best success marketing library, as opposed to individual, subscriptions, putting out two issues per year starting in 1973. By 1980, Hickson, who had assumed primary responsibility for the journal after Stacks and he left the Army, decided that it was time for a change. He placed an advertisement titled, "Journal for Sale" in SCA's newsletter, *Spectra*, and the Department of Communication at the University of South Florida bought the journal from him. The new owners dropped the "s" from "Communications" in the journal's name, and a succession of department faculty members edited it. In 1990, the department transferred ownership of *The Journal of Applied Communication Research* to SCA, where it has remained an association-wide publication.

The second journal was titled, *Women's Studies in Communication*, and it was begun under the editorship of Sandra A. Purnell by members of the Organization for Research on Women and Communication (ORWAC), an affiliate organization of the Western Speech Communication Association. The journal was begun to provide an outlet for feminist scholarship in communication, and was started, in part, because women scholars found it difficult to publish in the "mainstream" journals. Initially, the journal was regional, but as it developed, it found editors from the other regions and became national in scope. It continues to be published by ORWAC.

1975: ICA PROFESSIONALIZES

In 1975, ICA, while amid a very fertile period that included the start of new publications, a first conference outside of the United States (1973, in Montreal) and a number of initiatives generated by its five divisions, decided that it needed a staff member. A search resulted in the selection of Robert Cox as executive secretary and the acceptance of an offer from the University of Texas at Austin of some modest office space. Cox worked solo in the early years, and he helped to launch both of the new publications and to hold the first conference outside of North America (1977, in Berlin).

An anonymously written essay on the association's history that appears on the ICA website (International Communication Association, 2020) described this period in ICA's history as one of relative stability but also one of frustration regarding the achievement of goals for internationalization. The membership remained primarily based in the United States, and the number of members varied depending primarily on whether individual members planned to present research at the annual convention. Attendance at conventions varied, with international conventions drawing the fewest people (though, sometimes attracting significant numbers of scholars from the region, which may well have contributed to long-range growth of communication as a discipline internationally).

1981–1982: AEJ PROFESSIONALIZES
AND CHANGES NAME

In 1981, the AEJ hired its first professional staff members, including Jennifer McGill, who would become the long-serving executive director. In 1982, the association voted to add "and Mass Communication" to its name, prompting one former president to comment that the addition was "way too long in coming." AEJMC remained in Columbia, South Carolina, home of the University of South Carolina, where it was based for years. In 1999, AEJMC purchased an office complex that would continue to serve its needs into the future.

SUMMARY: 1964–1982

My argument here is that communication developed as an academic discipline in the United States because of specific actions taken by staff and members of the three major scholarly societies in journalism and speech: the AEJ, the SAA, and the NSSC.

AEJ's 1964 revision of its constitution and bylaws marks the beginning of this period, and while the inclusion of "communications" in the name of AEJ was rejected, the action opened the way for mass communication scholars to become an official part of the AEJ organization. The ability to interact at AEJ-sponsored meetings, to develop specialized divisions and interest groups, and to start division-based scholarly journals undoubtedly led to the advancement of mass communication and media studies scholarship in academic journalism units throughout the United States AEJ did not professionalize until 1981, which undoubtedly held back its advancement as a scholarly society. While it revised its name in 1982 to include "and mass communication," its association-wide journals did not include "mass communication" in their names until the 1990s. Many of the divisional and interest group journals focused on more specialized topics and did not include the word, "communication," in their titles. All in all, the membership of AEJ became accustomed to the inclusion of mass communication scholars, but there remained a strong culture that "this is a scholarly society focused on journalism."

SAA professionalized in 1963, and by doing so generated a major project to bring communication into the speech discipline explicitly and oversee planning for the intellectual and curricular development of the rhetorical studies part of speech. The "big tent" of speech was covering fewer and fewer, as both theater and speech pathology and audiology were departing to their own scholarly societies. Consequently, the SAA leadership was very supportive of the development of communication as an area not only of interest to its members but also to the growth—and, in some case, survival—of speech as an area of study in U.S. colleges and universities. The New Orleans conference, led by volunteer members but supported by professional staff, had an enormous influence on the speech field, and SAA members responded quickly to add "communication" to curricula and names of college and university departments, schools, and colleges. The membership also acted quickly, as well, to change the SAA name to Speech Communication Association. Revisions to journal names followed, and the four independent regional associations also followed SCA's lead, some quicker than others. It is interesting that the middle part of the United States, where speech education was initially centered, was the slowest to incorporate "communication" into its association and journal title. Curricular recommendations generated from both the New Orleans and Pheasant Run conferences worked their ways into graduate and undergraduate curricula during the 1970s. By 1982, speech communication departments were poised for a large influx of students who would become majors during the 1980s.

NSSC's membership overlapped considerably with SAA, but it could take credit for starting the movement within speech toward communication scholarship. It could also take credit for starting the *Journal of Communication*, which, across its history, has never needed to change its name. If the "study section" organization of NSSC was a failure, enough members stayed engaged to figure out a way forward, with more traditional divisions and a shift to an international focus via the name change to ICA. Interestingly enough, two things from ICA's history may have brought speech communication and mass communication scholars closer together. One was that there was a mass communication division in the ICA structure from the beginning. The other was that the *Journal of Communication* was operated by the Annenberg School of Communication at the University of Pennsylvania for a considerable period, and George Gerbner, the school's dean and a well-known mass communication scholar, edited the journal during its entire tenure at his university. Gerbner's reputation not only attracted submissions from mass communication scholars, but the quality of what Gerbner published attracted submissions from across not only "journalism" and "speech" but from disciplines where some scholars maintained an interest in conducting communication research. Indeed, these developments helped ICA toward its goal of attracting an interdisciplinary group of scholars as members—or if not as members, then as submitters to *Journal of Communication*. ICA's professionalization was the result of a greater emphasis on the international mission and the realization that volunteer members couldn't do the work that was needed in that area.

By 1982, there was enough of a critical mass of academic units with "communication" in their names to claim a shift toward communication by both "journalism" and "speech," though the claim was more tenuous for the former than for the latter. With that critical mass, an academic discipline of communication had been formed, though clearly additional development would be needed to establish the credibility of this new discipline.

There were also strands of scholarship that emerged or were reinforced during the mid-1960s through the early 1980s. I have given these strands my own names; these were not the names in use during that period. My contention here is that these strands of scholarship began outside of "speech," "journalism," or "communication," but they were built upon by those who would come to identify with a discipline of communication.

As I laid out in chapter 1, I've given the following names to these five strands: (1) *Communication as Shaper of Individual and Public Opinion*; (2) *Communication as Language Use*; (3) *Communication as Information Transmission*; (4) *Communication as Developer of Relationships*; and (5) *Communication as Definer, Interpreter, and Critic of Culture*. In chapters 4–8, I will provide more detail regarding each of these strands, including examples of scholarship published in communication journals during this period.

REFERENCES

Berelson, B. (1959). The state of communication research. *Public Opinion Quarterly, 23*, 1–17. doi:10.1086/266840

Berlo, D. K. (1960). *The Process of Communication*. New York: Holt, Rinehart and Winston.

Beth, E. F. (1965). Official minutes of the 1964 convention, Association for Education in Journalism. *Journalism Quarterly, 42*, 149–160. doi:10.1177/107769906504200122

Bitzer, L. F. (1968). The rhetorical situation. *Philosophy & Rhetoric, 1*, 1–14.

Bitzer, L. F. & Black, E. (eds.) (1971). *The Prospect of Rhetoric: Report of the National Development Project*. Englewood Cliffs, NJ: Prentice-Hall.

Blankenship, J. (2004). Marie Hochmuth Nichols (1908-1978): A retrospective. *Review of Communication, 4*(1/2), 75–85. doi:10.1080/1535859042000250295

Bowers, T. A. (1977, August). *A history of the Division of Communication Theory and Methodology of the Association for Education in Journalism*. Presented at the annual meeting of the Association for Education in Journalism, Madison, Wisconsin.

Cissna, K. N., Eadie, W. F. & Hickson, III, M. (2009). The development of applied communication research. In Frey, L. R. & Cissna, K. N. (eds.), *Routledge Handbook of Applied Communication Research* (pp. 3–25). New York: Routledge.

Dance, F. X. (2006). Frank E. X. Dance, 1982 President, National Communication
    Association. *Review of Communication, 6,* 221–227. doi:10.1080/15358590
    600918714

Daniel, J. L. (1995). *Changing the Players and the Game: A Personal Account of
    the Speech Communication Association Black Caucus Origins.* Annandale, VA:
    Speech Communication Association.

Dietrich, J. E. (1968). Conference background and procedures. In Kibler, R. J. &
    Barker, L. L. (eds.), *Conceptual Frontiers in Speech-Communication* (pp. 3–15).
    New York: Speech Association of America.

International Communication Association (2020, March 27) *History.* https://www
    .icahdq.org/page/History

Kibler, R. J. & Barker, L. L. (1968). *Conceptual Frontiers in Speech Communication:
    Report on the New Orleans Conference on Research and Instructional Development.*
    Annandale, VA: Speech Association of America.

McLuhan, M. (1964). *Understanding Media: The Extensions of Man.* New York:
    McGraw-Hill.

Roever, J. E. (1974). New Orleans, Wingspread, and Pheasant Run briefly revisited.
    Western Speech, 38(1), 7–12. doi:10.1080/10570317409373803

Scott, R. L. (1967). On viewing rhetoric as epistemic. *Central States Speech Journal,
    18,* 9–17. doi:10.1080/10510976709362856

Smith, D. H. (1972). Communication research and the idea of process, *Speech
    Monographs, 39,* 174–182. doi:10.1080/03637757209375755

Thonssen, L. & Baird, A. C. (1948). *Speech Criticism: The Development of Standards
    for Rhetorical Appraisal.* New York: Ronald Press Company.

Weaver, C. H. (1973). *History of the International Communication: The First
    Twenty-Three Years.* Unpublished Manuscript, Ohio University. Currently held by
    the International Communication Association, 1500 21st Street, NW, Washington,
    DC 20036 USA.

Weaver, C. H. (1977). A history of the International Communication Association. In
    Ruben, B. D. (ed.), *Communication Yearbook I* (pp. 607–618). New Brunswick,
    NJ: Transaction Books.

Work, W. & Jeffrey, R. C. (1989). Historical notes: The Speech Communication
    Association, 1965-1989. In Work, W. & Jeffrey, R. C. (eds.), *The Past is Prologue:
    The 75th Anniversary Publication of the Speech Communication Association* (pp.
    39–67). Annandale, VA: Speech Communication Association.

Chapter 4

Communication as the Formation and Change of Individual and Public Opinion

So far, I have described the basis for considering communication as an academic discipline. I have traced three histories of this discipline: a journalism history, a speech history, and an interdisciplinary communication history, driven primarily by individual scholars who were interested in some aspect of communication study. I have also laid out a series of events occurring between 1964 and 1982 where speech and journalism took on "communication" as a basic concept for both curriculum and scholarship.

While it is evident that individual academic units worked during this period to focus curricular offerings on communication, as well as to add the word "communication" to their titles, it is beyond the scope of my argument to detail the progress of those changes. Rather, I contended that the process was aided by the three major scholarly societies that came to be identified with communication: The Association for Education in Journalism and Mass Communication, the National Communication Association, and the International Communication Association. These activities intensified as each association moved from volunteer to professional staffing, but level of enthusiasm of the membership for communication study drove both the professional and volunteer efforts. Speech was clearly more enthusiastic than journalism, though speech scholars exhibited a broader scope of interests in communication, while journalism scholars focused on a narrower range of mass communication study and made more scholarly progress as a result.

I have contended that five strands of communication scholarship were evident between 1964 and 1982, some more evident than others. Each strand has roots in scholarly work that was done in communication by the individual and teams of scholars who became interested in particular issues. I have organized the strands roughly in the order as the work on each developed. Speech and mass communication scholars continued and expanded the work in each area, and their work on these strands has continued to serve as a basis for the discipline.

There is overlap in the content areas of these strands. One of the strands, information transmission, might purport to explain any findings from most or all the others. Most importantly, each strand differs in terms of how it might define "communication" and how it might judge what is "effective communication." While this diversity of definitions bothered Dance and Larson (1976) in their early attempt at theorizing communication, I am convinced that the lack of agreement about the definition of the core concept is actually a strength. Communication, it turns out, is a rich concept that can be approached productively from a number of different perspectives. We may worry, as did Craig (1999), that these differences work to create "silos" where scholars of one strand of communication have little or nothing to say to scholars of another strand, but I would contend that those who try to understand the work of another strand will find their own scholarship to be enriched more than confused.

In the five chapters that follow, I will outline the scholarship that led to the work that was done on that chapter's strand, and I will describe examples of the major work that was done between 1964 and 1982 on the strand. My intent here is not to provide a review of the literature for each strand during this period, as doing so would quickly prove to be dated. I will instead provide examples of the ways in which communication scholars advanced the work of others from a specifically communication perspective.

PUBLIC OPINION

As I summarized in chapter 2, the advent of electronic media spurred scholarly interest in how those media would affect audiences. The development of media such as film and radio would come to have a substantial impact on the populace, particularly those in urban areas. Frazier and Gauziano (1979) credited University of Chicago sociologist Robert Park as "a founder of the sociological study of mass communication and public opinion and the field's first theorist" (p. 5). Park, who at one point worked as a journalist, saw news as a basis for public discussion, as well as social control, a concept that would become important in the 1960s and 1970s.

Walter Lippmann, another journalist, wrote *Public Opinion* (1922), which was considered the pre-eminent book on the topic for many years. Lippmann wrote that we rely on news to help us interpret the complicated environment in which we live. Because news gathering and presentation is subject to stereotypes and self-censorship, as well as susceptible to manipulation of facts by others, public opinion can be shaped both by a process Lippmann called the "manufacture of consent." This process can be influenced both by truthful reporting and by propaganda.

I have already discussed how Paul Lazarsfeld and associates studied propaganda extensively from the 1930s onward, as well as how this research established the two-step flow theory of mass communication, which states that not everyone pays close attention to the news but those who do become opinion leaders for those who don't. Opinion leaders filter news reports, form opinions, and influence others through personal persuasion. There was a substantial amount of work on this theory in the 1940s and 1950s, and that work was summarized by Klapper (1960). Klapper concluded that media have minimal direct effects on individuals' attitudes and opinions, serving more to reinforce what others already think. Klapper's book seemed to settle the issue of media effects until two additional developments cast doubt on the efficacy of the minimal effects theory.

MEDIA AND AGENDA SETTING

As mass communication scholars in journalism programs carried on research on how media influence individual and corporate attitudes, an empirical study of the 1968 U.S. election provided new findings regarding media influence. These findings would lead to a revision of existing theory that would become a dominant model for continued research.

These findings were detailed in McCombs and Shaw's (1972) article, "The Agenda Setting Function of Mass Media." After collecting data during the 1968 presidential campaign, the authors were able to conclude that there was a very high correlation between the major issues covered by news media and what undecided voters perceived were the major issues in the campaign. The voters were not simply parroting news media coverage, however. McCombs and Shaw wrote, "while the three presidential candidates [Hubert Humphrey, Richard Nixon, and George Wallace] placed widely different emphasis upon different issues, the judgments of the voters seemed to reflect the *composite* of the mass media coverage" (p. 181). This interest in constructing the composite of mass media coverage led to the oft-repeated formulation, originally attributed to Bernard Cohen (1963), "the press may not be successful much of the time in telling people what to think, but it is stunningly successful in telling its readers what to think about" (p. 13).

Thus, while McCombs and Shaw acknowledged that voters were influenced by opinion leaders, as well as by casual conversations, at least those who were undecided not only sought out news coverage but were directly influenced by that news coverage.

Agenda-setting quickly became a well-researched theory, and in a way, it put mass communication scholarship "on the map" in terms of public opinion research. The 1970s brought several replications of McCombs and Shaw's study (Funkhouser, 1973; Shaw & McCombs, 1977; Palmgreen & Clarke, 1977), and by 1981, longitudinal studies began to appear (Winter & Eyal, 1981). Agenda-setting did what a good theory should do: it explained actual events in insightful ways, and it predicted future events, at least to some degree.

MEDIA AND CULTIVATION

Cultivation analysis is a broader theory of media effects than it is a theory of public opinion. In fact, it might be called a theory of media effects, generally, which could include the formation and change of both individual and public opinion.

Cultivation originally arose from attempts to account for how violence influenced mass audiences, and it, too, was, in part, a response to Klapper's minimal effects hypothesis. Focusing on television, the predominant electronic medium of the 1960s and 1970s, cultivation begins by positing that television had become not only ubiquitous but was serving as society's storyteller. In order to compete for a mass audience, television employed a common set of patterns and images, which, in turn, influenced how viewers understood the stories. The fact that, during this time, there was a limited selection of national programming, so that programming had to aim at the broadest possible audience. In doing so, television storytelling promulgated a set of what were called "cultural indicators" (Gerbner & Gross, 1976) that could cue audience reactions.

A cultural indicators analysis typically begins with content analysis of television programming, with the goal of finding images that are used repetitively and over time. This work is designed to yield hypotheses about viewers' attitudes, opinions, and behaviors, and these hypotheses are then tested through survey construction and administration. Surveys may be designed to yield what the "television answer" might be to certain questions, as well as discerning any differences in demographic or behavioral patterns of television watching. What television "cultivates" is an established social order, what theorists working from other perspectives would call "hegemony."

Gerbner and Gross (1976) published a definitive report on ten years of work on violence in television programming. The research team initially developed and kept refining a Violence Index for television programs. Eventually, the team concluded that "television is essentially different from other media and that research on television requires a new approach" (p. 174).

That new approach incorporated how television "cultivates" its viewers, providing meaning beyond what one might expect from simple exposure to violence.

Rejecting simple measures of attitude or behavioral change, Gerbner and Gross contended, "The substance of the consciousness cultivated by TV is not so much specific attitudes and opinions as more basic assumptions about the 'facts' of life and standards of judgment on which conclusions are based" (p. 175). Rather, they wrote,

> As any mythical world, television presents a selective and functional system of messages. Its time, space, and motion-even its 'accidents'-follow laws of dramatic convention and social utility. Its people are not born but are created to depict social types, causes, powers, and fates. The economics of the assembly line and the requirement of wide acceptability assure general adherence to common notions of justice and fair play, clear-cut characterizations, tested plot lines, and proven formulas for resolving all issues. (p. 182)

To draw appropriate conclusions requires not short-term experiments, the authors argued, but large datasets collected over time. Analysis focused on the context of the programming examined, including genre and the major and minor characters involved, measures of violence, as developed and honed over time, and insights about cultural indicators.

Findings indicated that violence episodes have a remarkable similarity within the context of the storyline. There is also stability over time regarding who perpetrates the violence and who is the victim of it.

The remarkable finding, however, was that there were significant differences between "heavy" viewers of television (four or more hours per day) as opposed to "light" viewers (two hours a day or fewer). Heavier viewers are more likely to provide the "television answers" to survey questions about the situation, particularly the ones about how much television programming reflected reality. These differences can be moderated by education level and regular newspaper readership. But, the differences persisted even with these moderators, just not at as extreme a level.

So, the authors concluded, television viewing cultivates a perception of social reality that influences individual opinions, and, collectively, public opinion. This contribution was made explicit by Gerbner's research team (Gerbner et al., 1982).

Like agenda-setting, cultivation became a major theory that was commonly researched by mass communication scholars. The Gerbner team continued to publish the major advancements through the 1982 cut-off date for this chapter (c. f., Gerbner et al., 1979, 1980, 1981; Morgan, 1982; Signorielli, 1982). A few other researchers offered comments and alternate perspectives on the theory (c.f., Hughes, 1980; Hawkins & Pingree, 1981). A greater variety of scholars would become involved in cultivation research as the 1980s progressed.

PERSUASION RESEARCH AND THE FORMATION
AND CHANGE OF INDIVIDUAL ATTITUDES

Speech scholars became interested in social science approaches to both speech and communication following the close of World War II, and they were aware of the developments in other disciplines on topics of traditional interest, including ability to persuade in a face-to-face setting and the dynamics of interacting with others, even when overt influence was not the goal. Speech scholars followed the work of the Yale Program in Communication and Attitude Change. The publication of Berlo's *The Process of Communication* provided a working model of dimensions for speech scholars to conduct social sciences research, even if Berlo had cautioned against taking his model as anything other than a conceptual framework.

Even so, it was convenient to tease out individual effects of sources, messages, and channels on receivers, as long as one also examined how the various elements worked together to form a process. But, at the beginning at least, focusing on one aspect of the process seemed to be somehow "cleaner." I will focus this section on three scholars who engaged face-to-face persuasion in major ways: James C. McCroskey, Dale Hample, and Gerald R. Miller.

LEADING RESEARCHERS IN PERSUASION

James McCroskey was one of the leading researchers to examine the individual parts of the Berlo model (Levine & Park, 2017). He was one of the early speech scholars to publish persuasion research, with titles such as "Scales for the Measurement of Ethos" (McCroskey, 1966), "The Credibility of Reluctant Testimony" (Arnold & McCroskey, 1967), and "A Summary of Experimental Research on the Effects of Evidence in Persuasive Communication" (McCroskey, 1969).

"Scales for the Measurement of Ethos" set a pattern for McCroskey's scholarship. Whenever McCroskey would develop an interest in a particular concept, he would set about creating one or more measures for that concept. He would develop a set of potential items and hone them to create a questionnaire that would fit the theoretical components of that concept. He would then administer his items to a large number of respondents, often manipulating the description that the respondents would read so that ratings would be variable. In the case of ethos, McCroskey relied on Aristotle's description of the term as characteristics of the source that would contribute to persuasion of the receivers. In this case, McCroskey would invent a source that would be seen by his student subjects as having high levels of ethos and another source that would have low levels of ethos. Sometimes, he would also invent a source whose levels of ethos would fall between the high and low source.

For the 1966 report, McCroskey conducted seven experiments, each time analyzing the quantitative data he collected. His experiments yielded several scales that might be used to measure ethos, or "source credibility," as McCroskey would later call the concept. His analyses yielded a major dimension McCroskey called "authoritativeness," and a secondary dimension he labeled "character." The establishment of scales would set in motion a series of studies, many conducted by McCroskey and his students, qualifying the dimensions of source credibility and the workings of this concept in public-speaking situations.

"The Credibility of Reluctant Testimony" was an early example of this kind of study. Arnold and McCroskey reviewed textbook advice about the use the opinions of others to bolster a speaker's claims and concluded that, while unbiased sources might seem best, sources that seem to speak against their best interests might be better. There was no research to warrant theorizing, however, so the authors started with a question about the conditions under which "testimony" might be considered to help or hurt the credibility of speakers' claims.

Arnold and McCroskey conducted two studies of similar design to generate answers to their question. In both studies, student respondents read either a pro-labor or an anti-labor message that was attributed to sources that the researchers considered to be pro-labor, anti-labor, or unbiased. Students were asked to rate the authoritativeness and character of the source, based on the message. The ratings they generated indicated that the unbiased and reluctant sources scored higher than the biased source on both authoritativeness and character, but the unbiased source was rated higher than the reluctant source only on the character dimension. The second study replicated the first one with more respondents and some minor design revisions. In this study, the unbiased source was rated higher than the reluctant source, who, in turn, was rated higher than the biased source on the authoritativeness dimension, while there were no differences on the character dimension.

Based on these two studies, the authors concluded that both unbiased and reluctant sources were superior in evincing judgments of authoritativeness but that the potential of enhanced credibility for reluctant sources was not supported. The results on judgments of character were mixed at best.

McCroskey would go on to conduct hundreds of studies on various aspects of persuasion, including message characteristics. He summarized some of that early work in a 1969 article published in *The Quarterly Journal of Speech.*

"A Summary of Experimental Research on the Effects of Evidence in Persuasive Communication" (McCroskey, 1969) reviewed twenty-two studies on the effects of good-quality evidence on audience attitude change, of which thirteen were conducted by McCroskey and his associates. Starting from the other nine studies, McCroskey identified a pattern of weak to non-existent associations between use of evidence in a persuasive speech and audience attitude change. He went on to identify and report data on several reasons why evidence might not matter.

First, following on the work he did with Arnold, evidence must be perceived by the audience to be unbiased, part of which is contained in audience judgments of the quality of the source of the evidence and part of which is generated by audience judgments of the insight the evidence provides. Indeed, evidence with which the audience is already familiar often has little to no effect on its persuasibility.

Second, audience perceptions of the speaker interact with its perception of the evidence. If a speaker already has high credibility with the audience, judgments of the quality of evidence seem not to matter much. A speaker who does not initially have high credibility, however, can use quality evidence to gain credibility with the audience.

Third, speakers can damage the judgment of the quality of evidence, through poor speaking abilities or bad speaking habits. Audiences who lose interest in the speech also don't attend to the evidence being presented.

But, even a judgment of quality evidence may not produce immediate attitude change unless the speech is well presented and the audience judges both the speaker's position and the evidence presented as new and insightful. Over time, however, judgments of the quality of the speaker's performance seem to become less important, and the quality of the evidence can lead to a greater acceptance of the speaker's advocated position.

Dale Hample was influenced by McCroskey's work on evidence while he was a graduate student. He focused his doctoral dissertation on exploring argumentation as a cognitive activity, building models of the effectiveness of arguments based on the work of psychological theorists and testing them by gathering and analyzing quantitative data. Hample published a series of these studies (1977, 1978, 1979, 1981) that were characterized by similar methods as well as by the kind of theory-building that they accomplished. At a time when nascent communication scholarship started with a set of variables and little to no theory, Hample's work was clearly a model of the kind of quantitative scholarship that could gain respect among speech communication scholars, as well as others interested in the study of argumentation, many of them European scholars from other disciplines.

Hample's project took psychological theories of belief change, reduced them to mathematical models, and created messages that he could present to student respondents in a form where he could measure and analyze their reactions quantitatively. Each of his studies featured a similar method, and each built on the others.

The initial study (1977), titled, "Testing a Model of Value Argument and Evidence," was based on Hample's dissertation research. The theories tested were those of Fishbein (1967), McGuire (1960), and Wyer (1974). Hample hypothesized that each of the theories would predict "adherence to the claims and warrants" of the argument. He also hypothesized that prediction would improve on the second measurement, with salient topics, with salient evidence, and with multiple arguments in the message. Finally, he hypothesized that amount of attitude change would graph as curvilinear.

Hample generated from a sample of students two salient topics (inflation and the job market) and constructed arguments using beliefs about these topics that the student sample generated. He presented messages containing the arguments to another group of students, while a control group responded only to the scales he constructed to measure opinions about the beliefs presented in the messages. He administered the scales a second time a week later. Results indicated that the formulation of the Fishbein theory did not predict adherence adequately, while the McGuire formulations predicted adherence to claims adequately but not adequately for warrants on the first administration. The predictions for claims held steady for the second administration, and the warrant predictions did not improve. The Wyer formulations predicted adherence to claims and warrants only marginally on the first administration, but prediction levels improved for both claims and warrants on the second administration. Topic and evidence saliency did not improve prediction for any of the theories tested.

In 1978, Hample tackled the problem of evidence head on by publishing the second in his series, titled "Predicting Immediate Belief Change and Adherence to Argument Claims." Rather than define evidence as had been traditional, Hample (1978) made certain that the use of evidence was interwoven with argument, and he measured the predictive power of what he called "probative force," the measurements he created for the previous study. Again, he used the McGuire and Wyer theories, but not Fishbein, as his previous research had shown it to predict adherence to neither claims nor warrants adequately.

The method was modified slightly as well. Instead of employing an immediate post-test and a delayed post-test, he used a pre-test/post-test model. The topics for the arguments were the job market, which had been used in the first study, and additionally bike paths and tenant rights. The statistical model attempted to predict belief change pre-test to post-test, as well as belief in the claim that was being made by the argument. Student participants in the control condition took only the pre-test and the post-test but did not read the argument. Participants were in the experimental condition for two of the three arguments and in the control condition for one of the arguments.

Results indicated that the predictive models did reasonably well at predicting belief change and adherence to the claim in the experimental conditions and less well in the control condition. Evidence played a substantial role in predicting both belief change and less of a role in adherence, though arguably adherence might have been predicted better had a delayed post-test been administered. The three topics produced different weights of the predictor variables, though, indicating that these predictors were not universal in their power but would vary from argument to argument. In this study, the McGuire model did somewhat better at prediction than the Wyer model. Hample suggested that the different topics may have hindered the effectiveness of the Wyer model.

Hample's 1979 study, titled, "Predicting Belief and Belief Change Using a Cognitive Theory of Argument and Evidence," set out to fix the problems encountered in the previous study. Hampel (1979) replicated the study using a larger sample and adding a delayed post-test to measure belief change over time. His results found that probative force, the measure of the combined effects of arguments interwoven with evidence, was an excellent predictor of belief change and could also predict adherence, especially over time, given that the other predictors, related to the salience of the argument to each respondent, could be loaded into a stepwise multiple regression.

Hample's final study in this series (1981), titled "The Cognitive Context of Argument," attempted to elaborate on the salience elements of the prediction model. Replicating, with improvements, his previous study, Hampel refined his message salience measurements and his methods so that his control group could be used to claim that the three experimental messages produced belief change. Salience of the argument was able to predict some magnitude of belief change, but the student respondents put the most weight on judgments of the quality of the argument and evidence and less weight on previously held opinions about the general topics of the arguments they read.

In 1980, Hample published a theoretical description of the work he had been doing. Titled "A Cognitive View of Argument," it was published in a journal whose readership was heavily invested in teaching and coaching competitive debate. Hample presented his "view" as a different way of looking at argumentation, and he was careful to state that he was not calling for the substitution of his perspective for traditional ways of understanding the topic.

Hample's (1980) "cognitive view" centered argument in the minds of receivers rather than in messages and evidence that could be found in public statements and whose texts could be analyzed and critiqued. He regarded those elements as means by which receivers would construct their own arguments about a topic, evaluating claims, warrants, and quality of support in the process. Receivers filtered their perceptions through what Hample labeled as "schemata," and these filters served to create order and coherence among elements and establish a baseline for judging what does and does not count as consistency. He identified three types of consistency: evaluative consistency, probabilistic consistency, and semantic consistency, and he stipulated that these three types overlap as they function to manage beliefs and arguments regarding those beliefs. Hample then detailed the mathematical formulations for each kind of consistency, consistent with the theories of Maguire and Wyer that had guided his empirical research. Hample concluded by reiterating,

My purpose here has not been to refute other common views of argument. Thinking of argument as being rhetoric, or social control, or interpersonal relationship is useful, and I have no wish to see those perspectives abandoned. I only hope to add another to the list. To view argumentation as cognitive belief-processing, as I do, opens a well-developed research tradition to us. We can add to our understanding of how choices are made, how values are related to purpose, how people create and move through their worlds. (p. 158)

Hample would continue to do this work throughout his career.

In 2016, he had an opportunity to provide a perspective on it, and here are excerpts of what he concluded:

Much of our research was originally stimulated by external work done in psychology, but it remains distinct from the studies done in social and cognitive psychology . . . Cognitive scientists are interested in how people approach deductive (or inductive, abductive, and causal) reasoning problems, but those problems are ordinarily presented in schematic ways without the idiosyncrasy or flourish that give color to actual interactions. These researchers sanitize the people out of the arguments . . . The social psychological approach to persuasion focuses largely on the internal cognitive or attitudinal processes of a single message recipient. Questions surrounding the producer (and even the production) of persuasive messages are rarely raised, and even the descriptions of the persuasive messages are often frustratingly vague. It is quite rare for a psychologist to describe the evidence and arguments that were used in persuasive stimuli, or to do any systematic manipulation of these argument features. Nonetheless, we continue to study this work with profit, and have recently added evolutionary

psychology to our reading lists . . . Our distinctiveness derives from our commitment to the idea that "arguments are in people," to quote Brockriede. This
leads to our simultaneous study of content and person, supplemented by our
understanding that both are contextualized within situations and phases of both
personal and relational development. (Hample, 2016, p. 269)

Gerald Miller was also one of the early speech scholars who researched
persuasion. While he was a fine researcher, a major strength of his as a
scholar lay in summarizing, critiquing, and articulating insights about the
work that he and others had done, including a review of research on the logical validity of arguments (Miller, 1969) that provided a basis for Hample's
scholarship. It was no accident that he was selected as the first editor of
the ICA journal, *Human Communication Research*, as those duties coin-
cided with his strengths. I will summarize two of Miller's review essays:
"Communication and Persuasion Research: Current Problems and Prospects"
(Miller, 1968) and "Persuasion research: Review and commentary" (Miller
& Burgoon, 1978).

Miller (1968) began his review by acknowledging the pioneering work
of Carl Hovland and his associates. Miller found three qualities worth noting about this work: (1) much of the Hovland group's early work focused
on interpersonal influence, using the SMCR (Source, Message, Channel
Receiver) model that Berlo (1960) had famously presented; (2) the early work
by Hovland and associates focused on manipulating a single variable, typically the source or the message, to see what effect it had on the receiver; and
(3) this early research typically relied on what Miller called "captive audiences," typically students or military recruits who did not have much choice
about participating in the research, and thus provided data under conditions
of "forced exposure."

Moving beyond this early work, Miller acknowledged the rise of cognitive
consistency theories, which affected research other than persuasion as well.
He outlined bodies of research that went beyond the initial Hovland work,
including self-persuasion, where the source's opinion changes after publicly
advocating for another position; overheard conversations, which presumably
have no persuasive intent; and immunization research, the study of what
inhibits persuasion, rather than what facilitates it.

Advances in research design and statistical analysis also allowed persuasive communication scholarship to become more sophisticated. Miller
pointed to refinements in one-sided versus two-sided arguments and how fear
appeals interact with qualities of the source to moderate the generalities about
the use of fear in messaging that the early Hovland research had promulgated.

Miller went on to select two areas of research for more detailed focus.
He looked at the concept of selective exposure, where cognitive consistency

theories would predict that individuals would avoid inconsistency by seeking out messages that agreed with already-held beliefs. Noting that this idea had yielded inconsistent research results, Miller offered an alternative explanation, drawing on Berlyne's (1960) work on a "curiosity motive" that could potentially override a desire to avoid cognitive inconsistency. He also offered what would later be called "counterattitudinal advocacy," where speakers may be induced to speak against their previously articulated positions, resulting in either a rationale for resolving inconsistency ("I was asked to speak on this position") or opinion change as a result of self-persuasion.

Elaborating on the phenomenon of self-persuasion, Miller outlined three competing positions in the social psychology literature on how and why self-persuasion occurs. These positions, labeled "justification," "learning-incentive," and "self-perception," were personified by the now familiar $1/$20 series of experiments where students received payment to tell other students that an assigned boring task was actually interesting.

Concluding with the questions, "How can we know that our results reflect actual effects and not some artifact of the research situation," and "How can we assure that what we measure as belief or opinion change will be reflected in behavior change," Miller offered his opinion that communication and persuasion research was "still in an embryonic stage" but also that "neither intellectual interest nor scientific manpower [sic] is lacking" (1968, p. 276).

Ten years later, Miller and his co-author, Michael Burgoon (1978), revisited the state of persuasion research in a review essay published in ICA's *Communication Yearbook*. Oddly enough, the review began with a provocative question: "Can a persuasive case currently be made for persuasion research?"

The evidence for the panicked tone of the teaser question emanated from researchers in social psychology having abandoned cognitive consistency in favor of other master theories of human behavior. But there had also been a revolt against the kinds of experimentation that had dominated the 1960s. Deception of research subjects was out. Scholarship that tore through variables in pursuit of vita-building, as opposed to theory-building, had been criticized. Some of that sort of scholarship was even offensive: one male-led study investigated the effect that female breast size would have on speaker credibility.

Miller and Burgoon identified four research practices that they believed had made persuasion research "'out-of-sync' with its relevant scholarly community" (p. 31). The first was "persuasion as a linear, unidirectional communicative activity." This perspective tells only part of the story and ignores how parties typically influence each other reciprocally. It also privileges the potential power of the persuader, and even though corporations or political campaigns may spend a good deal of money on persuasive campaigns, such campaigns may well be resisted and thus unsuccessful.

The second practice was "persuasion as a one-to-many communicative activity" (p. 32). While many traditional persuasion experiments presented messages to respondents as if they were part of a mass audience, research done in this manner ignores the effects of others on public-speaking or media audiences. In the time since Miller's 1968 review, there had been many studies conducted of interpersonal influence, but typically they were not labeled as "persuasion," but instead as "negotiation," "bargaining," or "conflict management."

The third practice was "persuasion as an action-centered or issue-centered activity" (p. 33). While a number of studies focused on promotion of healthy behaviors, such as smoking cessation or seatbelt wearing, Miller and Burgoon argued that persuaders most often "sell themselves" to others, as opposed to actions that are "good for you" in some way. Once again, though, studies of this kind of influence had come to fall under rubrics such as "interpersonal attraction" and "social desirability."

The fourth practice was "persuasion as an attitude change-centered activity" (p. 34). While much persuasion research focused on achieving attitude change, in the short or long term, there has always also been much evidence that attitude change does not always equate to behavior change. In fact, Fishbein and Ajzen's (1975) work had succeeded in shifting focus of such work to beliefs and intentions to behave as equal or better predictors of shifts in behavior.

Miller and Burgoon labeled these four "out-of-sync" practices as yielding "an impoverished view" of persuasion research. As an alternative, they proposed what they called "an expanded view" of the persuasion process.

This expanded view focused more on how individuals manage themselves, others, their environments, and other situational factors to achieve desired outcomes. The authors cited several studies in current interpersonal communication research that they argued would fit into this expanded model. They also focused their attention on the development of typologies of message strategies (e.g., Marwell & Schmitt, 1967), which they believed would prove fruitful in rejuvenating persuasion research under the rubric of "compliance gaining." In sum, the authors concluded, persuasion research was still a strong force in communication scholarship, except that it was being conducted under other labels.

CONCLUSION

Communication scholarship in the 1960s and 1970s was heavily invested in studying how people, organizations, and media entities were influential in individual and corporate lives. It was an area of obvious public interest, and it promised to produce not only powerful theoretical explanations but also results that could be applied to improved communication practices. Mass communication scholars were, in a sense, better organized in this area than were their colleagues in speech communication. They were fortunate to have a small number of influential scholars who picked up the mantle that Lazersfeld and his associates had discarded and were able to relate their theories to overturning the dominant model of the "two-step flow" with powerful alternative explanations for which they could provide focused data.

Speech communication scholars first had to deal with how to emphasize "communication" without alienating "speech" in the process. This process was not always an easy one to navigate. They were also heavily dependent on, at the beginning, carrying on the work of Hovland and the Yale Group, as a means of achieving some legitimacy. Eventually, they moved away from imitation and began to find other sources of inspiration in disciplines, such as sociology and anthropology.

They were also, to some degree, focused on building the International Communication Association as an independent entity from the Speech Communication Association, especially from the point of view of scholarly publication. George Gerbner, as long-serving editor of the *Journal of Communication* quickly built that publication's reputation as a premiere media journal that could compete favorably with *Journalism Quarterly*. *Human Communication Research*, under Miller's leadership, quickly became competitive with *Communication Monographs*. The *Communication Yearbook* series helped ICA to become known as a group that could summarize communication scholarship and, to some degree, set agendas for future scholarship. Scholars such as Dale Hample were supported in demonstrating how focused theory-building could yield significant results. Miller's talent at producing review essays would cement his standing as intellectual leader, not only in persuasion but also in moderating theoretical and methodological disputes among speech communication scholars.

REFERENCES

Arnold, W. E. & McCroskey, J. C. (1967). The credibility of reluctant testimony. *The Central States Speech Journal, 18*, 97–103. doi:10.1080/10510976709362870

Berlo, D. K. (1960). *The Process of Communication*. New York: Holt, Rinehart and Winston.

Berlyne, D. (1960). *Conflict, Arousal, and Curiosity*. New York: McGraw-Hill.

Cohen, B. (1963). *The Press and Foreign Policy*. Princeton, NJ: Princeton University Press.

Craig, R. T. (1999). Communication theory as a field. *Communication Theory, 9*, 117–161. doi:10.1111/j.1468-2885.1999.tb00355.x

Dance, F. E. X. & Larson, C. E. (1976). *The Functions of Human Communication: A Theoretical Approach.* New York: Holt, Rinehart and Winston.

Fishbein, M. & Ajzen, I. (1975). *Belief, Attitude, Intention and Behavior: An Introduction to Theory and Research.* Reading, MA: Addison-Wesley.

Fishbein, M. (1967). A behavior theory approach to the relations between beliefs about an object and the attitude toward the object. In, Fishbein, M. (ed.), *Readings in Attitude Theory and Measurement* (pp. 257–265). New York: Wiley.

Funkhouser, G. R. (1973). The issues of the sixties: An exploratory study in the dynamics of public opinion. *Public Opinion Quarterly, 37,* 62–75. doi:10.1086/268060

Gerbner, G. & Gross, L. (1976). Living with television: The Violence Profile. *Journal of Communication, 26,* 172–194. doi:10.1111/j.1460-2466.1976.tb01397.x

Gerbner, G., Gross, L., Morgan, M. & Signorielli, N. (1980). The "Mainstreaming" of America: Violence Profile No. 11. *Journal of Communication, 30*(3), 10–29. doi:10.1111/j.1460-2466.1980.tb01987.x

Gerbner, G., Gross, L., Morgan, M. & Signorielli, N. (1981, May/June). Scientists on the TV screen. *Society, 18*(4), 41–44. doi:10.1007/BF02701349

Gerbner, G., Gross, L., Morgan, M. & Signorielli, N. (1981, October 8). Health and medicine on television. *New England Journal of Medicine, 305*(15), 901–904. doi:10.1056/NEJM198110083051530

Gerbner, G., Gross, L., Morgan, M. & Signorielli, N. (1982). Charting the mainstream: Televisions contributions to political orientations. *Journal of Communication, 32*(2), 100–127. doi:10.1111/j.1460-2466.1982.tb00500.x

Gerbner, G., Gross, L., Signorielli, N. & Morgan, M. (1980). Aging with television: Images on television drama and conceptions of social reality. *Journal of Communication, 30*(1), 37–47. doi:10.1111/j.1460-2466.1980.tb01766.x

Gerbner, G., Gross, L., Signorielli, N., Morgan, M. & Jackson-Beeck, M. (1979). The demonstration of power: Violence profile No. 10. *Journal of Communication, 29*(3), 177–196. doi:10.1111/j.1460-2466.1979.tb01731.x

Hample, D. (1977). Testing a model of value argument and evidence. *Communication Monographs, 44,* 106–120. doi:10.1080/03637757709390121

Hample, D. (1978). Predicting immediate belief change and adherence to argument claims. *Communication Monographs, 45,* 219–228. doi:10.1080/03637757809375967

Hample, D. (1979). Predicting belief and belief change using a cognitive theory of argument and evidence. *Communication Monographs, 46,* 142–146. doi:10.1080/03637757909376000

Hample, D. (1981). The cognitive context of argument. *Western Journal of Speech Communication: WJSC, 45,* 148–158. doi:10.1080/10570318109374037

Hample, D. J. (1980). A cognitive view of argument. *Journal of the American Forensic Association, 16,* 151–158. doi:10.1080/00028533.1980.11951168

Hawkins, R. P. & Pingree, S. (1982). Uniform content and habitual viewing: Unnecessary assumptions in social reality effects. *Human Communication Research, 7,* 291–301. doi:10.1111/j.1468-2958.1981.tb00576.x

Hughes, M. (1980). The fruits of cultivation analysis. A re-examination of the effects of television watching on fear of victimization, alienation, and the approval of violence. *Public Opinion Quarterly, 44,* 287–302. doi:10.1086/268597

Klapper, J. T. (1960). *The Effects of Mass Communication.* New York: Free Press.

Levine, T. R. & Park, H. S. (2017). The research of James C. McCroskey: A personal and professional remembrance. *Communication Research Reports, 34,* 376–380. doi:10.1080/08824096.2017.1368474

Marwell, G. & Schmitt, D. R. (1967). Dimensions of compliance-gaining behavior: An empirical analysis. *Sociometry, 30,* 350–364. doi:10.2307/2786181

McCombs, M. E. & Shaw, D. L. (1972). The agenda-setting function of mass media. *Public Opinion Quarterly, 36,* 176–187. doi:10.1086/267990

McCroskey, J. C. (1966). Scales for the measurement of ethos. *Speech Monographs, 33,* 65–72. doi:10.1080/03637756609375482

McCroskey, J. C. (1969). A summary of experimental research on the effects of evidence in persuasive communication. *The Quarterly Journal of Speech, 55,* 169–176. doi:10.1080/00335636909382942

McGuire, W. J. (1960). A syllogistic analysis of cognitive relationships. In Rosenberg, M. J., [and others], *Attitude Organization and Change: An Analysis of Consistency Among Attitude Components* (pp. 65–111). New Haven, CT: Yale University Press.

Miller, G. R. (1968). Communication and persuasion research: Current problems and prospects. *Quarterly Journal of Speech, 54,* 268–276. doi:10.1080/00335636809382900

Miller, G. R. (1969). Some factors influencing judgments of the logical validity of arguments: A research review. *Quarterly Journal of Speech, 55,* 276–286. doi:10.1080/00335636909382954

Miller, G. R. & Burgoon, M. (1978). Persuasion research: Review and commentary. In Ruben, B. (ed.), *Communication Yearbook 2* (pp. 29–47). New Brunswick, NJ: Transaction Books.

Morgan, M. (1982). Symbolic victimization and real world fear. *Human Communication Research, 9,* 146–157. doi:10.1111/j.1468-2958.1983.tb00689.x

Palmgreen, P. & Clarke, P. (1977). Agenda-setting with local and national issues. *Communication Research, 4,* 435–452. doi:10.1177/009365027700400404

Signorielli, N. (1982). Marital status in TV drama: A case of reduced options. *Journal of Broadcasting, 26,* 585–597. doi:10.1080/08838158209364027

Winter, J. P. & Eyal, C. H. (1981). Agenda-setting for the civil rights issue. *Public Opinion Quarterly, 45,* 376–383. doi:10.1086/268671

Wyer, R. (1974). *Cognitive Organization and Change: An Information Processing Approach.* Potomac, MD: L. Erlbaum Associates.

Chapter 5

Communication as Language Use

Language use has been a staple of communication scholarship, and both speech and journalism scholars explored the nature of language and how it is used as their disciplines developed before adopting communication as a major concept in their scholarly work. For journalism scholars, "language use" provided more of a method for exploring other questions of interest, such as conducting content analysis of newspaper articles to learn about how news was presented. For speech scholars, "language use" proved to be a primary means of understanding the communication enterprise, often from the perspective of rhetoric, but also from other perspectives. This chapter, then, will focus primarily on the various understandings of language use from the speech scholar's perspective, as "speech" transitioned to "speech communication."

There were several approaches to this scholarship. I will begin with John Stewart's (1972) seminal *Quarterly Journal of Speech* essay on the topic, titled, "Concepts of Language and Meaning: A Comparative Study." Stewart reviewed what he called the "Speech Communication Approach" to language use before focusing his essay on several types of what he called the "Ordinary Language Philosophy Approach." I'll then skip ahead to Brian L. Ott and Mary Domenico's (2015) essay, "Conceptualizing Meaning in Communication Studies," which appeared in the volume that Pat J. Gehrke and William M. Keith were commissioned to produce for the celebration of the one hundredth anniversary of the founding of what by then was called the National Communication Association. Ott and Domenico, working primarily with material produced either prior to 1964 or during the 1964–1982 period, divided their analysis into seven sections. I will summarize the sections and will then present a journal article to illustrate each one.

CONCEPTS OF LANGUAGE AND MEANING

John Stewart was just starting his career at the University of Washington when he published "Concepts of Language and Meaning: A Comparative Study" in the *Quarterly Journal of Speech*. He began his survey of language by referencing directly three "traditions" in speech communication. First, he quoted I. A. Richards' (1936) rhetorical definition, "study of misunderstanding and its remedies;" then the New Orleans conference "spoken symbolic interaction" definition to represent what he called the "scientific analysis" tradition; and third, the "mutual struggle for common ground between two distinct and inviolable identities" (Matson and Montagu, 1967), which represented the emerging humanistic tradition that Stewart would embrace in his later work.

Stewart divided his analysis into two parts. The first he labeled the "Speech Communication Approach," and the second he called the "Ordinary Language Approach."

The section titled the "Speech Communication Approach" provided a summary of ways in which speech communication scholars had historically studied language, including reference to scholars who influenced those different concepts. This approach, Stewart argued, treated words as representing things in some manner. They were symbols, rather than the "signs" that some language philosophers discussed. Stewart referenced Suzanne Langer's (1951) distinction that while animals can learn to use signs to indicate one thing causing another, it is humans who are able to move beyond indication to representation. Interestingly, Langer (1960) had published a *Quarterly Journal of Speech* article analyzing the relationship between speech and communication.

Steward posited three theories of meaning within the Speech Communication Approach: referential, ideational, and behavioral. Referential theories included General Semantics (Korzybski, 1948; Lee, 1941; Hayakawa, 1944; Johnson, 1946), which focused on how working to eliminate abstraction would yield words that could be used scientifically, that is, referring directly or indirectly to one's personal experience. The referential approach was informed by Ogden and Richards' (1946) analysis of meaning, where symbols are associated with what they represent via a mental state that is, in turn, influenced by the coordination over time of speaker and hearer images evoked by the word.

The ideational theory of meaning is more specific about Ogden and Richards' ideas about how words must be mediated in referring to things. In the ideational theory, mediation takes place through the idea that the speaker has about the word. Speakers shade meaning through word choice, because similar words will call up different ideas about a thing. Stewart quoted Langer

(1951, p. 61) in this vein, echoing the argument that words are the vehicles for the conception of objects.

Stewart associated the behavioral theory of meaning with the work of Charles Osgood (c.f., 1953). Osgood took the idea that people respond to language in much the same way as they respond to other stimuli in their environments, then improved it by theorizing that words mediate responses, because a word can elicit the same response as the thing the word was supposed to represent.

All told, Stewart summarized, speech scholars' approaches to language and meaning are similar, in that they "accept the assumption that language is fundamentally a system of symbols" (p. 128).

Stewart clearly found the "Ordinary Language Approach" to be superior to the "Speech Communication Approach." He first summarized the basic tenants of the approach, and then he compared them to what at the time had been standard ways of thinking about language use in speech communication.

Stewart presented four propositions that distinguish ordinary language approach. First, "language does not naturally and cannot accurately represent a calculus" (p. 129). In other words, there is no such thing as an ideal language, as the scholars reviewed in the Speech Communication Approach had posited. Second, "ordinary language philosophers argue that, since language is not mathematically consistent, words do not function in any single way; specifically, meaning is not simply reference and words are not simply names" (p. 130). This position directly contradicts Stewart's characterization of the Speech Communication Approach's conclusion that ultimately words represent things. Stewart also referenced J. L. Austin's (1961) note that meaning is adequate at a minimum at the sentence level. Third, Stewart wrote, "virtually all generalizations about language unnecessarily distort its nature" (p. 130). In other words, understanding is not a function of "getting inside the speaker's head" and coming to the exact same meaning as the speaker. Finally, "language-using is ordinary behavior" (p. 131). In other words, the best way of looking at language is not via what it means but what it does, as in Austin's concept of a "speech act."

Stewart concluded, "(1) knowledge of ordinary language philosophy can be used by the speech communication scholar to examine his [sic] presuppositions about the nature of language"; (p. 132) "(2) analysis from an ordinary language philosophy perspective also reveals weaknesses in the approach to meaning taken by speech communication scholars"; (p. 132) and "(3) speech communication scholars could profitably employ the ordinary language method of close, detailed analysis of many examples of ordinary utterances used to talk about an important concept. This methodical analysis might well clarify such problematic concepts as rhetoric and communication" (p. 133).

PERCEPTION AND MEANING

Before moving on to Ott and Domenico's look at how language use developed in speech communication, I would be remiss if I didn't acknowledge Gary Cronkhite's (1984) review essay titled, "Perception and Meaning," that was published in the *Handbook of Rhetorical and Communication Theory*. Though it was published outside of the time period I set for consideration, the book was a major landmark in the development of the idea that communication, along with rhetoric, was central to the study of speech communication, and it drew heavily on scholarship that was published between 1964 and 1982. Chronkhite's essay, covering 178 pages of an 891-page volume, was a scholarly tour de force. Approximately half of the review focused on perception, and half on meaning. Cronkhite's perspective was a cognitive one, and the major headings in the meaning section provide a precise of the scope of the essay. They were as follows:

Meaning: The Attribution of Symbolic Significance

I. The Semantic Nature of the Cognitive System
    a. Traditional Theories of Meaning
    b. Rule-Defined Meaning
    c. Contextual Meaning
    d. The Cognitive Connection
II. The Pragmatic Nature of the Cognitive System
    a. Subjective Expected Utility Models
    b. The Conceptual Structure of Pragmatic Discourse
III. The Pragmatic Meanings of Some Symbolic Alternatives
    a. Clarity
    b. Connotation and Conditioning
    c. Intensity and Obscenity
    d. Aesthetic Language Style
    e. Dialects: Social Causes and Effects
    f. Meaning and Verbal Reasoning
    g. Communication Competence and Interaction
IV. Ecological Functions of Symbolic Processes
    a. A Theory of Designer Genes
    b. Ideological Evolution
    c. Play, Recursion, Negentropy, and a Mind for the Planet

I will return to an example of the cognitive approach to language use later in the chapter.

HOW MEANING HAS BEEN CONCEPTUALIZED

Writing from the perspective of the 100th anniversary of what had become the National Communication Association, Ott and Domenico (2015) summarized seven approaches to how communication scholars had conceptualized meaning. Some of the approaches overlapped Stewart's (1972) review, others emerged with different names. I will summarize the seven approaches identified by Ott and Domenico, focusing primarily on those that are unique.

General Semantics

Ott and Domenico relied on Stewart's characterization of general semantics as part of the referential approach to meaning. They provided more detail on the theory itself, namely that Korzybski saw "time-binding" as a unique characteristic of humans. That is, humans can organize knowledge over generations and observe how meanings change rather than just react to the changes. They also highlighted Korzybski's idea of extensional and intentional meanings, or the difference between a word as representative of an object and a word as formed in individual people's minds. Both kinds of meaning are inherently abstract, though extensional meanings by their nature come closest to concrete meaning. Nevertheless, the authors quoted Krozybski's dictum that "the map is not the territory" to indicate that a word can never entirely represent the thing that it purports to represent. Ott and Domenico also noted that general semantics was a common part of the speech communication curriculum in the 1960s and 1970s, but that it lost popularity, even though it never completely disappeared from the theoretical canon.

The New Materialism

This approach has more in common with the cognitive approach than any other. The basic idea, according to Ott and Domenico, is that "meaning is grounded in the materiality of the body" (p. 237). The theory draws on a combination of developmental learning as language is acquired, along with a growing appreciation of "higher cognitive processes such as intellectual feelings and reflective thinking" (p. 239). The cognitive work is carried out via image schemata and metaphorical projections. "Image schemata are basic patterns or recurring gestalts of embodied (visual, auditory, kinesthetic, or cross-modal) experience typically formed during infancy and early childhood, and metaphorical projections are the abstract concepts and inferences derived from those patterns" (p. 239).

I will represent this approach later in the chapter by analyzing a cognitively based study of language use.

The New Rhetoric

In Ott and Domenico's view, "The New Rhetoric" refers to the writings of I. A. Richards and Kenneth Burke. I have alluded to the ideational approach to meaning that Richards constructed with C. K. Ogden. Ott and Domenico elaborated on that discussion by showing that Richards' (1936) book, *The Philosophy of Rhetoric* pulls rhetoric away from persuasion by defining it as "a study of misunderstanding and its remedies" (p. 3). Richards' work, Ott and Domenico argued, situates meaning in context rather than in words themselves.

Burke also situated rhetoric away from persuasion, claiming in *A Rhetoric of Motives* (1950) that its key term is identification. As Ott and Domenico wrote, "Identification is critical to Burke's new rhetoric because, like Richards, he regards division (or alienation) and conflict to be endemic to the human condition. But whereas Richards locates the source of conflict in misunderstanding, Burke locates it in social hierarchy and human motives. Thus, Burke's rhetoric is more concerned with attitudes than with comprehension" (p. 242, italics from the authors).

In Burke's view, language constructs a social world rather than reflects it. Consequently, like Richards, Burke saw meaning as what Ott and Domenico termed "radically contextual in character" (p. 242).

Ordinary Language

Ott and Domenico followed Stewart's analysis of ordinary language rather closely. Where they departed was to elaborate on J. L. Austin and John Searle's work on speech acts as units of meaning. The authors referenced Searle's development of indirect speech acts, where literal meaning and non-literal meaning may be at odds with each other. This sort of meaning may arise when multiple elements of the speech act may be operating at once, such as in a joke or in sarcasm.

Semiotics

Semiotics as an approach to study of language dates to the founding of the journalism and speech disciplines. Ott and Domenico noted that Ferdinand de Saussure's pioneering lectures on a system where the study of words was replaced with the study of *words in relation to other words* were published posthumously in 1959. Saussure essentially proposed an academic discipline titled Semiology, and he posited that its study consisted of two parts: a "structure or system of rules and conventions that makes speech possible" (p. 246), called *la langue*, and "the actual use of language by speakers" (p. 246), called *la parole*. "For Saussure, it is the conceptual structure of *la langue* and not the social use of *la parole* that determines the meanings of words" (p. 246).

Saussure's semiology was elaborated into the study of semiotics by the philosopher of pragmatism Charles Sanders Peirce. Peirce focused on the study of what he called "signs." Peirce extended the use of signs beyond words and posited three levels of consciousness for understanding signs: an immediate sensation level, a level where signs are related to each other, based on one's experience with the world, and a level where experience of the sign relations leads to understanding and formulating concepts and theories.

Roland Barthes built on both theories by designing a signifying system. This system encompasses the entirety of the sign itself, how it looks and sounds, and the concept with which the sign is associated. Barthes' key contribution was to distinguish between denotative meaning, which is literal or expressive, and connotative meaning, which operates on a cultural level, incorporating ideology and myth. Barthes' contributions provided the basis for semiotics to become associated with the study of media in its various forms.

Symbolic Forms

Drawing on perspective that comes from the passage of time, Ott and Domenico reclassified Susanne Langer's work by pairing it with that of Ernst Cassirer. While this work may still be considered to represent Stewart's concept of ideational meaning, as opposed to representational or behavioral meaning, the addition of Cassirer complicates this notion somewhat, particularly because it uses similar words in different ways.

Cassirer's 1944 book, *An Essay on Man* [sic], outlined the idea of symbolic forms. These forms essentially provide a framework consisting of sets of rules through which experience may be made meaningful. These forms differ substantially by the kind of thing being experienced. For example, art and science are experienced in entirely separate ways and by separate sets of rules. Commonly used language is experienced in its own way, but because it is common, the rules for experiencing it are more widely understood.

Cassirer provided forms of meaning to match his explanations of the differences among art, common language, and science. He called the symbolic form for art expressive, the one for science significative, and the one for common language representative. Here's where there might be confusion: the representative symbolic form embodies rules for understanding common language. The type of theory is ideational, however, not referential, as Stewart labeled it (accurately) a different language philosophy.

Ott and Domenico's explanation of Langer's approach added concepts that helped to clarify Cassirer's ideas. Langer (1954) differentiated between discursive and presentational meanings. Discursive meaning describes how we interpret common language, via understanding the rules underlying vocabulary, and syntax, as well as understanding the context in which the language is used. Presentational meaning covers how we understand the art and other forms of what Langer called wordless symbolism.

Symbolic forms provided a means of moving away from what speech scholars considered to be acceptable texts for analyzing rhetoric and provided a basis for the rhetorical analysis of casual conversation, media, and other more presentational uses of symbols.

Symbolic Interactionism

Symbolic interactionism arose from George Herbert Mead's (1934) ideas about mind, self, and society, which were published from lecture notes after his death. For Mead, communication invokes what he called a "conversation of gestures" which are intended to indicate each person's ideas (mind) about themselves (self) and the roles they play in relation to the roles that others play (society). A basic act of meaning for Mead involves three gestures: an initial gesture, a response gesture, and a third gesture that responds to the interpretation of the second gesture. Therefore, meaning is created in conversation and is always, as Ott and Domenico put it "collaborative and conditional" (p. 252).

Herbert Blumer (1969) published a refined version of Mead's ideas. He advanced three main premises: first, that human action is based on meanings those people have formed over time; second, that the formation of those meanings is derived from social interaction; and third, that meanings are modified through an interpretive process generated through additional social interaction.

As Ott and Domenico noted,

> symbolic interactionism sees meaning as contingent, co-constructive, and crucial to all human behavior. This view of meaning also contests the belief that meaning is a personal or private affair . . . In fact, for symbolic interactionists, both the concepts of self and mind are social constructions that develop out of . . . symbolic interaction. (p. 352)

In the sections that follow, I will review a scholarly publication that illustrates each of these approaches to meaning in language use, in the process showing how fertile this approach to the study of communication was between 1964 and 1982.

SCHOLARLY ARTICLES ILLUSTRATING APPROACHES TO THE STUDY OF COMMUNICATION AS LANGUAGE USE

General Semantics

While the principles of general semantics were taught in the 1960s and 1970s, particularly in the speech communication classroom, little scholarship attempting to develop general semantics as a theory was published in the mainstream journals in speech communication or journalism. The journal, *Etc*, was devoted to articles about general semantics, however, and to some extent published original scholarship.

Alvin Goldberg (1965), University of Denver, published an example of early scholarship on general semantics. His study, titled, "The Effects of a Laboratory Course in General Semantics," was, by the author's admission, a means of testing the potential for more sophisticated study based in general semantics.

Using a design that did not include a control group, Goldberg investigated how taking an experiential course based on the principles of general semantics might impact short-term change on the participants. The qualities measured were "authoritarianism," "dogmatism," "opinionation," and "rigidity."

Thirty-one secondary teachers completed the course, which was taught by Goldberg's colleague, Elwood Murray. The course consisted of twenty sessions of three hours each, offered over a period of five months. Participants were administered standardized measures of the four qualities at the beginning of the course and again at the end of the course.

Data analysis focused on the degree to which the scores changed between the two administrations of the measures. Goldberg reported that two of the four measures, for dogmatism and rigidity, moved to a statistically significant degree in the predicted direction. Scores for opinionation moved in the predicted direction, but not to a statistically significant degree. Scores for authoritarianism were low in the first administration of the test and remained low in the second administration.

Goldberg admitted that his design could not produce conclusive results, nor did his measures provide information about what aspects of the general semantics approach to understanding communication as language use might have impacted the movement of scores on dogmatism and rigidity. He argued that these initial results were promising enough to warrant a follow-up. From results of a database search of communication journals, Goldberg never published the follow-up study.

Indeed, what little was published on general semantics were critiques of its theoretical formulations (c.f., Benjamin, 1976; Gorman, 1967). Nevertheless, general semantics has proven to be a topic of continued interest, though largely outside of the academic study of communication. *Etc*, its journal, continues to be published quarterly by the Institute of General Semantics.

The New Materialism

Liska, Mechling, and Stahas (1981) studied how deferential and nondeferential language influenced listener perceptions of the characteristics of speakers who used each style of language. The authors drew on what had become a rich literature analyzing differences between women's and men's speech (c.f., Berryman & Wilcox, 1980; Bostrom & Kemp, 1969; Kibler, Barker, & Cegalia, 1970; Kramer, 1974; Lakoff, 1975).

The authors posed four questions for study:

(1) What characteristics do raters attribute to deferential language users? (2) To what extent do raters discriminate on feminine/masculine scales between those who do or do not use deferential language? (3) To what extent do raters discriminate on believability scales between those who use these two styles? (4) To what extent do raters' perceptions of deferential language users depend on the sex of the rater? (p. 40).

To answer these questions, the researchers settled on three topics of interest to both male and female students and composed scripts for each topic. Each script portrayed a four-person group discussing the topic, where two of the group members used deferential language and two of the group members used nondeferential language. There was one of each type of language user on each side of the issue posed by the topic.

Once the scenarios had been developed, undergraduate students read and rated each of the four participants on scales measuring believability and masculinity vs. femininity. One-third of the participants read each of the three scenarios.

The findings of the data analysis indicated that while there were differences in how men and women raters perceived the deferential versus nondeferential styles, there were more similarities between the male and female raters than differences. The deferential language users were perceived to be less assertive, more submissive, more tentative, less believable, more caring, and more feminine than nondeferential language users. Interestingly, the researchers reported that those who were judged as dominant were also judged as masculine rather than those judged as masculine being judged as dominant. Men saw the deferential language users as more friendly and indicated that they would be more willing to accept the opinion of the deferential language user. Women, on the other hand, saw deferential language users as more sincere and more honest, but they were also less likely to accept the deferential language users' opinions. Overall, men and woman raters agreed that deferential language style users had less power but more personal warmth. They also associated femininity with the deferential language style, though the researchers argued that the strength of this judgment of femininity deserved additional research.

All in all, this study characterized the approach of The New Materialism, in that it used a cognitive method for studying language use, and it drew on measuring raters' schemata regarding particular styles of language use to generate its findings.

The New Rhetoric

Scott (1967) took on a classic debate in his article, "On Viewing Rhetoric as Epistemic." He wanted to know of what good rhetoric might be if knowledge consisted only of absolute truths that were predetermined and waiting to be discovered. If such were the case, Scott argued, rhetoric would have very little function, except "a persuasive leading of inferiors by the capable" (p. 10).

Taking off from the work of Stephen Toulmin (1958), Scott urged readers not so much to concentrate on how one knows what one knows, the classical definition of epistemology, but rather to examine the argument behind coming to know something. Toulmin contrasted analytic arguments, ones based on a kind of manipulation of words, as in a classic syllogism, with substantial arguments, whose premises are based on a shift in time. Something may be true at one point but not at another. One cannot assume, for example, that I have gray hair, because there remains the possibility that I could dye my hair so that it more closely matched the brown hair I had growing up.

Scott then turned to his colleagues, Douglas Ehninger and Wayne Brockreide (1963), whose book on debate described it as "cooperative critical inquiry," a position Scott described as "normative" rather than "descriptive" of the actual practice of the activity. Indeed, the process of cooperative critical inquiry would lead to the conclusion that it is the only way in which truth might be agreed upon. Even then, truth is subject to change as agreements change.

Scott concluded that, "At best (or least) truth must be seen as dual: the demands of the precepts one adheres to and the demands of the circumstances in which one must act" (p. 17). The role of rhetoric is to become a way of knowing, despite the uncertainty that results from treating it as such. As Scott wrote, "The uncertainty of this way may seem too threatening to many. But the other way of looking at the world offers no legitimate role to rhetoric; if one would accept that way, then one may be called upon to act consistently with it" (p. 17).

Writing a decade later, Fisher (1978) continued the conversation in a manner that was grounded in what had become known as "The New Rhetoric." His 1978 essay, titled "Toward a Logic of Good Reasons," attempted to insert the role of values into making judgments about the worth of reasons that are proffered in an argument.

Fisher did not originate the topic he was considering. He built on earlier essays published by Wallace (1963) and Booth (1974). He claimed that this earlier work was deficient, in that its definitions of how reasons were "good" were circular ones and too narrowly focused. To remedy this concern, Fisher proposed to widen the traditional means by how one arrives at a judgment that reasons are good ones, by incorporating values into the analysis. Drawing on Toulman's system of claims and warrants, Fisher proposed, "that good reasons be conceived of *as those elements that provide warrants for accepting or adhering to the advice fostered by any form of communication that can be considered rhetorical*" (p. 378, author's italics).

Fisher contrasted what he considered to be the current logic of reasons with what he proposed. First, current practice advised evaluating how "facts" presented in support of an argument have been judged to be facts. Fisher compared this step with one where the analyst identifies what are the implicit and explicit values that are part of the message. Second, the analyst should identify how relevant the facts presented are to the argument and whether any pertinent facts have been omitted or distorted. He refocused this consideration of relevance on the values that had been identified, rather than the facts. Third, the traditional analyst would evaluate the patterns of reasoning employed, while Fisher's formulation would call on the analyst to look instead at the consequence of having the values involved influence all of one's self-concept, behavior, and relationships with others, and society should the reasoning be judged as "good." Fourth, instead of assessing the soundness of the arguments themselves, Fisher would ask the analyst to examine consistency of the values involved in the argument, not only internally but with the ability of the audience member to confirm them against personal experience or understanding of the experience of others. Finally, instead of making a judgment about whether the message addresses the "real" issues in the argument, Fisher asked the analyst to consider the transcendence of the values underlying the message, whether they represent what he called "the ideal basis for human conduct" (p. 380).

The remainder of Fisher's essay was devoted to implementation issues, as well as to the extended analysis of a sample case. Fisher also considered the possibility of a universal hierarchy of values and argued that the ones in the literature were not convincing. Values may recur as underlying arguments, but each set of values is discerned from examining arguments, particularly when applying the tests of consistency, consequence, and transcendent issue to the analysis of values underlying those arguments, somewhat unique to the situation being analyzed.

Fisher concluded,

> Since the time of Francis Bacon, knowledge has been conceived largely as power over people and things. In my judgment, we have lost a sense of wisdom. To regain it, I think, we need to reaffirm the place of value as a component of knowledge—and that, too, is a function of a logic of good reasons. (p. 384).

Ordinary Language

Gerry Philipsen's (1975) *Quarterly Journal of Speech* article, "Speaking 'Like a Man' in Teamsterville: Culture Patterns of Role Enactment in an Urban Neighborhood," ushered in a new era in communication scholarship. Mixing ethnographic methods developed in cultural anthropology with macro-level language analysis, Philipsen used extensive field study in a working-class white community in the south side of Chicago to portray the cultural patterns of men and boys in a neighborhood that was relatively closed to outsiders.

Before summarizing this article, I will provide some background on Gerry Philipsen, taken from an interview I conducted with him in 2007 (A Conversation with Gerry Philipsen, 2007). Philipsen's background is important to the understanding of how his article influenced the development of nonquantitative, nonrhetorical, methods of communication study.

Philipsen contended that as an undergraduate at the University of Denver, he focused on competitive debate more than on the study of speech or communication.

> I was a college debater for four years at the University of Denver. During that time I had over 300 judged debates. I think one of the things that you learn from 300 judged debates is it gets wired into your DNA—that you try to see both sides of a subject because you're forced to debate both sides—and about 150 of those were on the affirmative and about 150 on the negative.

Debating also led to discussion, and Philipsen noted, "I ended up getting what you might call a mini-specialization in group discussion at the University of Denver and took four different courses in the department, in that area." Studying discussion changed him:

One of the things that I learned through that process is that this was a different mode of communication, a different type of experience and that the idea was to get the wisdom of the group to prevail. This was quite a startling thought to me, and quite an attractive and interesting one. So that had a very powerful impact on me.

Moving on to Northwestern University for doctoral work, Philipsen found that his interests didn't fit well with the program. What saved him, in a way, was coming under the influence of Ethel Albert, who would eventually become his adviser. Albert was a philosopher of science by training, who had done work in anthropology as a graduate student. She had written what Philipsen called "quite an influential piece on rhetoric, logic and poetics in Burundi."

Philipsen took Albert's class, titled "Culture Patterns of Communication," and then he started to work in the field: "I'm working as a director of group work for this organization, this Salvation Army settlement house in the near south side of Chicago." Having registered as a conscientious objector during the Vietnam War, he received a call to perform alternative service in lieu of being drafted into the military.

I will quote extensively from his interview here:

I thought, well, this would be a job that would satisfy my Alternative Service requirement and that I'd be working with all of these groups and group workers, would be leading all of these groups and that there could be even some learning that I would do there.

What I didn't realize, what my learning would be, would be about culture. So, I got into this neighborhood and I was directing this program, and the program was in a crisis because several of the staff had either been fired or quit, including the director. I had to go in there and restore order because the kids were out of control, the kids in the program, and they were locking people—the staff—in the building and writing on the walls and so forth.

The character-building mission was a little bit in disarray, at that point. So, I had to come in and build character fast. What I had learned—and this had worked quite well for me, in other situations—is you come into a situation, you talk to the people and you engage in communication. So, I would bring these kids in to my office and talk with them.

After a couple months of this I realized, quite profoundly, that was not working. That's what I'd learned in school, in my major, and it had worked, and it was working for me in other aspects of my life and of my work. I had been director, a program director, of a summer camp for a couple of years and it worked there. To make a long story short, I failed; I was failing, quite objectively. I was failing because there was something I didn't know.

I had to either admit failure and walk away or I had to learn something. What I feel I had to learn was, I was coming into contact with a different culture— people who spoke the English language and understood the English language, as I understand it, but for whom the meaning of, the mode of activity that we think of as speaking, meant something different. The problem was that I was dealing with this, as a man, I was dealing with this problem through communication and through speech, and that violated the sensibilities, the moirés [patterns?] and understandings of the people in that community. It took me a long time to figure that out, but I first had to figure it out on a practical level.

Philipsen worked at this position for two years and then returned to Northwestern to finish his coursework and write a dissertation. He recalled his conversation with Ethel Albert about a dissertation topic:

When it came time to propose my dissertation topic to Professor Albert, who was quite an imperious woman, I was sitting in her office and she had told me to bring in three topics. I gave her the three and I said, One, I would develop a cognitive model of how people process messages, and she was very interested in cognitive models. Or I would do a quantitative study of two communities using the kind of questionnaires that the sociologist Basil Bernstein was using at that time, to study social class differences in modes of speech, and Frederick Williams in the Communication field; a very influential article to me, in *Speech Monographs*. Or I would do an ethnographic study of this community that I had told her about.

She took a drag on her cigarette and blew a smoke-ring or two and she said, "It'll be the third one."

So I said, "Thank you Professor Albert. I'll get started on that right away. Just for my own illumination, why did you pick that one?"

She blew another smoke-ring and then said, "That's the one I want to read."

So, Philipsen went off to a small community on the south side of Chicago and did field work for a total of twenty-three months, and the result was a dissertation that became "Speaking 'Like a Man' in Teamsterville." Philipsen saw it as a work on communication in culture, but it was well grounded in how language was being used (or not used) in that community.

Philipsen started with the premise that performance of manliness was essential to one's identity as male in this community. Parameters for such performances were well known by the actors, as well as when actions would speak louder than words. Because these parameters were well known, Philipsen chose to analyze examples of violation of those expectations.

Particularly, the quantity and quality of male speech depends on relationships that are symmetrical: that is, where the pair of speakers is approximately the same age, ethnicity, and occupational status. In contrast, actions, as opposed to speech, are the hallmark of relationships that are asymmetrical—that is, not matching on those same identity characteristics. Philipsen chose three situations for analysis: (1) responding to an insult, either to himself or family members; (2) influencing the behavior of a "status inferior," such as a child; and (3) taking positions regarding politics or economics.

Regarding insults, Philipsen recounted observing an adult who worked with a group of neighborhood boys respond to a conversation the boys had regarding fighting as a response to insults. The adult, who was not native to the boys' community, opined that he would try to talk with the offender, and his opinion made the boys visibly nervous, so much so that they felt unsafe to visit Chicago's Old Town, which is where the adult was driving them. The group ended up turning back and returning to the community.

Regarding influencing the behavior of the status inferior, Philipsen described a series of episodes that took place over several weeks between the director of a settlement house with boys in the youth program who were habitually behaving in an unruly manner. The director used communication strategies that had worked in similar situations elsewhere, strategies that focused on collaborating with the boys to help them to take ownership of the operation of the program. Instead, the boys became even more rebellious. One of the older boys, in an effort to help the director, at first advocated that the director beat the boys into submission. When that strategy didn't work, he rationalized that the director had to be legally constrained from hitting the boys. When that rationalization proved not to be the case, the older boy concluded that the director must be a saint. All of the explanations were couched in moral terms. Indeed, one of the boys balked at even talking to a younger child before physically punishing the child for misbehavior.

In the third case, Philipsen noted that boys who wished to join the Settlement House program inevitably enlisted the aid of the boy who was already a member to plead with the director to let him in. In applying this observation to other situations, Philipsen noted that both boys and men in the community tried to find an intermediary for assistance when they wanted to advocate with higher status individuals. Philipsen concluded, "in Teamsterville, speech and group action are not regarded as effective methods for attaining difficult goals, and sometimes speech is thought to be counterproductive" (p. 20).

Recall that these situations apply only to speech where the other person is not a peer. With peers, the expectations were considerably different, both in terms of quantity and quality of speech. Philipsen also noted that men in this community had a similar sense of "knowing their place" as did women in the same community. Philipsen also noted that the Black community nearby had very different speaking styles than did Teamsterville men—and that the nearby white middle-class community had different speaking standards than either of the other communities as well. Philipsen would later report that some of the "Teamsterville" research was auto-ethnographic, as he had worked as both the adult who made the group of boys nervous during a field trip and as the director of the program.

Philipsen's work in Teamsterville provided not only insightful findings, but it also laid out a method for conducting scholarship that was different from either the traditional quantitative approach of many of communication scholars but was also different from the, clearly evolving, approach of rhetorical scholars of the period. Ethnographic methods would come to be regarded as an approach to communication scholarship that could yield rich results to reward the dedication and time needed to conduct individual studies.

Semiotics

Farrell Corcoran (1981) tackled the issue of the structure of film and television and the extent to which it can be said to constitute a grammar in his essay titled, "Towards a Semiotic of Screen Media: Problems in the Use of Linguistic Models." Corcoran introduced readers to the terms, "vidistic," a play on "linguistic," and "cinevideo," which, fairly or unfairly, conflates cinema and video as media languages.

Corcoran took as his purpose to elucidate the ability of traditional linguistic models to be superimposed onto cinevideo. To do so, he delved into the capability of semiotics to have a grammar, using Noam Chomsky's (1968) distinction between a taxonomic grammar and a generative grammar as a guide. A taxonomic grammar focuses on surface structures, while a generative grammar focuses on deep structures, making it the clear choice to form the basis for semiotic analysis.

But, Corcoran argued, selecting a generative grammar approach raises more issues than it solves. The chief problem is that a generative grammar assumes that what is grammatical and what is not can be judged by an ideal version of a native speaker of the language. There would certainly be dispute around finding a native speaker of any sort of language underlying cinevideo.

Corcoran concluded,

> It may well be that film resembles a mode of expression like poetry, rather than a fully-coded system of communication like speech, i.e., film may not constitute a full language but rather a code having some linguistic properties though lacking the generative power based on recursion that natural languages have. (p. 187)

An additional problem Corcoran considered was what constitutes a minimal unit in cinematic language. In speech, linguists have defined phonemes as minimal units, but that works only because spoken language is, for the most part, arbitrary and relies on competent speakers for understanding. Some elements of cinematic structure (e.g., lighting, shooting angles, camera placement, movement, and distance from objects) are much less arbitrary, however, and their use would be recognized by experienced viewers.

In a concluding section, Corcoran returned to the roots of semiotic theory, noted that even if linguistic models cannot be imposed on media directly, media is still a "coded system." Corcoran contended that media scholars had become overly concerned with what he called "psychological and sociological effects of messages." He suggested instead that scholars focus on four attributes of media: "all media convey (1) contents which are structured by (2) symbol systems; they use (3) technologies for the gathering, encoding, sorting, and conveying of their contents, and they are associated with different (4) situations in which they are typically used. (p. 191) He further suggested, "Semiotics suggests a fruitful direction of research in delineating the blend of symbol systems a medium uses (p. 192)."

Symbolic Forms

The study of discourse developed as another alternative to approaching communication study from solely a "scientific" perspective. Typically, this approach focused on conversation and social interaction, as opposed to more traditional "rhetorical" texts. The approach drew on similar area of study in sociology, and, at least initially, it took as a goal to discover rules of conversational interaction.

Nofsinger's (1976) paper elaborated conversational examples of indirect speech, a topic that had been mined earlier by sociologists studying varying form of speech. Like others researching language use during this period, Nofsinger declared that his goal was to contribute to a grammar of conversation by elucidating rules underlying how utterances are connected and how speakers make sense of those connections.

Specifically, Nofsinger collected examples of sequences of conversation where direct questions were answered indirectly. Generally, the connection that drives understanding of an indirect response is found in understanding the relationship of the speakers and shared history that helps to supply the meaning. For example, Nofsinger explained that the answer, "Do I dress like this to go fishing?" to the question, "Having lunch with the dean?" makes sense if one knows that the person answering typically dresses casually but not sloppily.

Questions may be answered legitimately in numerous ways. The answer to the question, "Are you going to be working at the office?" may be as direct as,

"No," or as indirect as "The kids are sick," or somewhere in between, such as "When the kids are sick. I work at home." The question may also be answered in an exaggerated form designed to be emphatic, such as "When hell freezes over," or "Is the Pope Catholic?"

Nofsinger concluded with a brief discussion of how this question-answer process was similar in function to the enthymeme in rhetorical reasoning. Elements of the reasoning may be left out because the speakers co-create the meaning through their interaction and their understanding of the rules underlying that interaction.

Symbolic Interactionism

Hart and Burks (1972) observed that the terms of "ideal" communication had changed with the *Zeitgeist* of the 1960s. Communicators were encouraged to be authentic, direct, sometimes to the point of being brutal. Hart and Burks took issue with these prescriptions for speakers to be expressive, reasoning that a kind of instrumental "rhetoric-in-action" was a better approach to building effective interpersonal relations. The authors labeled this instrumental approach as "rhetorical sensitivity," and they laid out five characteristics of it, based primarily in symbolic interactionist principles: (1) accepting role-taking as part of the human conditions; (2) avoiding stylized verbal behavior; (3) willingness to undergo the strain of adaptation; (4) distinguishing between all information and information acceptable for communication; and (5) knowing that ideas can be rendered in multiform ways.

In discussing role-taking, Hart and Burks drew directly on Mead and Dewey to assert that people have many roles available to them, that they consciously make choices as how to adapt their roles to a given situation, and that the notion of a "true self" from which one can speak authentically is antithetical to the ability to creating rhetorical definitions of one's roles in various relationships through ongoing interaction.

Regarding stylized verbal behavior, Hart and Burks defined it as dogged adherence to "sure fire" verbal formulations (such as Dale Carnegie's advice to smile and use the other person's name regularly in conversation) or adhering to consistency for the sake of consistency. Rather, they argued, effective interpersonal relationships are formed out of struggle in the moment, when the speaker makes decisions about what to say and how to say it based on an assessment of how the conversation can best be coordinated and how ideas can be best expressed.

Regarding the strain of adaptation, Hart and Burks argued that adaptation is both necessary and a strain, because it arises out of what they called "interaction consciousness." Such consciousness arises out of not only an assessment of the current moment but from an understanding of the history of the relationship and the capabilities of each person involved in the interaction. Adaptation, too, does not lead to a position of other-directedness. Rather, it involves making choices about when and how to defend the self, as well as how to acknowledge the other without encouraging domination by the other.

Adaptation necessarily involves making choices about what to say and how to say it. Here is where the fourth principle of rhetorical sensitivity comes to the fore. One need not say whatever one thinks to be true to oneself. Rather, an interaction consciousness requires saying things in a way that will achieve the speaker's ends while still maintaining the integrity of the relationship. Sometimes, this process will warrant saying nothing rather than saying something that will potentially damage the relationship. Self-disclosure for the sake of self-disclosure can be damaging, not only to the relationship but to the individual making the disclosure as well.

Related to making choices is the dictum that there are multiple ways of saying the same thing, and rhetorical sensitivity involves an ability to understand how to choose ways of saying things that will contribute most productively to the development of the relationship. This ability also includes how to recognize when one has said something in a less-than-effective way and to make amends for doing so.

Rhetorical sensitivity implies that individuals are "always unsure, always guessing, continually weighing" (p. 91). But, such a strenuous intellectual and emotional exercise is essential to the ongoing development of effective interpersonal relationships, as well as to the sharing of responsibility for the outcomes of the relationships in which individuals are engaged.

CONCLUSION

Language use was central to the speech communication understanding of communication. It proved to be the theme that drove the diversification of the study of rhetoric away from a focus on public address, and it also provided a means of implementing more than one qualitative means of conducting research that could yield rich and interesting data on a variety of speech acts and communication episodes. Rather than spark a duel that had already begun between rhetoricians and "behavioral scientists," the qualitative study of language use eventually proved to become accepted as a means of advancing knowledge in the communication discipline. The period between 1964 and 1982, however, was a time when these qualitative methods were being discovered by speech communication scholars, and most of the scholarship during this period consisted of introducing colleagues to these other approaches and, in addition, to building on the work of the group of sociologists who were studying conversation and generating theory regarding speech acts and communication episodes as new units of analysis.

Some media scholars found semiotics to be appealing, with its emphasis on images and metaphors serving as "signs" that could potentially produce a vocabulary of film or television. Semiotics would prove to become a basis for a discipline of film studies, one that focused on how audiences understood various types of film. This study helped understand film as art, as opposed to film as communication. As we shall see, many media scholars interested in film as communication would come to embrace British cultural studies as a basis for what would become "media studies," as opposed to "mass communication."

Language use was central enough to communication study that it would prove to overlap with the other strands of research I have identified. Particularly, language scholars were interested in how language use influenced the development of interpersonal relationships and how language intertwined with the development of culture. Philipsen's ethnographic work pushed the boundaries of language use and culture and showed speech communication scholars that the study of culture did not have to transcend national boundaries to be insightful.

Quantitative scholars were refining their work as well during this period, and the next chapter returns to how their scholarship evolved from applying information theory to understanding cognitive processes that underlie communication effects.

REFERENCES

Austin, J. L. (1961). *Philosophical Papers*. Oxford: Clarendon Press.

Benjamin, J. (1976). The viability of general semantics. *Speech Education, 4*, 155–160.

Berryman, C. L. & Wilcox, J. R. (1980). Attitudes toward male and female speech: Experiments on the effects of sex-typical language. *Western Journal of Speech Communication, 44*, 50–59. doi:10.1080/10570318009373985

Blumer, H. (1969). *Symbolic Interactionism: Perspective and Method*. Englewood Cliffs, NJ: Prentice-Hall.

Booth, W. C. (1974). *Modern Dogma and the Rhetoric of Assent*. Notre Dame: University of Notre Dame Press.

Bostrom, R. M. & Kemp, A. P. (1969). Type of speech, sex of speaker, and sex of subject as factors influencing persuasion. *Central States Speech Journal, 20*, 245–251. doi:10.1080/10510976909362975

Burke, K. (1950). *A Rhetoric of Motives*. Berkeley, CA: University of California Press.

Cassirer, E. & Yale University. Louis Stern Memorial Fund. (1944). An essay on man: An introduction to a philosophy of human culture (Yale paperbound). New Haven: London: Yale University Press; H. Milford, Oxford University Press.

Corcoran, F. (1981). Towards a semiotic of screen media: Problems in the use of linguistic models. *Western Journal of Speech Communication, 45*, 182–193. doi:10.1080/10570318109374040

Cronkite, G. (1984). Perception and meaning. In Arnold, C. C., & Bowers, J. W. (eds.) *Handbook of Rhetorical and Communication Theory* (pp. 51–229). Boston, MA: Allyn and Bacon.

Ehninger, D. & Brockriede, W. (1963). *Decision by Debate*. New York: Dodd, Mead.

Fisher, W. R. (1978). Toward a logic of good reasons. *Quarterly Journal of Speech, 64*, 376–384. doi:10.1080/00335637809383443

Goldberg, A. (1965). The effects of a laboratory course in General Semantics. *ETC: A Review of General Semantics, 22*, 19–24. Retrieved September 5, 2020, from http://www.jstor.org/stable/42574076

Gorman, M. (1967). A critique of general semantics. *Western Speech, 31*, 44–50.

Hart, R. P. & Burks, D. M. (1972). Rhetorical sensitivity and social interaction. *Speech Monographs, 39*, 75–91. doi:10.1080/03637757209375742

Hayakawa, S. I. (1944). *Language in Thought and Action*. New York: Harcourt, Brace.

Johnson, W. (1946). *People in Quandaries: The Semantics of Personal Adjustment*. New York: Harper & Row.

Kibler, R. J., Barker, L. L. & Cegala, D. J. (1970). Effect of sex on comprehension and retention. *Speech Monographs, 37*, 287–293. doi:10.1080/03637757009375680

Korzybski, A. (1948). *Science and Sanity: An Introduction to Non-Aristotelian Systems and General Semantics* (3rd edition). Lakeville, CT: International Non-Aristotelian Library Pub. Co.

Kramer, C. (1974). Women's speech: Separate but unequal? *Quarterly Journal of Speech, 60*, 14–24. doi:10.1080/00335637409383203

Lakoff, R. (1975). *Language and Woman's Place*. New York: Harper and Row.

Langer, S. K. (1951). *Philosophy in a New Key: A Study in the Symbolism of Reason, Rite and Art*. Cambridge: Harvard University Press.

Langer, S. K. (1960). The origins of speech and its communicative function. *Quarterly Journal of Speech, 46*, 121–135. doi:10.1080/00335636009382402

Lee, I. J. (1941). *Language Habits in Human Affairs: An Introduction to General Semantics*. New York: Harper & Brothers.

Liska, J., Mechling, E. W. & Stathas, S. (1981). Differences in subjects' perceptions of gender and believability between users of deferential and nondeferential language. *Communication Quarterly, 29*, 40–48. doi:10.1080/01463378109369388

Matson, F. & Montagu, A. (1967). *The Human Dialogue: Perspectives on Communication*. New York: The Free Press.

Mead, G. H. (1934). *Mind, Self & Society from the Standpoint of a Social Behaviorist*, edited by Charles W. Morris. Chicago, IL: University of Chicago Press.

Nofsinger, R. E., Jr. (1976). On answering questions indirectly: Some rules in the grammar of doing conversation. *Human Communication Research, 2,* 172–181. doi:10.1111/j.1468-2958.1976.tb00709.x

Ogden, C. K. & Richards, I. A. (1946). *The Meaning of Meaning: A Study of the Influence of Language Upon Thought and of the Science of Symbolism.* New York: Harcourt, Brace.

Osgood, C. E. (1953). *Method and Theory in Experimental Psychology.* New York: Oxford University Press.

Ott, B. L. & Domenico, M. (2015). Conceptualizing meaning in communication studies. In Gehrke, P. J. & Keith, W. M. (eds.), *A Century of Communication Studies: The Unfinished Conversation* (pp. 224–260). New York: Routledge.

Philipsen, G. (1975). Speaking "Like a Man" in Teamsterville: Culture patterns of role enactment in an urban neighborhood. *Quarterly Journal of Speech, 61,* 13–22. doi:10.1080/00335637509383264

Richards, I. A. (1936). *The Philosophy of Rhetoric.* New York: Oxford University Press.

Saussure, F. de. (1959). *Writings in General Linguistics.* Translated by Wade Baskin. New York: Columbia University Press.

Scott, R. L. (1967). On viewing rhetoric as epistemic. *Central States Speech Journal, 18,* 9–17. doi:10.1080/10510976709362856

Stewart, J. (1972). Concepts of language and meaning: A comparative study. *Quarterly Journal of Speech, 58,* 123–133. doi:10.1080/00335637209383108

Toulmin, S. (1958). *The Uses of Argument.* Cambridge [England]: University Press.

Wallace, K. R. (1963). The substance of rhetoric: Good reasons. *Quarterly Journal of Speech, 49,* 239–249. doi:10.1080/00335636309382611

Chapter 6

Communication as Information Transmission

Communication as information transmission is arguably the most familiar of the strands of research in the academic discipline of communication. The models and ideas that drove it were replicated and taught in basic communication courses for many years. The idea that a message gets from a sender to a receiver is a simple and direct way of understanding communication, even though it was clear that message transmission was typically much more complex than the model suggested. Trying to adapt a machine model to human communication proved to be difficult, as little was known about human capacity to process information. This cognitive function was, in the early days, represented as a "black box": scholars knew that something went on, but they weren't sure what it was. Still, it was appealing to pick one or more variables and measure their effects on one or more other variables. Often, there was little to no theory involved in the variable selection, though generally the idea was to build theory bit by bit, eventually arriving at universal truth, or what might be called a law.

Communication scholars would incorporate concepts from social psychology into their research, as these concepts had already been developed and used productively in related scholarship. This borrowing occurred both in research on face-to-face communication and in mass communication scholarship.

Fairly early on, some communication scholars distinguished between information transmission and information systems. Basing this distinction in General Systems Theory (Bertalanffy, 1969), these scholars attempted to move beyond variable analysis by incorporating system thinking into how information flows, as opposed to transmission. Systems thinking allowed a variety of additional concepts to be added to a model of communication that incorporated principles of information systems.

In this chapter, I will summarize articles and book chapters that helped to define how the information transmission approach was distinguished from the information systems approach. I will provide examples of variable analytic research, both in face-to-face and mass communication, and I will especially focus on mass communication scholarship that became known as Uses and Gratifications research (Katz, Blumler, & Gurevitch, 1973). I will also summarize a theory of human organizing that, while not from the communication discipline, incorporated information system principles and became very influential with communication scholars (Weick, 1969).

NONSYSTEM'S APPROACHES TO
INFORMATION TRANSMISSION

Klaus Krippendorff (1975, 1977) wrote influential essays on information theory, as it was maturing in communication research. Krippendorff's essential point was that information transmission only makes sense when viewed as part of a system, but he did distinguish between nonsystems and systems approaches to the concept of information in his 1977 essay for the first volume of ICA's *Communication Yearbook* series.

Krippendorff listed several examples of nonsystems study based primarily in models of information transmission. His first example took an unique event and described it from a variety of perspectives. Krippendorff attributed this method of study to historians but was then quick to point out that such study could yield interesting insights. Those insights would be the scholar's own, however.

A second example would be the study of individual variables in a model of the information transmission process. By manipulating only one variable and holding others constant, Krippendorff argued, ignores too much of what is going on in the information transmission process. Krippendorff especially hearkened back to a revised version of Lasswell's model of communication: "Who" "Says What" "In What Channel" "To Whom" "With What Effect," as yielding insights about how individual communicators control the transmission; how content analysis may yield insights about messages; how media analysis might provide ideas about differences between mediated and face-to-face transmission, as well as differences in effectiveness of a variety of transmission technologies; how audience analysis can describe characteristics of various groups of receivers; and how effect analysis can look for predictable and unpredictable impacts of the transmission process. While these insights may well be useful, Krippendorff argued that they do not describe appropriately communication as the result of information transmission.

Krippendorff (1975) also summarized information theory's mathematical base as a means of describing its potential for explaining information as a concept at the syntactic, semantic, and pragmatic levels. Stipulating that information is primarily measured in bits (at the simplest level, whether a column of data contains a 0 or a 1), the more bits of information, the more predictable the transmission becomes.

There is the possibility of no information, according to Krippendorff. If no alternatives exist, no decision is necessary and the environment is, for the moment, completely certain. Of course, it doesn't stay that way for long. We live in a world where we are always making choices and need information to reduce uncertainty by the choices we make. Over time, patterns develop, and it becomes possible to assign probabilities to the occurrence of one choice over another. Krippendorff posited that these probabilities can be assigned statistically, as well as what he called "semantically," as language itself is substantially predictable, or, in information theory terms, redundant. The technical term for the measurement of uncertainty is "entropy," but Krippendorff contended that "uncertainty" was better, because there is not a complete fit between the mathematical basis of mechanical systems and human systems.

And, besides, human information processing doesn't occur in a vacuum: information flow always occurs in a context. Even if one simple message is highly important, the reason we know it is important is due to understanding the context in which it occurs.

There are two sources of interference with the message transmission process, Krippendorff, wrote. "Noise" is one, and it was included in Shannon and Weaver's original model. Krippendorff added "equivocation" as a form of interference. Noise was originally understood as interference in the channel, as messages passed from sender to receiver. As forms of mechanical communication developed, one of the key engineering problems to tackle was how much noise could be tolerated before the sender's message would not be understood by the receiver. From the engineer's perspective, improvements to the means of transmission, ranging from better cables or finding means of transmission, such as via satellites, where the fidelity of the signal might be improved.

Equivocation, the other source of interference, is a semantic, rather than a mechanical, concept. Hearers may have a variety of interpretations of what speakers say, including inferences that do not coincide at all with the speaker's intent. The remedy for this sort of interferences is repetition. "In other words" serves as a key that the speaker is trying to improve message fidelity by using different language to say what had already been said. To the extent that perfect transmission is the desired goal of the message-sending-and-receiving process, its outcome is achieved when "redundancy equals or exceeds the noise in the transmission" (1975, p. 381).

It is possible for information systems to contain too much uncertainty, requiring a higher level of information processing than an individual can handle, cognitively. This phenomenon, known as "information overload," can be handled by finding ways of combining information into more general units, as well as by ignoring aspects of the transmission. Krippendorff called this phenomenon a "shift of attention from what a message means to what it doesn't mean" (p. 387).

Krippendorff concluded his survey of information theory with these words:

> Any information theory requires a clear differentiation of elements, signals, messages, events, etc., whose flow, causes, or effects are being assessed. In human communication, this is not always given naturally. The workings of the human mind are often quite amorphous and diffuse, and numerous interpretations of its expressions are possible. But occasionally clear thoughts and mutually exclusive categories and distinctions grow out of it, which become at once amenable to formal analysis. Social science data satisfy this formal requirement most obviously; hence, information theory can contribute to the formation of data-based social theory. Technology, engineering in particular but also managerial decision-making, also has this rational quality; hence, the initial success of information theory in these fields. Where distinctions between what is and what is not cannot be easily made, any theoretical comprehension is difficult. In such situations, information theory can hardly exhibit its power as a calculus, but it can still be a source of ideas for understanding communication and control in complex systems. (pp. 387–388)

CHARACTERISTICS OF AND MISCONCEPTIONS ABOUT SYSTEMS IN COMMUNICATION SCHOLARSHIP

In the essay on Information Systems in *Communication Yearbook 2*, B. Aubrey Fisher (1978) lamented the lack of common understanding of how systems approaches could be used in communication scholarship. Fisher contended that "most misconceptions [of system theory] result from unfairly delimiting system approaches so that a rejection of system theory relies on reasons which are generally superficial" (p. 82). Fisher offered four misconceptions about systems approaches, and then outlined relevant concepts of system theory and particular concepts of information systems, offering broad categories of information systems research as well.

The first misconception was, "Systems are mere analogies without explanatory value." Fisher wrote, "systems approaches to communication inquiry are not merely metaphors. Rather, they are attempts to establish a heuristic basis for the discovery of generalizations, laws or rules which serve to explain the phenomena of human communication" (p. 82). He went on to say,

Clearly, systems research relies on analogies, models, or metaphors developed from principles of much greater generality. Concepts such as structure, homeostasis, equifinality, wholeness, etc., do not "belong to" communication. But, in their application to the phenomena of communication, they go beyond their metaphorical existence and become principles which serve to explain and have a referent in the phenomena of human communication. (p. 83)

In other words, systems perspectives provide a "framework for organizing empirical phenomena and generating research questions" (p. 83).

The second misconception was "The goal of system theory is to provide a general theory for the unification of all science—physical and social." While such a goal was stated as General System Theory was being formatted—and was carried out through attempting to impose the mathematics of physics on individual disciplines, Fisher dismissed this idea as of little relevance to the study of communication. While he purported to like the tenents of systems approaches, and he found systems approaches to be useful to the study of communication, he thought the idea of unification to be a dead end as a goal for communication scholarship. I should note that there had been a time when the study of speech was argued to be an integrator of the arts and sciences (Hefferline, 1955), so Fisher's assertion of a "misconception" more than twenty years later announced a shift in disciplinary thinking.

The third misconception was that "System Theory is a rigid logical formalization which imposes structure on the empirical world." I should note here that Fisher was writing amidst a debate among whether covering laws, systems, or rules presented the most viable means of theory building in communication. The laws approach had been disparaged (c. f., Bochner, 1977) but rules approaches were being debated regarding their ability to be akin to covering laws (c. f., Adler, 1978). Fisher contended that such rigidity should not be imposed on a "communication theory" that was yet in its early stages of development.

Fisher's final misconception was that "Systems approaches are dependent upon the purposes of inquiry." Here, Fisher was specifically responding to Cushman and Pearce (1977), who advocated for rules approaches, *vis-a-vis* systems. Fisher cited Berlo (1960) to contend that reality is created rather than discovered. Fisher argued that systems approaches are certainly a function of the purpose of inquiry. But, he concluded, "Because systems approaches to communication emanate from the purposes of the inquiry does not imply that they employ a specific or limited method of performing inquiry. Like other perspectives, systems approaches reflect a methodological and conceptual disparity" (p. 86).

Fisher also discussed several characteristics of System Theory that are useful to understanding the distinctiveness of this approach. These characteristics were: holism and nonsummativity, or, in more common parlance, "The whole is greater than the sum of its parts"; and openness, including equifinality (the same state may be reached by different paths), decreases in entropy (the amount of randomness in the system), evolutionary processes (which lead to increased complexity), and self-regulation. Fisher elaborated on hierarchical organization to mean that systems exist within sub-systems and supra-systems, and these systems need a method of communication to continue the hierarchy. Fisher explained organized complexity, which implies that systems will have structures and functions and those are likely to be related in non-simple ways. Self-regulation, according to Fisher, implies that feedback processes exist within systems that allow choice of how the system interacts with its environment.

In terms of information and communication systems, Fisher contended that they are both social and complex. They are social, in that humans are their basic components, though humans not only exchange information and communicate with other humans but with technology as well. Fisher's description of the levels of these systems maps well onto what many have called "context," such as intrapersonal, dyadic, interpersonal, group, organizational, and mass communication. I should note here that these levels of system analysis are structural, though they have implications for system functions. I should also note that I have eschewed hierarchical analysis in defining the five strands of communication scholarship I discerned occurring between 1964 and 1982. While the labels I've given to these five strands do not make them entirely distinctive from each other, they, ideally at least, exist on equal levels of legitimacy in communication scholarship. Thus, they add complexity to our understanding of the concept of "communication" without a claim that any are "superior" or "subordinate" to each other.

Fisher concluded that communication systems are frustrating for scholars, because they imply choices that scholars would rather not make. So, systems might not bring a coherent theory of particular communication phenomena, but it might serve as a good organizing principle for study of the implications of communication in society.

LISTENING RESEARCH: AN EXAMPLE OF SCHOLARSHIP USING AN INFORMATION THEORY PERSPECTIVE

Listening is a topic that almost begs to be studied from an information theory perspective. It requires some ability, and there are multiple potential factors that might influence retention of content, which is what is typically measured in listening studies of this period.

Charles R. Petrie, Jr. and Susan Carrel (1976) published a study in *Communication Monographs* titled, "The Relationship of Motivation, Listening Capability, Initial Information, and Verbal Organizational Ability to Lecture Comprehension and Retention." Sorting through the title provides understanding of what would be the independent and dependent variables in this research. The dependent variable was comprehension of a university-level lecture, both immediately after hearing it and a couple of weeks later. The independent variables were motivation, listening capability, initial information, and verbal organization ability.

The authors formulated three hypotheses to guide the study. First, they hypothesized that the following variables would best account for immediate comprehension of a 20-minute lecture: listening comprehension ability, extrinsic motivation, verbal organization ability, initial information, aroused interest, and intrinsic interest in the topic. Second, they hypothesized that listening comprehension ability and extrinsic motivation would be the most influential variables for understanding immediate comprehension, as they anticipated that the other variables would be correlated with these two. Third, they anticipated that immediate comprehension and initial information would be most related to delayed retention of the lecture content, as individuals who already knew at least some of the material contained the lecture would better be able to answer questions about the lecture later.

To test these hypotheses, the researchers selected 100 males in a first-year communication course and randomly assigned them to experimental and control conditions. All of the students took tests measuring their verbal organization ability, their listening comprehension ability, their level of information about radio and television speaking, the topic of the lecture, as well as their initial level of interest in this topic. The students then watched a male lecturer present the content via a video recording for twenty minutes. Immediately thereafter, the students completed measures of their interest in and immediate comprehension of the lecture material. Two weeks later, the students completed another measure of retention of the lecture content.

The difference between the experimental and control groups was that the experimental group was told that they were selected especially for viewing this lecture, based on instructor recommendations, and that they could earn additional course credit if they did well on the test that would be given after viewing the lecture. Students in the control group were asked to watch the lecture, were told that the material would not count in their course grade, and were not told that they would be tested on the content after they watched the video.

Data analysis indicated that listening ability and extrinsic motivation were the two major variables that predicted immediate lecture comprehension, while the other variables measured accounted for only a small amount of the overall predictive ability. Delayed comprehension of the lecture was influenced most by the initial interest in the topic, the intrinsic interest in the lecture, and the aroused interest from watching the lecture. The two variables named in the hypothesis, initial information and immediate comprehension, had little value in predicting delayed comprehension.

The authors concluded that these results were more confusing than helpful in understanding listening comprehension. While it makes sense that general listening ability and extrinsic motivation affected immediate comprehension of the lecture, the other variables made only a minor contribution. And the variables affecting delayed comprehension were even more confusing, as someone with low interest but considerable information about the lecture topic did no better in comprehending the lecture immediately after listening to it, what that person did learn was retained better than other students who participated in the study.

The problem may well have come from how "listening" was conceptualized. Rather than trying to measure how an individual processed information, the researchers looked for results of tests of social psychological factors that they could measure and which they thought affected the listening process. The cognitive activity involved remained in the "black box." As a result, listening research during this period produced more confusion than clarity.

USES AND GRATIFICATIONS AS AN INFORMATION PROCESSING APPROACH TO MASS COMMUNICATION

Mass communication researchers were interested in the amount people used various media and for what purposes they used it. Some of this research was related to studying media as influencing individual and public opinion (c.f., chapter 4, this volume), but other research examined how people processed information presented by various media. The desire to account for motivations for consuming various media led to the Uses and Gratifications lines of research (Katz, Blumler, & Gurevitch, 1973). The study I selected as an exemplar focused on using media as a means of processing information for later use.

Charles Atkin (1972) wanted to see what media his college student subjects consumed and how they used the content in conversations with others. To explore the relationship between media consumption and proclivity to talk about media content with others, Atkin did two secondary analyses and conducted an experiment.

The first secondary analysis examined data collected for another purpose, but which asked questions of interest to Atkin. The questions involved the number of groups with whom adult subjects discussed news content and the number of newspapers read daily, along with the daily time devoted to newspaper reading and weekly time devoted to magazine reading. The subjects were also asked how frequently they were asked their opinion of topics in the news. Both the number of groups for news discussions and the number of times others asked for the individual's opinion were related to the number of newspapers read daily, the amount of daily time spent reading newspapers, and the weekly amount of time spent reading magazines.

The other secondary analysis examined data from a study of Wisconsin voters' perceptions of a political campaign. Atkin had data on four predictor variables and the levels of media exposure to newspaper and magazine coverage of the campaign, television coverage of the political conventions associated with the campaign, and television news and public affairs programming. The analysis indicated that levels of exposure to newspaper and magazine coverage of the campaign exhibited the strongest positive relationships with (1) frequency of discussing the election campaign, (2) level of interest in the election campaign, (3) amount of the respondent's education, and (4) income of the respondent's family. Levels of exposure to both the television coverage of the political convention and to television news and public affairs programming were positively related to these four variables but at lower levels of strength. Atkin attributed these findings to wanting to be prepared for discussions about these political events. Clearly, reading newspapers provided opportunities to process information that would be useful in these discussions to a more complete extent than watching television, no matter whether the content was specific to the election or more general news and public affairs programming.

Atkin also conducted an experiment, using local high-school seniors. The students were enrolled in a class on social problems and current events. They were divided into three groups to discuss different types of problems for the study. One group discussed national problems, a second group discussed problems local to the city where they lived, and a third group discussed problems within the school the students attended. As part of a longer questionnaire, students also reported their media use patterns, both for a typical day and for the past two days, when they were preparing for the discussion group to which they had been assigned. The analysis focused on how students prepared for the national problems group, as compared to the local and school problems groups. The students in the national and local groups paid more attention to news that would be relevant for them in their upcoming discussions, but they did not consume more news media in total. Rather, they paid better attention to the stories that would be relevant for the class assignment.

Atkin concluded that anticipating that one will need to communicate with others about media content fosters greater attention to that content,

particularly for reading newspapers. He added that the anticipated circumstances of the communication, along with whether the person anticipated
either agreement or disagreement with another on the topic played a role
in how much and to what content the person paid attention. Finally, people
often anticipated that they would have conversations about the news, citing
newspaper reading in particular as playing a substantial role in "keeping up"
so that the anticipated conversations would be productive ones.

AN EVOLUTIONARY THEORY OF ORGANIZING

Karl Weick (1969), a management professor at the University of Minnesota,
published a book that revolutionized management theory. Rather than
focusing on the nature of organizations, Weick focused on the process of
organizing, shifting the emphasis from what the organization (and, by extension, management) did to what people do when they want to make sense
of their environments. Weick focused on process rather than on individual
behavior, and his theory was rooted in information systems concepts and
principles. Implicit in this process was how organizing could be seen as a
sophisticated use of these ideas. Once discovered by communication scholars,
Weick's work quickly became popular with those studying organizational
communication, and Weick himself saw how his ideas fit with the idea of
communication.

Weick's concise summary of his idea of organizing was as follows:
"Organizing consists of the resolving of equivocality in an enacted environment by means of interlocked behaviors embedded in conditionally related
processes" (p. 91). Given the terminology, we can determine that Weick used
systems ideas in constructing his theory, and in fact, the mechanism by which
his theory works is information processing. I will backtrack here to explain
how information processing works in Weick's account of the organizing
process.

Weick worked from the notion that when equivocality presents itself in a
system, the system works to recognize it and remove it. Recall that "equivocality" is a synonym for "entropy" or "uncertainty," and open systems make
a priority of reducing equivocality so that an equilibrium of randomness and
predictability is achieved. There is always randomness in a system, and the
counterforce to randomness is organization, which is accomplished by creating predictably.

Predictability is created through behavior, according to Weick, and behavior isn't individual. Rather, it's dependent on relationships, which arise from
communication. Weick described the basic unit of this relational behavior
as the "double interact": that is, Person A enacts something that potentially

makes a change in the system, Person B responds to Person A (Weick calls this an "Interact"), and Person A takes into account Person B's response and makes a determination how to act further (the "double interact"). These actions help both Person A and Person B to make sense of the current state of the system, and doing so reduces equivocality. Weick calls each set of double interacts a "cycle," and as "cycles" proliferate, the people involved in creating them select those that make sense and interpret them in terms of "rules" for enacting them again. Those rules help the participants make further sense of the environment and allow for the reduction of equivocation to proceed more efficiently.

The patterns of behavior that "work best" over time are retained, while those that spawn more equivocation, which may threaten the equilibrium of the system, are candidates for being discarded. The people involved in the process make sense of it retrospectively: that is, they come to understand it after the fact. Weick borrowed an aphorism, attributed to E. M. Forster, "How do I know what I think until I see what I say?" to summarize how the process of meaning creation works.

The stages of enactment, selection and retention were borrowed from the theory of evolution, and Weick saw organizing as an evolutionary process. Over time, what is organized tends to become more and more complex, and this trend toward complexity helps keep the system open to its environment and processing the resulting equivocation in a manner that exerts increasing control over the system. Indeed, Weick contended that it is backward thinking to assume that organizations have begun to achieve certain goals. Rather, he argued that while such goals may exist, they are overshadowed by the goals that emerge from the sense people make of the organizations in which they are participating. Those overarching goals may be as simple as, "I want to stay employed," which can drive both behaviors that facilitate the enactment-selection-retention process and behaviors that can inhibit it or send it off in a different direction.

In any case, communication, as conceptualized as systemic processing of information by two or more people, is the heart of the organizing process. Weick illustrated how the organizing process works in practice with five "practical suggestions": (pp. 106–108)

1. *Don't panic in the face of disorder.* Too much rationality and order is a sign of trouble rather than a sign of prosperity. Disorder is the system's way of feeding back on the choices made in the enactment-selection-retention process and prompting an ongoing reconsideration of the "sense" that the organization makes.
2. *You can never do one thing all at once.* In a system, enactment always leads to adjustment. The system reacts to an individual's attempt to

"complete" a task. Sometimes, these reactions are immediate, sometimes, they are delayed.

3. *Chaotic action is preferable to orderly inaction.* Recalling that sensemaking is retrospective, "chaotic" action is, by definition, that which introduces equivocation into the system, causing it to engage in the "healthy" process of registering and reducing that equivocation.

4. *The most important decisions are often the least apparent.* As Weick wrote, "decisions made in the selection process have less to do with the fate of a system than do the decisions made concerning retention. This means that the retention process and the persons who mediate between it and the selection and enactment processes are the most crucial points in terms of organizing" (p. 107).

5. *You should coordinate processes rather than groups.* Behavior, as defined as cycles of double interact among at least two people, is what begins the enactment-selection-retention process. Groups may form around these cycles, but it is the behavior the groups engage in, via the relationships among the group members, that drives the organizing process. But, at the organizational level, Weick wrote that the functioning of the overall system is guided by a control network, "and this network comprises relationships among processes, not among groups" (p. 108).

CONCLUSION

It was clear from relatively early on that engineering conceptions of "communication" would be limited in explaining human interaction. The question became how the linear formulation of the transmission model might be modified to account for the oftentimes nonlinear progress of human interaction. There was a drive to impose a "scientific" veneer to communication study, but that drive was criticized by scholars who saw that studying how variables interacted with each other sometimes led to more confusion than to clarity. There was considerable scholarly debate in the 1970s particularly about the utility of "laws" versus "systems" and "rules" as ontological and epistemic frameworks for studying communication, and I have only glossed that debate.

As usual, mass communication scholars proved to be more closely knit and, consequently, as a group, generated a relatively small number of theoretical approaches, each of which attracted a relatively large number of individual published studies. There was also, during this era, more agreement among mass communication scholars not only about what to study but also about how to study it than there was among speech communication scholars. Some of the mass communication unity was driven by societal concerns about the rapid development of nonprint media and how that development might affect both individuals and society as a whole. In other words, the general public worried about how mass communication was affecting them in ways that it did not worry about for face-to-face communication.

Systems proved to be a popular way of conceptualizing communication, but the systems approach also proved to be a somewhat problematic way of actually studying communication. Weick's breakthrough, by focusing on the process of organizing, rather than the organization as a context of communication, assisted communication researchers to see some alternatives for their scholarship from a man who was an eloquent mix of empirical scientist and phenomenological philosopher. That combination proved to be an appealing one, though the publication of relatively atheoretical, variable analytic, scholarship continued to be the lifeblood of some communication journals.

Weick's ideas about the importance of relationships as means of organizing experience served to moved "interpersonal communication" beyond a context-driven variable-analytic approach as well. I shall explore the development of "relational communication" scholarship in chapter 7.

REFERENCES

Adler, K. (1978). On the falsification of rules theories. *Quarterly Journal of Speech, 64*, 427–438. doi:10.1080/00335637809383448

Atkin, C. K. (1972). Anticipated communication and mass media information-seeking. *Public Opinion Quarterly, 36*, 188–199. doi:10.1086/267991

Berlo, D. K. (1960). *The Process of Communication.* New York: Holt, Rinehart and Winston.

Bertalanffy, L. (1969). *General System Theory: Foundations, Development, Applications* (International library of systems theory and philosophy). New York: George Braziller.

Bochner, A. P. (1977). Whither communication theory and research? *Quarterly Journal of Speech, 63*, 324–332. doi:10.1080/00335637709383392

Cushman, D. P. & Pearce, W. B. (1977). Generality and necessity in three types of human communication theory — Special attention to rules theory. In Ruben, B. D. (ed.), *Communication Yearbook 1* (pp.173–182). New Brunswick, NJ: Transaction Books. doi:10.1080/23808985.1977.11923679

Fisher, B. A. (1978). Information systems theory and research: An overview. In Ruben, B. D. (ed.), *Communication Yearbook 2* (pp. 81–124). New Brunswick, NJ: Transaction Books.

Hefferline, R. F. (1955). Communication theory: I. Integrator of the arts and sciences. *Quarterly Journal of Speech, 41*, 223–233. doi:10.1080/00335635509382071

Katz, E., Blumler, J. G. & Gurevitch, M. (1973). Uses and gratifications research. *Public Opinion Quarterly, 37*, 509–523. doi:10.1086/268109

Krippendorff, K. (1975). Information theory. In Hannenman, G. J., S. & McEwen, W. J. (eds.), *Communication and Behavior* (pp. 351–389). Reading, MA: Addison-Wesley.

Krippendorff, K. (1977). Information systems theory and research: An overview. In Ruben, B. D. (ed.), *Communication Yearbook 1* (pp. 149–171). New Brunswick, NJ: Transaction Books.

Petrie Jr., C. R. & Carrel, S. D. (1976). The relationship of motivation, listening capability, initial information, and verbal organizational ability to lecture comprehension and retention. *Communication Monographs*, *43*, 187–194. doi:10.1080/03637757609375931

Weick, K. E. (1969). *The Social Psychology of Organizing*. Reading, MA: Addison-Wesley Publishing Company.

Chapter 7

Communication as Developer
of Relationships

As speech transitioned to communication, it also transitioned from a focus on public speaking to other kinds of speaking. Early in this transition, there was some speculation about how these other forms of speaking were different from public address, but attention quickly turned to person-to-person communication as a context for study. While considerable attention had been paid to how people solved problems in groups, sometimes in a public forum—or a kind of group public speaking—it was clear that what became known as "interpersonal communication" was something different.

What made it different, speech scholars soon concluded, was an emphasis on the relationship that was being developed, both positively and negatively, between the people engaged in the communication. Theory development among speech researchers was perhaps at its most fertile in this strand of research, and while the term "interpersonal communication" persisted for quite a while, the term, "relational communication" also came into use.

Mass communication scholars made progress on understanding audiences during this period as well, and not solely from an "effects" perspective. Studies of interactions between media and their audiences paved the way for more sophisticated theory-building in the 1980s and beyond (c.f., Jackob, 2010).

In this chapter, I will provide sample studies on various kinds of relational communication research, including how the appearance of a volume laying out a sophisticated theory of human communication, the publication of a popular book on relationship development and decay, and the start of the ICA *Communication Yearbook* series contributed to the development of research on communication from a relational perspective.

It seems best to start with how "interpersonal communication" was assessed in the first volume of *Communication Yearbook* (1977). The *Yearbook* was initially conceptualized to provide annual review essays for each of ICA's divisions, along with sample studies, also organized by division. Charles R. Berger (1977), who wrote the overview essay on interpersonal communication, began with, "Had this overview been written 10 years ago, the characterization of the area of interpersonal communication would have been vastly different from the present one" (p. 271).

Berger acknowledged that communication scholars had a debt to pay to social psychologists for generating early work on face-to-face communication. But he noted that much of this work was focused on persuasion, while such studies had waned by the time his review was published. They had been replaced, he contended, by scholarship on negotiation and cooperation, and he speculated that some of this shift had been brought about by the rise of the "humanistic psychology" movement led by scholars and practitioners such as Carl Rogers (1961).

Berger also noted the various ways that interpersonal communication had been defined, including by numbers of persons interacting, by a distinction between "interpersonal" and "noninterpersonal" communication (Miller & Steinberg, 1975), or by rules approaches, such as Pearce's "coordinated management of meaning" (Pearce, 1976). In addition, Berger referenced his own work on what he called deductive and/or axiomatic theories (e.g., Berger & Calabrese, 1975).

In outlining the research directions taken by interpersonal scholars, Berger identified several main themes, including communicator style (e.g., Norton, 1978), communicative competence (e.g., Littlejohn & Jabusch, 1982), social influence processes (e.g., Seibold, 1975), nonverbal communication (e.g., Knapp, Hart, & Dennis, 1974), and self-disclosure (e.g., Delia, 1974). Berger also anticipated a shift toward relational communication (e.g., Parks, 1977) as the defining term for research in this area, along with a move from individual studies to process-oriented studies (e.g., Hewes, 1975). As a first try at summarizing interpersonal communication research and anticipating developments in that research, Berger succeeded admirably.

AN EXAMPLE OF "NON-RELATIONAL" INTERPERSONAL COMMUNICATION RESEARCH

Person perception was a strong strand of research in social psychology in the 1950s and going forward (Hastorf, Schneider, & Polefka, 1970). While the process of person perception might not be constitutive of interpersonal communication, it would be considered a foundational element worth studying in the context of interpersonal communication.

Such a study was undertaken by Jesse Delia and his associates at the University of Illinois at Urbana–Champaign. Working from a cognitive perspective, Delia and colleagues published a series of studies on differences in how individuals formed first impressions based on casual conversation.

An example of this research may be found in Delia, Clark, and Switzer (1974). Drawing on Kelly's (1955) work on factors influencing perception and Crockett's (1965) work on impression formation, the authors investigated how differences in individual levels of cognitive complexity influenced the impressions they formed when meeting a new person for the first time.

The authors divided student volunteers into pairs and put the two students in a room together. They were told that the study would begin shortly and left together to converse on their own, with a hidden tape recorder running. After ten minutes, the students were separated and told that the study was about how people formed impressions of individuals they just met. The students were asked to write as much as they could about the other person, as well as what they believed that the other person would write about them. They also filled out a survey where they could rate their impressions, and they were given some contradictory information about their partner and asked to write how their impression had changed. In addition, the students completed a measure of cognitive complexity, which asked them to generate as many terms as they could about two individuals they knew: one they liked and one they didn't like. Cognitive complexity was determined by counting the unique qualities that the students were able to write about the two people they knew.

Students were divided into a "high" and a "low" group by cognitive complexity scores. The two groups were compared on three composite measures: differentiation, level of organization, and evaluation. Each measure generated differences between the two groups. As the authors wrote, those students high in cognitive complexity "more differentiated, more abstract, more highly organized impressions after ten minutes of unstructured interaction with a stranger" (p. 306). The authors also concluded that persons with different levels of cognitive complexity "spontaneously structure their interpersonal environments in different ways" (p. 308). What is left unresearched, of course, is how these first impressions play out should the two decide to continue their communication. Impressive as studies such as this one were, they are open to criticism that communication is really in the background. The knowledge gained is more about individual differences and social psychological processes than it is about communication.

BEGINNINGS OF RELATIONAL COMMUNICATION AS AN ALTERNATIVE TO INTERPERSONAL COMMUNICATION

In 1967, three researchers at the Mental Research Institute in Palo Alto, California, published what would become a landmark book on communication theory. These three researchers had been pursuing techniques of treating communication dysfunction from a mental health standpoint, and their work initially was not well-known by professors in the emerging discipline of communication.

The earliest reference to *Pragmatics of Human Communication* (Watzlawick, Beavin, & Jackson, 1967) in a communication journal appeared in an article authored by Gerald Miller, in which he called readers' attention to several books of interest to scholars of communication theory (Miller, 1971). *Pragmatics of Human Communication* was reviewed toward the end of the article, and while Miller admired some of its way of analyzing its topic, he was not entirely convinced. Here's his assessment:

> Reading this book is a strange experience, for it is at once fragmented, yet whole. The axioms dealing with the impossibility of not communicating and with symmetrical and complementary interaction, the discussion of the punctuation of human interaction, the consideration of the family as a communication system, the explication of the double bind theory, these and numerous other lines of argument fit together to form a coherent viewpoint toward human communication. Moreover, the viewpoint differs drastically from what most students of communication have typically encountered. While the reader may choose to reserve judgment on the utility of the approach, he is at least likely to agree that Watzlawick et al. have managed to conceptualize the process of human communication in a novel way. (p. 9)

Miller's review may well have alerted communication scholars to this "novel way" of conceptualization, because, aside from one brief mention in another review (Smith, 1971) and one additional mention as part of an essay on new ways to conceptualize communication (Hawes, 1971), the next mention (Stewart, 1972) was taking Watzlawick, Beavin, and Jackson's basic ideas as axiomatic. By 1982, Watzlawick, Beavin, and Jackson's book had been cited in thirty-six articles in communication journals, including a comprehensive review of the Palo Alto group's perspective on communication (Wilder, 1979).

For the most part, however, communication scholars focused on chapter 2 of the text, which was titled, "Some Tentative Axioms of Communication." The authors advanced five such axioms, which, in formal theory, are building blocks that need no further defense. These axioms were (1) One cannot not communicate (p. 51); (2) Every communication has a content and a relationship aspect such that the latter classifies the former and is therefore a metacommunication (p. 54); (3) While, to an outside observer, a series of communications can be viewed as an uninterrupted sequence of interchanges, the participants in the interaction always introduce what Whorf, Bateson, and

Jackson have termed the "punctuation of the sequence of events" (p. 54); (4) Human beings communicate both digitally and analogically—digital language has a highly complex and powerful logical syntax but lacks adequate semantics in the field of relationship, while analogic language possesses the semantics but has no adequate syntax for the unambiguous definition of the nature of relationships (pp. 66–67); and (5) All communicational interchanges are either symmetrical or complimentary, depending on whether they are based on equality or difference (p. 70).

This "novel" approach was not always understood by communication scholars. Some thought that the idea that "one cannot not communicate" implied that everything was communication, thus rendering the term "communication" undefinable. Some took the notion of the "content" and "relationship" aspects of messages to mean verbal and nonverbal communication, while the authors' view was that messages contained both the text and information about how to interpret the text, in terms of the relationship that the speaker was implying with the hearer. The ideas of punctuation and digital and analogic language took some working through, but scholars eventually interpreted them as the perception of communication not as individual messages but as consisting of episodes that had beginnings, middles, and ends. And the idea that there were power differences in communication and that those differences could be accepted or resisted seemed clear to communication scholars. It was this idea that attracted the focus of research using these axioms as a base.

Frank Millar was one of the early doctoral students to take up the ideal of symmetry and complementarity, in his 1973 doctoral dissertation. He described that work in a volume of essays that helped to set a research agenda for scholars in communication (Millar & Rogers, 1976).

Millar and Rogers' article began with an interesting claim: "People become aware of themselves only within the context of their social relationships" (p. 87). The article went on to cite Gregory Bateson (1958) as the origin of the idea that messages have both content and relational characteristics, and, indeed, Bateson had been credited by Watzlawick, Beavin, and Jackson as having mentored their process of writing *Pragmatics of Human Communication*.

With that in mind, the authors declared that their purpose was to present a means of understanding relational communication at the interpersonal level. To do so, they would discuss the relational dimensions that would come into play in interaction, as well as a means of measuring those dimensions and some findings from initial work in the area.

Millar and Rogers described their work as transactional, meaning that while behavior is "made up of individual actions, [it has] a 'life' of its own, which goes beyond its constituent parts" (p. 90). They then posited that there were three "transactional dimensions of relationships" that were of interest: control, trust, and intimacy. While all three dimensions were necessary for the work that was reported, the control dimension, with its two-dimensional continua of "rigid/flexible" and "stable/unstable" seemed the most important.

The coding system that the authors presented attempted to measure control via coding a series of two-message exchanges. The first dimension of the scheme was the identity of the speaker (A or B), the second was the form of Speaker A's message (assertion, question, talk-over, noncomplete, or other), and the third was a means of categorizing Speaker B's response (support, nonsupport, extension, answer, instruction, order, disconfirmation, topic change, and initiation-termination). The authors went to some care to describe how these patterns of interaction fit into symmetrical/complementary relational control schema.

Millar and Rogers discussed results of initial analyses of the conversation of married couples. Couples with stable/rigid relationships featured the wife as the dominant partner and reported the highest levels of satisfaction with the relationship. Couples with unstable/rigid relationships tended to "give speeches" to each other and featured more challenges by husbands of their wives' dominance. Stable/flexible couples featured more dominance by the husband than in the other types. Unstable/flexible couples seemed to be in a "holding pattern" and gave the impression of being defensive in much of their interactions with each other. Millar and Rogers concluded that these initial findings were suggestive of more to be learned, and, indeed, this program of research investigating relational control persisted.

There was a fair amount of excitement about the prospects for relational communication research. Parks (1977), for example, wrote a review essay for *Human Communication Research* that summarized in detail the work that led to the publication of *Pragmatics of Human Communication*, as well as research that had been done on various aspects of symmetry and complementarity. Parks summarized the kinds of symmetry and complementarity that had emerged from this work in terms of "one-up," "one-down," and "one-across" symbols. Here are the classifications that he synthesized from the research:

a. Competitive Symmetry: (one-up, one-up)
b. Submissive Symmetry: (one-down, one-down)
c. Neutralized Symmetry: (one-across, one-across)
d. Complementarity: (one-up, one-down)
e. Transitory-Dominant: (one-across, one-up; one-up, one across)
f. Transitory-Submissive: (one-across, one-down; one-down, one-across)
   (p. 374)

Using this terminology, Parks offered the beginnings of a formal theory of power and control in communication, consisting of a series of fifteen axioms and twelve theorems:

Axioms:

1. The greater the competitive symmetry, the greater the frequency of unilateral action in a relationship.
2. The greater the competitive symmetry, the lower the probability of relationship termination.
3. The greater the role discrepancy, the greater the competitive symmetry.
4. The greater the competitive symmetry, the greater the frequency of open conflict.
5. The greater the competitive symmetry, the greater the frequency of threat and intimidation messages.
6. The greater the competitive symmetry, the greater the frequency of messages of rejection.
7. The less competitive symmetry, the greater the satisfaction with communication.
8. The greater the external threat, the less competitive symmetry.
9. The greater the role discrepancy, the less frequent is communication about feelings toward the other.
10. The greater the complementarity, the less empathy.
11. The greater the complementarity, the greater the role specialization.
12. The greater the complementarity, the greater the mutual envy.
13. The greater the complementarity, the greater the frequency of disconfirming messages.
14. The greater the rigidity, the greater the probability of psychopathology.
15. The greater the rigidity, the less frequent are attempts to explicitly define the relationship. (pp. 375–376)

Theorems:

1. The greater the role discrepancy, the greater the frequency of unilateral action in the relationship.
2. The greater the role discrepancy, the lower the probability of relational termination.
3. The greater the role discrepancy, the greater the frequency of open conflict.
4. The greater the role discrepancy, the greater the frequency of threat and intimidation messages.
5. The greater the role discrepancy, the greater the frequency of messages of rejection.

6. The greater the role discrepancy, the less satisfaction with communication.
7. The greater the external threat, the greater the frequency of mutual or joint action in a relationship.
8. The greater the external threat, the higher the probability of relationship termination.
9. The greater the external threat, the lower the frequency of open conflict within the relationship.
10. The greater the external threat, the lower the frequency of threat and intimidation messages within the relationship.
11. The greater the external threat, the lower the frequency of messages of rejection within the relationship.
12. The greater the external threat, the greater the satisfaction with communication within the relationship. (p. 377)

Parks concluded that this approach, while still diffuse, though mostly focused on descriptive studies, showed great promise for understanding not only relational dynamics but also how power and influence operate in relationships.

PHASE MODELS OF RELATIONSHIP
DEVELOPMENT AND DECAY

It seems intuitive that communication changes as relationships change. We don't speak to someone we know well in the same way we speak to someone we've never met or are just getting to know. There were a couple of models of communication in different phases of relationship put forth in the 1970s. One was anchored by Berger and Calabrese's (1975) formal theory of communication in initial interaction, and the other was Knapp's (1978) less formal but more comprehensive description of communication as relationships develop and decay. I'll summarize each of these authors' work in this section.

Berger and Calabrese (1975) noted that many interpersonal communication scholars have grounded their work in social psychology theory. These authors proposed to work more from the perspective of uncertainty reduction, which is most prevalent in initial interactions. They did, however, speculate on what a phase model of interpersonal communication might look like. They articulated three such phases, an entry phase, where communication is often ritualized and more formal, a personal phase, where talk about attitudes and values was more likely to be heard, and an exit phase, where decisions are made about continuing the relationship, and plans are made to exit both the extant conversation and, potentially, future interactions.

For this particular piece of scholarship, the authors focused on detailing the salient variables for initial interactions and their relationships with one another. By grounding the theory in uncertainty reduction, the authors envisioned that communicators were simultaneously trying to predict what their interaction partner might say and assessing what that person actually said. In doing this work, the authors acknowledged the recent analysis of interpersonal relationships development by social psychologists Irving Altman and Dalmas Taylor (1973).

Berger and Calabrese put forth seven axioms and twenty-one theorems as part of their formal theory:

Axioms:

1. Given the high level of uncertainty present at the onset of the entry phase, as the amount of verbal communication between strangers increases, the level of uncertainty for each interactant in the relationship will decrease. As uncertainty is further reduced, the amount of verbal communication will increase.
2. As nonverbal affiliative expressiveness increases, uncertainty levels will decrease in an initial interaction situation. In addition, decreases in uncertainty level will cause increases in nonverbal affiliative expressiveness.
3. High levels of uncertainty cause increases in information-seeking behavior. As uncertainty levels decline, information-seeking behavior decreases.
4. High levels of uncertainty in a relationship cause decreases in the intimacy level of communication content. Low levels of uncertainty produce high levels of intimacy.
5. High levels of uncertainty produce high rates of reciprocity. Low levels of uncertainty produce low reciprocity rates.
6. Similarities between persons reduce uncertainty, while dissimilarities produce increases in uncertainty.
7. Increases in uncertainty level produce decreases in liking; decreases in uncertainty level produce increases in liking. (pp. 101–107)

Theorems:

1. Amount of verbal communication and nonverbal affiliative expressiveness are positively related.
2. Amount of communication and intimacy level of communication are positively related.
3. Amount of communication and information-seeking behavior are inversely related.

4. Amount of communication and reciprocity rate are inversely related.
5. Amount of communication and liking are positively related.
6. Amount of communication and similarity are positively related.
7. Nonverbal affiliative expressiveness and intimacy level of communication content are positively related.
8. Nonverbal affiliative expressiveness and information seeking are inversely related.
9. Nonverbal affiliative expressiveness and reciprocity rate are inversely related.
10. Nonverbal affiliative expressiveness and liking are positively related.
11. Nonverbal affiliative expressiveness and similarity are positively related.
12. Intimacy level of communication content and information seeking are inversely related.
13. Intimacy level of communication content and reciprocity rate are inversely related.
14. Intimacy level of communication content and liking are positively related.
15. Intimacy level of communication content and similarity are positively related.
16. Information seeking and reciprocity rate are positively related.
17. Information seeking and liking are negatively related.
18. Information seeking and similarity are negatively related.
19. Reciprocity rate and liking are negatively related.
20. Reciprocity rate and similarity are negatively related.
21. Similarity and liking are positively related. (pp. 107–109)

Berger and colleagues (Berger et al., 1976) elaborated on Berger and Calabrese's initial findings. The focus shifted from initial interaction to how people come to understand their relationships through communication, a process dubbed "interpersonal epistemology." Sticking with the idea that uncertainty reduction was key to understanding relationship development, the authors began by outlining three levels of interpersonal knowledge: (1) descriptive statements, such as height and weight; (2) the person's beliefs, which are more difficult to ascertain than the readily observable physical qualities—and which may never be fully known; and (3) the ability to explain another person's actions and beliefs, which takes sustained interaction to achieve. The authors summarized these three levels as involving description, prediction, and explanation, respectively (pp. 150–152).

The authors chose to elaborate types of prediction and explanation. Prediction first involves being able to surmise an individual's attitudes and beliefs. Doing so typically is associated with initial interactions. Second, communicators make predictions about an individual's enduring qualities, based on several encounters but also based on second-hand information from those who know the individual better. Third, communicators make predictions about under what conditions an individual's behavior might vary from established expectations. These predictions increase in accuracy over time interacting with the other individual. Explanations may be either external or internal, that is, behavior may be a function of situational expectations, such as a job, or the individual's preferred manner of behaving (pp. 152–154).

To achieve interpersonal understanding, the authors argued, requires sustained interpersonal communication where the parties are engaged in all levels of prediction and explanation. If one party stops participating in this manner, the relationship will decay. To support these processes, communicators employ a set of strategies: (1) interrogation, or asking the "right" questions; (2) self-disclosure, if engaged in a manner appropriate for the state of the relationship; (3) deception detection, particularly to determine how ingratiation is occurring; (4) environmental structuring so that there are as few barriers to interaction as possible; and (5) deviation testing, to determine whether someone is deliberately violating expectations and for what purpose. (pp. 156–163)

The authors presented some data to illustrate how their theory might be studied, and they concluded that continuing to study these processes should prove to be productive for seeing more specifically how interpersonal communication influences relationship development.

In a third essay, Berger (1979) elaborated on elements of the conceptualization put forth in Berger, Gardner, Parks, Schulman, and Miller. Specifically, he clarified that "when cognitive uncertainty is decreased, persons are more likely to assert that they know and understand each other" (p. 126). He also indicated that individual levels of awareness, ability to self-monitor, and incentives present to continue interaction would influence how an individual decides to interact with another. A commitment to continue interacting was a necessary element for enacting the strategies Berger and associates had outlined earlier. Berger concluded,

> when people develop what they call 'meaningful relationships' with others, they usually say that these relationships involve a high level of understanding. And, when significant relationships disintegrate, the persons involved are frequently heard to say that they lacked understanding. While such constructs as knowledge and understanding are difficult to conceptualize and operationalize, this very difficulty suggests their potential importance in relational growth and disintegration, (p. 144, emphasis omitted)

The other major phase model of relationship development and decay was put forth by Mark Knapp (1978). Laid out in what became a popular undergraduate textbook, Knapp proposed a model of how relationships develop, combined with a model of how relationships decay. The models specified the kinds of talk that occurred in each phase of the relationship and offered advice on how to move between stages, as well as strategies for reversing signs of relationship decay.

Knapp also worked from the conceptualization put forward by Altman and Taylor (1973), particularly the notion that both breadth and depth of relationships were dependent on the amount and frequency of communication that the participants undertook. Like Berger, Knapp acknowledged that not all relationships needed to be close or intimate, and his model took into account the idea that relationships could find a comfortable plateau at any of the stages of development he proposed.

Knapp's stages of "coming together" were: (1) initiating, where people first interact; (2) experimenting, where they looked for common interests and topics of conversation that both would enjoy; (3) intensifying, where the participants would more openly express feelings, particularly about each other; (4) integrating, where the participants began to refer to their relationship as a partnership of some sort; and (5) bonding, where the participants made some sort of commitment for the relationship to become permanent. His stages of "coming apart" proceeding in the opposite direction: (1) differentiating, where the relationship partners started to assert individual identities as being more important than their joint identity; (2) circumscribing, where topics of communication would become less intimate; (3) stagnating, where the partners communicated less frequently and found less to talk about; (4) avoiding, where partners deliberately found reasons not to interact; and (5) terminating, where one or both partners decided to abandon the relationship altogether. Knapp also proposed five rules for understanding his stage model: (1) movement is generally systematic and sequential; (2) movement may be forward; (3) movement may be backward; (4) movement occurs within stages; and (5) movement is always to a new place (p. 32).

Knapp acknowledged that his stages were situational and that those situations would dictate choices that the participants made about how to enact each stage. Situational components Knapp identified were time, space, quantity, substance, code, medium, flexibility, and duration, and he argued that there were norms and values associated with each of these components. A fair amount of the material that followed elaborated on these dimensions and how they are enacted. Knapp drew on the research of others in presenting his insights, though he did illustrate how each of his stages might be enacted. Particularly interesting were his ideas about how people "said goodbye," not only at the end of a conversation but at the end of a relationship. These ideas were drawn from his own research (Knapp, Hart, Friedrich, and Shulman, 1973).

Knapp's conceptualization was not based primarily on scientific data that he had collected and analyzed but on a synthesis of others' work. Its strength was in the synthesis: Knapp had a talent for providing cogent examples of communication that would illustrate his descriptions of the various phases of his model. His ideas would not guide his own future scholarship, but they would serve as a starting point for the scholarship of a variety of other relational communication researchers.

THE MEDIA–AUDIENCE RELATIONSHIP

Media scholars were focused on finding effects of various kinds that media had on audiences. In some ways, audiences were taken for granted and studied for reasons other than the nature of the media–audience relationship. Ball-Rokeach and DeFleur (1976) contended that such an approach was wrong-headed and proposed as a corrective what they called a "dependency model" of media effects.

Ball-Rokeach and DeFleur began their analysis by criticizing the stimulus-response model that had dominated media effects research. They claimed, "It can be suggested that one of the reasons that there is such a lack of clarity as to whether or not the media have effects is that researchers have proceeded from the wrong theoretical conceptualizations to study the wrong questions" (p. 4). To set things right, Ball-Rokeach and DeFleur proposed focusing on what they called "the high level of dependence of audiences on mass media information resources in urban-industrial societies" (p. 5).

Ball-Rokeach and DeFleur began by positing an interrelationship among media and audiences, both of which are part of a larger social system. People, who make up audiences, understand their realities by interacting with each other, as well as with the structural aspects of their societies. Media are one of the primary structural aspects of society, and people become more or less dependent on media based on how complex they perceive society to be at any given time. Media serve to make societal complexity palatable, thus engendering dependency.

The authors defined dependency in terms of needs. The more audience members rely on media to satisfy their information needs, the more effect media messages have on those audience members. Needs can range from information about prospective purchase, information about the world in which audience members live, and even the need for fantasy and escape. As Ball-Rokeach and DeFleur posited, "The greater the need and consequently the stronger the dependency in such matters, the greater the likelihood that the information supplied will alter various forms of audience cognitions, feelings, and behavior" (p. 6).

Audience interest predicts attention to media content and vice versa. This relationship drove the authors' first hypothesis: "the greater the number and centrality of the specific information-delivery functions served by a medium, the greater the audience and societal dependency on that medium." The second hypothesis was related to the ebb and flow of societal change: "in societies with developed media systems, audience dependency on media information increases as the level of structural conflict and change increases" (p. 7). This relationship is also reciprocal, in that audiences can influence how structural conflict and change periods in societies are resolved and in what ways those changes are implemented.

The authors described cognitive, affective, and behavioral effects that media dependency can produce. Such dependency relationships are particularly salient during times of societal conflict, which will tend to be reflected in message ambiguity. Media reports may be incomplete or conflicting until they can be clarified. Because media tend to identify and resolve ambiguous messages, audiences learn to become more dependent on media during periods where messages may conflict. They are less likely to pay attention or be influenced when messages are less ambiguous or when their content is in line with audience expectations.

Media also influence audience attitudes by selectively portraying the society of which both are a part. Media do not necessarily evoke the same attitudes in each person, but they do serve to facilitate attitude formation, especially as dependency increases. And media do serve an agenda-setting function by helping audiences understand what's important in their immediate world—as well as what isn't important. In addition, media expand the scope of their audience's beliefs, creating the possibility that such beliefs will change over time. Finally, media may not influence beliefs and values that audience members hold close, but they can serve as a means of clarifying audience values by presenting how society is changing.

At the time of writing, the authors were not convinced that sufficient evidence existed for exactly how media influence the feelings of audience members. They posited, however, that it was clear that audiences react to media content on an affective level, and they advocated for additional scholarship to determine just how those reactions were a function of audience dependency. It is also clear that media can promote a feeling of "we-ness" within audiences and that such a feeling can have positive effects on morale and negative effects on potential alienation.

In terms of potential changes of behavior, the authors chose to address how media work to activate or de-activate behavior change. They noted that there were many examples of how media information activated behavior, motivated, at least in part, to the feeling of "we-ness" that media can create. The authors also noted that audiences can become frustrated with similarity of messages day in and out, and the boredom created can cause apathy and resistance to take positive action.

The authors concluded that the dependency model can account for media effects ranging from none that are measurable to significant reaction leading to social changes. They summarized their position as follows:

> When media messages are not linked to audience dependencies and when people's social realities are entirely adequate before and during message reception, media messages may have little or no alteration effects. They may reinforce existing beliefs or behavior forms. In contrast, when people do not have social realities that provide adequate frameworks for understanding, acting, and escaping, and when audiences are dependent in these ways on media information received, such messages may have a number of alteration effects. Media messages, in this instance, may be expected to alter audience behavior in terms of cognitive, affective, and/or overt activity. Thus, both the relative adequacy of the audience's social realities and the relative degree of audience dependency on media information resources must be taken into account to explain and predict the effects of media messages. (p. 19)

CONCLUSION

Communication as developer of relationships was studied mostly by speech faculty making the transition to communication during 1964–1982. The study began with a focus on how one-to-one communication was different from public speaking and sorting through those differences led to the realization that relationship development was the more important topic. Still, there was considerable research that focused on individual's reactions to their communication, and studies that focused on interaction between people often used power dynamics as the explanatory model for the scholarship. There was influential scholarship that attempted to understand the phases of relationship development and decay, as well as the dynamics that could be used to identify what phase the relationship was in at the time. This work would grow in sophistication as it became more established.

Media scholars began to study how audiences interacted with media, instead of assuming that audiences were passively acted upon by media. This idea of an active audience would become better developed after communication as a discipline became established.

REFERENCES

Altman, I. & Taylor, D. A. (1973). *Social Penetration: The Development of Interpersonal Relationships.* New York: Holt, Rinehart and Winston.

Ball-Rokeach, S. J. & DeFleur, M. L. (1976). A dependency model of mass-media effects. *Communication Research, 3*, 3–21. doi:10.1177/009365027600300101

Bateson, G. (1958). *Naven* (2nd edition). Stanford, CA: Stanford University Press.

Berger, C. R. (1977). Interpersonal communication theory and research: An overview. In Rubin, B. D. (ed.), *Communication Yearbook 1* (pp. 217–228). New Brunswick, NJ: Transaction Books. doi:10.1080/23808985.1977.11923682

Berger, C. R. (1979). Beyond initial interaction: Uncertainty, understanding, and the development of interpersonal relationships. In Giles, H. & St Clair, R. N. (eds.), *Language and Social Psychology* (pp. 122–144). Baltimore, MD: University Park Press.

Berger, C. R. & Calabrese, R. J. (1975). Some explorations in initial interaction and beyond: Toward a developmental theory of interpersonal communication. *Human Communication Research, 1*, 99–112. doi:10.1111/j.1468-2958.1975.tb00258.x

Berger, C. R., Gardner, R. R., Parks, M. R., Schulman, L. & Miller, G. R. (1976). Interpersonal epistemology and interpersonal communication. In Miller, G. R. (ed.), *Explorations in Interpersonal Communication* (pp. 149–171). Beverly Hills, CA: Sage Publications.

Crockett, W. H. (1965). Cognitive complexity and impression formation. *Progress in Experimental Personality Research, 2*, 47–90.

Delia, J. G. (1974). Attitude toward the disclosure of self-attributions and the complexity of interpersonal constructs. *Speech Monographs, 41*, 119–126. doi:10.1080/03637757409375827

Delia, J. G., Crockett, W. H., Press, A. N. & O'Keefe, D. J. (1975). The dependency of interpersonal evaluations on context-relevant beliefs about the other. *Speech Monographs, 42*, 10–19. doi:10.1080/03637757509375872

Delia, J. G., Clark, R. A. & Switzer, D. E. (1974). Cognitive complexity and impression formation in informal social interaction. *Speech Monographs, 41*, 299–308. doi:10.1080/03637757409375854

Hastorf, A., Schneider, D. & Polefka, J. (1970). *Person Perception (Topics in Social Psychology)*. Reading, MA: Addison-Wesley.

Hawes, L. C. (1971). Information overload and the organization of 1984. *Western Speech, 35*, 191–198. doi:10.1080/10570317109373703

Hewes, D. E. Finite stochastic modeling of communication processes: An introduction and some basic reading. *Human Communication Research, 1,* 271–283. doi:10.1111/j.1468-2958.1975.tb00274.x

Jackob, N. G. E. (2010). No alternatives? The relationship between perceived media dependency, use of alternative information sources, and general trust in mass media. *International Journal of Communication (19328036), 4*, 589–606.

Kelly, G. A. (1955). *The Psychology of Personal Constructs*. New York: Norton.

Knapp, M. L. (1978). *Social Intercourse: From Greeting to Goodbye*. Boston, MA: Allyn and Bacon.

Knapp, M. L., Hart, R. P. & Dennis, H. S. (1974). An exploration of deception as a communication construct. *Human Communication Research, 1*, 15–29. doi:10.1111/j.1468-2958.1974.tb00250.x

Knapp, M. L., Hart, R. P., Friedrich, G. W. & Shulman, G. M. (1973). The rhetoric of goodbye: Verbal and nonverbal correlates of human leave-taking. *Speech Monographs, 40*, 182–198.

Littlejohn, S. W. & Jabusch, D. M. (1982). Communication competence: Model and application. *Journal of Applied Communication Research, 10*, 29–37. doi:10.1080/00909888209365210

Millar, F. E. & Rogers, L. E. (1976). A relational approach to interpersonal communication. In Miller, G. R. (ed.), *Explorations in Interpersonal Communication* (pp. 87–103). Beverly Hills, CA: Sage Publications.

Miller, G. R. (1971). Readings in Communication Theory: Suggestions and an occasional caveat. *Today's Speech, 19*, 5–10. doi:10.1080/01463377109368958

Miller, G. R. & Steinberg, M. (1975). *Between People: A New Analysis of Interpersonal Communication*. Chicago, IL: Science Research Associates.

Norton, R. W. (1978). Foundation of a communicator style construct. *Human Communication Research, 4*, 99–112. doi:10.1111/j.1468-2958.1978.tb00600.x

Parks, M. R. (1977). Relational communication: Theory and research. *Human Communication Research, 3*, 372–381. doi:10.1111/j.1468-2958.1977.tb00541.x

Pearce, W. B. (1976) The coordinated management of meaning: A rules based theory of interpersonal communication. In Miller, G. R. (ed.), *Explorations in Interpersonal Communication* (pp. 17–35). Beverly Hills, CA: Sage Publications.

Rogers, C. (1961). *On Becoming a Person: A Therapist's View of Psychotherapy*. Boston, MA: Houghton Mifflin Company.

Seibold, D. R. (1975). Communication research and the attitude-verbal report-overt behavior relationship: A critique and theoretical reformulation. *Human Communication Research, 2*, 3–32. doi:10.1111/j.1468-2958.1975.tb00466.x

Smith, D. R. (1971). From id to information: A Biblogical (*sic*) view of communication. *Today's Speech, 19*, 11–16. doi:10.1080/01463377109368959

Stewart, J. (1972). An interpersonal approach to the Basic Course. *Speech Teacher, 21*, 7–14. doi:10.1080/03634527209377916

Watzlawick, P., Beavin, J. H. & Jackson, D. D. (1967). *Pragmatics of Human Communication: A Study of Interactional Patterns, Pathologies, and Paradoxes*. New York: W. W. Norton & Company.

Wilder, C. (1979). The Palo Alto Group: Difficulties and directions of the interactional view for human communication research. *Human Communication Research, 5*, 171–186. doi:10.1111/j.1468-2958.1979.tb00632.x

Chapter 8

Communication as Definer, Interpreter, and Critic of Culture

In many ways, the link between communication and culture was explicit before speech and journalism began the transition to emphasizing communication in 1964. This link had been pursued by scholars in other disciplines and even in fiction. For example, William J. Lederer and Eugene Burdick's (1958) novel, *The Ugly American*, had been a best seller. In fact, it is still in print. The tale of a physically ugly man who wanted to help develop a fictional Asian country but who faced many diplomatic challenges for which he was unprepared became iconic of American attitudes toward the "third world" in the 1950s. American travelers, even to countries far older than the United States, were cautioned to adapt to local customs so as not to be perceived as an "ugly American."

Other books describing the relationship between culture and communication were written by anthropologists. Most prominent among these were a series of books by Edward T. Hall, beginning with *The Silent Language* (1959) and continuing with *The Hidden Dimension* (1966) and eight additional books altogether. The books focused on aspects of nonverbal communication, with an emphasis on cultural differences in use of space and architecture. Another anthropologist, Alfred G. Smith (1966) published an anthology of works by well-known scholars that served to introduce the breadth of communication study to professors and students alike.

In the meantime, the influence of the Frankfurt School's work (see chapter 2) seems to have facilitated the development of what became known as the Birmingham School of Cultural Studies. Stuart Hall, one of the leading lights of this movement, would adapt the Frankfurt School's concept of Critical Theory to the study of media. The work of Stuart Hall and others presaged what would develop into a full-fledged critical/cultural approach to media

studies in the 1980s, but that work originated in the late 1960s and is important enough to present in this chapter.

Back to Edward T. Hall, whose influence on what would become known as
intercultural communication was so significant that communication scholars
would look back on it later. Wendy Leeds-Hurwitz (1990) published a history
of the beginning of the study of intercultural communication in *The Quarterly
Journal of Speech*. I shall begin my discussion of this topic with a summary
of her history.

According to Leeds-Hurwitz, anthropologists such as Hall became interested in intercultural communication for a practical reason: the training of
nascent diplomats by the U.S. Foreign Service Institute. Leeds-Hurwitz dated
this work as occurring between 1946 and 1956, and she documented how Hall
and his colleague, William Foote Whyte, came to revise the standard practice
of training diplomats specifically for the culture where they were going to be
placed. Instead, the training began to emphasize general principles that could
be applied across cultural contexts. Leeds-Hurwitz indicated that spelling
out these general principles in communication terms was an afterthought to
the work on developing the training, but it turned out to be one that became
important to scholars.

Interestingly, Leeds-Hurwitz found that the concepts of "communication" and "culture" are similar, in that they are both "patterned, learned, and
analyzable" (p. 263). Hall also chose to focus on what Leeds-Hurwitz called
"microcultural behaviors" that would potentially make a difference in practical situations. These behaviors included tone of voice, gestures, and use of
time and space. Sensitivity to these factors would assist diplomats in appre-
ciating the subtleties of the communication in which they would engage, and
Hall's insights formed the basis for communication scholars to test the effects
of these nonverbal cues (e.g., Holbrook & Hsiao-Tung Lu, 1969; Jamieson,
1976; Martin, 1981).

INTERCULTURAL COMMUNICATION

With interest in the relationship between communication and culture dating
to the post–World War II period, it is surprising that serious study of intercultural communication did not begin until the mid-1970s. "International
and Intercultural Communication" was the theme of William Howell's 1970
SCA convention, and while he apparently wished to highlight both, as stated
in his Presidential Address (1972), it was clear that the international part was
a proposal to hold the convention he planned in Hong Kong, while the intercultural part was close to his heart. But Howell was on the leading edge and
would go on to champion the development of intercultural communication

in the doctoral program at the University of Minnesota, where he served on the faculty. More typical of the period were journal articles such as one by the well-known public address scholar, Robert T. Oliver (1967), in which he recounted episodes from his extensive travel experiences to other countries.

SAA, the Speech association, held a summer conference on intercultural communication, and Becker (1969) offered a research agenda from the discussions at that event:

1. How can the United States assist in developing indigenous leadership through improving individual communication skills?
2. How does diffusion of innovations vary within individual cultures, and how it is similar between cultures?
3. What is the role of culture in distorting information?
4. What are the characteristics of "the culture of information seeking?"
5. How does culture shape common communication events, such as political news broadcasts?
6. How does culture influence ways that official information gets to people in nonofficial ways?
7. What are cultural differences and similarities in the acceptance of family planning?
8. To what extent do media promote ideas of how life might be different in different cultures? To what extent do cultural characteristics strengthen or weaken this effect?
9. How is empathic ability related to skill in intercultural communication?
10. How do media affect audiences in various cultures, how do those audiences affect media?
11. How is information about a particular country spread to individuals in other countries? By what process do individuals form impressions of countries other than their own?
12. What factors contribute to the success of U.S. government operations located in other countries and staffed by natives of those countries?
13. How can international cooperation be achieved through the use of new technologies? What are the factors that contribute to such cooperation?
14. What factors predict what media content from another country will be imported into the United States?

Becker concluded by allowing that this research agenda was quite overwhelming:

> Most of my comments have been directed at the extreme complexity of the task
> of Intercultural communication and Intercultural communication research. It
> would be completely understandable if everyone threw up his [sic] hands and

said that we might as well forget it; there really is not much that we can do or discover. However understandable, this response cannot be tolerated. The task is too important—the need is too great. I believe that we must follow the advice of one of the great men in the field of speech, my good friend A. Craig Baird. Whenever a graduate student of Craig's would encounter a seemingly impossible problem in his research, Professor Baird would say, "That's all right; just keep with it. Just do the best you can." This seems to me to be good advice. (p. 13)

The study of intercultural communication was a natural fit for the newly renamed International Communication Association. It should have been no surprise that ICA's initial four divisions (Information Systems, Interpersonal Communication, Mass Communication, and Organizational Communication) were soon joined by Division V–Intercultural Communication.

Intercultural Communication was somewhat warily represented in the first volume of *Communication Yearbook*, however. One of the essays in the "Communication" section dealt with the issue of how to conceptualize "intercultural communication" (Ellingsworth, 1977), and the section of the volume devoted to intercultural communication featured an overview essay (Saral, 1977). I will summarize both essays.

Ellingsworth offered five propositions, and then found fault with and revised each. He began by lamenting the existing confused state for the study of communication among people of different cultures. He catalogued with dismay several alternate terms for this study, including "culture and communication," "cross-cultural communications," "cross-national communication," "international communication," "intercultural interchange," "interracial communication," interethnic communication," "interculturation," and "male–female communication." He saw these terms as "well-intentioned, but not always functional" (p. 100).

Ellingsworth proceeded to describe his five propositions. The first was, "Intercultural communication is a unique dimension of communication which requires special labeling, attention, methodology, and instruction" (p. 100). But then he disagreed with himself, saying that the existence of intercultural communication implied the existence of "intracultural communication," where cultural differences between communicators are non-existent. The existence of intracultural communication would not yield much, if anything, of interest to study. Better to study "culture" as a continuous, as opposed to dichotomous variable. Plus, to assert that "all communication is intercultural" gets a scholar nowhere. Therefore, "the term *intercultural communication* should be used sparingly by scholars and then most properly as a post hoc description of encounters where cultural differences became manifest, were recognized, and were successfully compensated for" (pp. 101–102, italics in the original).

The second proposition was, "Cultural differences between communicators function as boundaries or barriers which must be overcome if understanding and satisfaction are to be achieved" (p. 102). In critiquing this proposition, Ellingsworth argued that the amount of cultural difference does not predict the difficulty of a particular communication encounter. He also observed that the "stakes" of a particular conversation make a substantial difference in the impact of culture. Low stakes conversations are likely to find the participants forgiving of cultural gaffes. Even when the stakes are higher, the participants may be motivated enough to come to a satisfactory conclusion by minimizing cultural differences. If a power differential is involved, the person with greater power will likely dictate how the conversation will proceed. Ellingsworth's modified this proposition to read, "Cultural differences signify the need for accommodation in communication, but they are not arbitrarily either barriers or facilitators" (p. 102).

The third proposition initially stated, "Any given member of a culture is a potential interactor with any member of another culture" (p. 102). This proposition might be appealing if one looks at technology as potentially creating a "global village" where communication among people of different cultures is made easy. But Ellingsworth observed that such interactions are difficult to arrange and are usually likely to occur between people who have more in common than not. He revised this proposition to read, "Training, research and theory in intercultural communication should reflect the probability that the population of participants is relatively small and identifiable" (p. 103). Going back to the success of the Foreign Service Institute, its training worked because the individuals being trained were planning to experience a particular kind of set of communication challenges, ones where learning a set of principles, coupled with language learning, could be used effectively.

In related fashion, the fourth proposition initially stated, "Learning about a cultural pattern is an important means of reducing uncertainty about the behavior of a member of that culture" (p. 103). Ellingsworth reviewed Hall's work and noted that there are enough exceptions to make this phrasing problematic. For example, countries making up what we call "Latin America" are significantly different from each other and so learning what amounts to stereotypes, even informed stereotypes, doesn't get one far. And there are "cultures" where differences are made less important by common technological savvy, a "third culture," as it were. Elliingsworth rephrased this proposition as follows: "Culture learning is a useful background for intercultural context: it may not predict behavior for a given situation, which is likely to occur in a synthetic third culture ambiance" (p. 104).

The final proposition initially read, "Culture is primarily a phenomenon of region or nationality." Ellingsworth countered that national boundaries often don't predict much, and that socio-economic status and education are often better predictors of behavior. He revised his proposition to read, "Nationality is one major dimension of cultural identity: it is not by itself a reliable indicator of the cultural behaviors of its citizens" (p. 104).

Ellingsworth concluded by arguing that the term, "intercultural communication" should be abandoned, at least for serious scholarship. He wrote,

> Research designs in communication would be complete only if they included the means of examining demographic and sociocultural characteristics as potential sources of variance and also of investigating the interaction of these differences with communicative purposes. The ultimate goal of such research would be the generation of middle-range theories with the power to predict process and outcomes where cultural variability is found. This would represent the ultimate convergence of intercultural and intracultural communication study. (p. 105)

Saral's (1977) essay provided a brief overview of intercultural communication theory and research for the initial volume of *Communication Yearbook*. Saral began his piece with what was almost an apology:

> The field of intercultural communication is relatively young, and its boundaries are not yet clearly identified. The newness of the field has attracted scholars from varying disciplines who, while enriching and broadening the area, have also rendered the field so diverse and discursive that it defies definition. Conceptualizations of intercultural communication range from those which regard intercultural communication as a subsystem of human communication to those that consider it as an independent and respectable area of study that cuts across various disciplines, including communication. (p. 389)

Saral went on to recite several different definitions of intercultural communication before declaring that both "culture" and "communication" were terms where there was not an agreed-on definition. Interestingly, a number of these definitions came from textbooks. Textbook production led intercultural communication into prominence—and then scholarship followed. This phenomenon was much like Hall's experience, where there was a need to train U.S. Foreign Service Officers before there existed a scientific basis for such training.

Finally, Saral wondered whether an "intercultural communication context" actually existed. He mused that definition of individual situations, using factors such as roles, norms, and institutional expectations, would be a better direction for research. He also expressed concern that creating a research paradigm to generate law-like predictions would be productive. Instead, he favored taking a more descriptive approach to understanding the complex dynamics of individual interactions.

As Leeds-Hurwitz noted, while a volume of intercultural communication scholarship had been published (Asante, Newmark, & Blake, 1979), it would not be until 1983 that a serious attempt at theorizing in intercultural communication appeared (Gudykunst, 1983). The work for that volume was completed at a conference SCA held in 1980.

SCA had published an annual volume on international and intercultural communication since 1974, and that annual volume had been devoted to printing the top-rated papers from what was then known as the Commission on International and Intercultural Communication. The 1980 SCA conference was brought together a set of scholars to consider the lack of theory in intercultural communication, as well as, coincidentally, to improve the quality of the annual volumes that SCA was publishing. The Gudykunst volume was officially number seven in SCA series, and it was the first one to be distributed by Sage Publications.

Conference participants were invited to submit their papers for publication. The submissions were peer reviewed, which had not been past practice.

Gudykunst organized the chapters under four headings. The first introduced the content of the volume and summarized the results of the conference from which the work was taken.

The second part of the volume was titled, "Theories Based on Traditional Communication Perspectives." The chapters in this section focused on constructivism, rules theories, intercultural relationships, rhetorical perspectives on intercultural communication, and systems theories. Interestingly, while Barnett Pearce was a co-author of the chapter on rules theories, his contemporaneous book, *Communication, Action, and Meaning: The Creation of Social Realities* (Pearce & Cronen, 1980) contained a chapter that provided a far more interesting perspective on different ways of viewing culture.

The third part of the volume was titled, "New Theoretical Developments." It began with a contribution on mass media and culture, and also included a chapter detailing a mathematical theory of cultural convergence, a chapter on interpersonal conflict, and a chapter from Professor Ellingsworth, whose perspective I already covered.

The final part was titled, "Contributions from Other Disciplines." This section consisted of six chapters whose topics included codes and contexts, language theory and linguistic principles, attribution processes as barriers to effective communication, phenomenology, grounded theory, and a concluding chapter arguing explicitly for doing descriptive work first and letting theory follow later. All the authors of the chapters in this section were communication scholars.

Gudykunst's volume called attention to the need for theory to make inter-cultural communication respected, instead of just popular, but its contents didn't resolve issues about how to constitute such theory.

CRITICAL THEORY, CULTURAL STUDIES, AND MEDIA STUDIES

Critical Theory would become a widely used basis for communication schol-arship, but it had barely started to appear in communication journals by 1982. The roots of critical theory popped up to a degree in the form of semiotic approaches, mostly in film studies. The most complete set of ideas, however, originated in what became known as "The Frankfurt School." An alternate perspective came from "British Cultural Studies," and it was this perspective that inspired communication scholars to move beyond Critical Theory and label their work "cultural studies." In addition, the idea of "culture" shifted from an approach grounded in anthropological theory and methods to socio-logical theory and methods.

Critical Theory arose from the Frankfurt School in the 1930s. It originated when Theodor Adorno was able to immigrate to the United States by being offered a job in Paul Lazersfeld's Radio Research program (Towers, 1977). The Frankfurt School influenced Speech Communication scholars to a greater extent than it did media scholars (though, see Blumler, 1978, for discussion of Critical Theory's influence on journalism scholarship).

Even so, it was speech communication scholars who introduced the work of Stuart Hall to the budding cultural studies community at the University of Illinois. That community provided Hall a residency where he delivered a series of lectures on cultural studies from the perspective of the group he had assembled in Birmingham.

Tracing the development of the Frankfurt School's theoretical work, Towers (1977) wrote that Adorno's views "came from the coalescing of an intellectual circle around [Max] Horkheimer, and featured an interest in the integration of philosophy and social analysis . . . This integration, with its stress on Hegelian dialectics and Marxian social conceptions, became known as critical theory, and its practitioners became identified as members of the Frankfurt School" (p. 135).

The rise of the Nazis in Germany forced many of these scholars to emigrate to Switzerland and then to the United States. Adorno was able to travel to the United States because his mentor, Horkheimer, had preceded him. Adorno immediately clashed with Lazarsfeld, however, and he was able to publish his work on critical theory through collaborating with Horkheimer while also working on what would become *The Authoritarian Personality*.

Towers made the point that Lazarsfeld was looking for data from which to build a theory. He wanted to find predictable regularities in the world. Adorno, on the other hand, was looking for analogies that would prove to be interesting examples of a theory he had already developed and accepted. Interestingly, Leonard Hawes took a similar position in his (1975) book on theory and model construction in communication. Hawes, wrote, "the use of analogues as models for theories is not mere scientific or intellectual window-dressing, but it is essential to the doing of social science . . . In short, the social scientist must be able to see similarities between phenomena where others see only differences." (p. ix)

Farrell and Aune (1979) introduced speech communication scholars to the work of the Frankfurt School via a book review essay they published in *The Quarterly Journal of Speech*. These authors made their readers cognizant of the likes of Horkheimer, Adorno, Marcuse, Walter Benjamin, Ernst Bloch, and, rating a brief mention, Habermas, whose work specifically on communication was not yet widely known in the United States (For an analysis of Habermas' concept of "legitimation crisis," from this period, see Held, 1982). They took some pains to show how Critical Theory had deviated from Marxist economic and social thought. Specifically, they wrote, "Critical Theory would question the material determinism of current Marxist thought and thereby reassert the import of consciousness formation in social change" (p. 95). Yet, Critical Theory was, perhaps, most effective in challenging the assumptions of empiricism. As the authors wrote, "In a bold synthesis of Marxist and Freudian assumptions, Critical Theory claimed as its purview of investigation *and* criticism the entire frame of social arrangements that impose themselves on the unconscious individual" (p. 96 italics by the authors).

Critical Theory, according to Horkheimer, characterized the Frankfurt School writers as sharing four assumptions:

> *First*, the concern with social reality as subject to conscious representation, and, therefore, as subject to rational criticism.
>
> *Second,* a concern with the exclusionary character of social and relational communication—that is, a preoccupation with the relationship of systems of domination to systems of thinking and acting.
>
> *Third,* the employment of a common dialectical mode of social exposition and critique.
>
> *Fourth,* the attempt to reunite, through the coordinated efforts of scholars, systems of thought with strategies for enlightened political action. (p. 97, italics by the authors)

Farrell and Aune noted that German Critical Theorists were fascinated with popular culture, particularly the structure and function of mass media. They concluded that a creative focus on the critique, particularly on the political implications of various texts, was a strength. However, Farrell and Aune noted, Critical Theory "seems to have been a dialectic in search of a rhetorical counterpart" (p. 107). They challenged scholars of rhetoric to provide that counterpart.

The other approach to cultural studies originated at the Centre for Contemporary Cultural Studies (CCCS) at the University of Birmingham. Led by Stuart Hall, the Center's work was grounded not in German theorists, such as Adorno, but in French scholars, such as Claude Levi-Strauss and Louis Althusser, as well as the Italian Marxist scholar Antonio Gramsci (White, 1983). Writing in the *Journal of Communication's* special issue titled, "Ferment in the Field," White characterized British Cultural Studies as concerned with how media assist capitalist power structures in promoting "hegemonic control" by ideological elites. Gramsci envisioned hegemony as a means of producing ideological leadership, resulting in cultural and moral expectations of society. Hegemonic control arises over struggles for dominance in various societal forces, and Hall observed that media play a crucial role in the dynamics of hegemony. As White wrote, "In Hall's view, mass media are the most important instrument of twentieth-century capitalism for maintaining ideological hegemony because they provide the framework for perceiving reality" (p. 291).

In particular, White continued, "Television, especially, gives the impression of a pluralistic diversity but in fact excludes some social images as deviant and subtly orders representations in news, drama, and documentary in the interests of the ruling coalition" (p. 291). This process Hall called "encoding," where media content is given a professional veneer of neutrality while, in fact, representing only the dominant ideology. This veneer of neutrality is embedded in genres of content, where audience expectations are formed over time and, when met, cue audiences to regard the content as "normal," ignoring its ideological bias. Discerning audiences may object, of course, but many times their objections can be either dismissed as minority opinions or incorporated into how media present themselves to audiences.

The role of the scholar/critic is to uncover the hegemonic control and expose its political implications. This work is especially important when hegemony reaches the level of cultural imperialism, where exposing hegemonic control may threaten the nature of capitalism itself. Exposing such imperializing may result in giving voice to oppositional movements demanding societal change. These oppositional movements, Hall thought, were most likely to arise out of the working class.

Hall was invited to give a series of lectures at the University of Illinois in 1983. The lectures were eventually compiled and edited by Jennifer Daryl Slack and Lawrence Grossberg and published by Duke University Press

(Hall, 2016). The volume drew the attention of *The New Yorker*, where a reviewer (Hsu, 2017) wrote for the magazine's online site (www.newyorker .com): "Many of the pieces in this collection orbit the topic of 'common sense,' how culture and politics together reinforce an idea of what is acceptable at any given time . . . This was the simple question at the heart of Hall's complex, occasionally dense work . . . Culture, after all, is a matter of constructing a relationship between oneself and the world."

CONCLUSION

Despite being a term of abiding interest for speech and, to a lesser degree, journalism scholars, "culture" has proven to have been a fuzzy concept in the period between 1964 and 1982. It seemed that "intercultural communication" became somewhat more of a curricular innovation than an area of scholarship as "speech" was transitioning to "communication." Howell's idea to make intercultural communication the theme of the 1970 SCA convention probably helped interest to coalesce, at least for speech scholars (journalism scholars had been interested in international communication, particularly in how media and journalism in other countries compared to the United States). Speech scholars may have also been energized by political movements in the 1960s, where awareness of communication between people of differing racial or ethnic groups came to the fore. What may have slowed down theoretical work was competition between the anthropological approaches of scholars, such as Edward Hall, and the sociological approaches of scholars, such as Stuart Hall.

Critical Theory, which was well established in the United States by the 1950s, was a product of Adorno and others in the Frankfurt School. While speech scholars were clearly interested in Adorno's work, the increasing interest in "culture" in the 1970s may have led to awareness of Stuart Hall's more "radical" ideas. The fact that "Cultural Studies" was starting to challenge the quantitative/empirical approach to communication scholarship may have intrigued both speech and journalism scholars, but it would not be until after 1982 when it would take hold as a framework for studying both interpersonal and mediated phenomena. This transition was clearly in progress in the early 1980s, though, as witnessed by the publication of the landmark issue of *Journal of Communication* (volume 33, number 3), which editor George Gerbner titled, "Ferment in the Field." The issue featured several articles comparing "administrative" research with "critical research," and the tone of the articles made it clear that "critical" approaches were fast advancing, particularly in what was coming to be known as "media studies." While "mass communication" would not disappear as a term (and, in fact, when the

Association for Education in Journalism changed its name in 1982, it would add "and Mass Communication," and not "and Media Studies"), "mass communication" would diminish in importance as a term of art, to be replaced by "media."

With this chapter, I conclude my discussion of the five strands of communication scholarship that I believe crystalized during the period between 1964 and 1982. In my concluding chapter, I will comment on how these five strands developed after 1982, discuss two strands that might have emerged after 1982, and reflect on how communication developed as a discipline after becoming established.

REFERENCES

Asante, M. K., Newmark, E. & Blake, C. A. (eds.) (1979). *Handbook of Intercultural Communication*. Beverly Hills, CA: Sage Publications.

Becker, S. L. (1969). Directions for inter-cultural communication research. *Communication Studies, 20*, 3–13. doi:10.1080/10510976909362945

Blumler, J. G. (1978). Purposes of mass communications research: A transatlantic perspective. *Journalism Quarterly, 55*, 219–230. doi:10.1177/107769907805500201

Ellingsworth, H. W. (1977). Conceptualizing intercultural communication. In Ruben, B. D. (ed.), *Communication Yearbook 1* (pp. 99–106). New Brunswick, NJ: Transaction Books.

Farrell, T. B. & Aune, J. A. (1979). Critical theory and communication: A selective literature review. *Quarterly Journal of Speech, 65*, 93–120. doi:10.1080/00335637909383461

Gudykunst, W. B. (1983). *Intercultural Communication Theory: Current Perspectives*. Beverly Hills, CA: Sage.

Hall, E. T. (1959). *The Silent Language*. Garden City: Doubleday.

Hall, E. T. (1966). *The Hidden Dimension*. Garden City: Doubleday.

Hall, S. (2016). *Cultural studies 1983*, edited and with an introduction by Jennifer Daryl Slack and Lawrence Grossberg. Durham, NC: Duke University Press.

Hawes, L. C. (1975). *Pragmatics of Analoguing: Theory and Model Construction in Communication*. Reading, MA: Addison-Wesley.

Held, D. (1982). Critical theory and political transformation. *Media, Culture and Society, 4*, 153–160. doi:10.1177/016344378200400205

Holbrook, A. & Hsiao-Tung Lu. (1969). A study of intelligibility in whispered Chinese. *Speech Monographs, 36*, 464–466. doi:10.1080/03637756909375641

Howell, W. S. (1972, February). Presidential address – 1971. *Spectra, 8(2)*, 2–7.

Hsu, H. (2017, July 17). Stuart Hall and the Rise of Cultural Studies, *The New Yorker*. Retrieved from https://www.newyorker.com/books/page-turner/stuart-hall-and-the -rise-of-cultural-studies.

Jamieson, K. (1976). The Rhetorical manifestations of *Weltanschauung*. *Central States Speech Journal, 27*, 4–14. doi:10.1080/10510977609367860

Lederer, W. & Burdick, E. (1958). *The Ugly American*. New York: Norton.

Leeds-Hurwitz, W. (1990). Notes in the history of intercultural communication: The Foreign Service institute and the mandate for intercultural training. *The Quarterly Journal of Speech, 76,* 262–281. doi:10.1080/00335639009383919

Martin, H. R. (1981). The prosodic components of speech melody. *Quarterly Journal of Speech, 67,* 81–92. doi:10.1080/00335638109383553

Oliver, R. T. (1967). Communication—community—communion. *Today's Speech, 15*(4), 7–9.

Pearce, W. B. & Cronen, V. E. (1980). *Communication, Action, and Meaning: The Creation of Social Realities*. New York: Praeger.

Saral, T. B. (1977). Intercultural communication theory and research: An overview. In Ruben, B. D. (ed.), *Communication Yearbook 1* (pp. 389–396). New Brunswick, NJ: Transaction Books.

Smith, A. G. (ed.) (1966). *Communication and Culture: Readings in the Codes of Human Interaction*. New York: Holt, Rinehart and Winston.

Towers, W. M. (1977). Lazarsfeld and Adorno in the United States: A case study in theoretical orientations. In, Ruben, B. D. (ed.), *Communication Yearbook 1* (pp. 133–145). New Brunswick, NJ: Transaction Books.

White, R. A. (1983). Mass communication and culture: Transition to a new paradigm. *Journal of Communication, 33,* 279–301. doi:10.1111/j.1460-2466.1983.tb02429.x

Chapter 9

After 1982

Communication's Development as a Discipline

Communication may have been established as an academic discipline by 1982, but its disciplinary status was not without skeptics and critics. In this chapter, I will review a sample of articles that commented on communication's disciplinary status in the 1980s and 1990s, I will provide examples of the kind of scholarship that continues in each of the five strands I identified, I'll discuss two additional strands that may have emerged after 1982, and I'll conclude with a consideration of communication's current disciplinary status.

ASSESSMENTS OF THE DISCIPLINARY STATUS OF COMMUNICATION

Negative commentary about the state of the discipline appeared in a 1982 issue of SCA's newsletter, *Spectra*, when Donald Ellis published a "research editorial" titled "The Shame of Speech Communication" (Ellis, 1982). Under the leadership of Roderick Hart, the SCA Research Board had decided to sponsor competitively selected editorials as a means of starting discussions that might lead to the improvement of the quality of members' scholarship. Ellis' position came through like a lit firecracker.

Ellis contended that while every academic discipline had its "quacks" Speech Communication had more than its share. Ellis believed that an entire set of specialties within the discipline were "narrow, theoretically vacuous, without a research base, and, just as an aside, morally degenerate and politically naive" (p. 1). Ellis specifically named organizational communication, public relations, and advertising as the objects of his scorn. In particular, he attacked what he considered to be a bias toward managerial points of view, a fascination with flashy presentations designed to make money for the consultant or trainer, and what he considered to be the lack of research support for these areas of study. Ellis commented, "The study of rhetoric and communication have a long and noble history and I can think of no quicker way to pervert that history than by packaging and selling ourselves as trade specialists."

These were harsh words designed to provoke a response—and they did. But they also set a tone for casual criticism of communication as a "true" academic discipline, a criticism that was offered in press accounts throughout the following years. It took a long time for communication to "shake" the rap of an easy and vacuous area of study. Mass communication suffered from the same complaints, journalism, which was clearly a professional major, less so.

The next critical assessment appeared in a volume of essays commissioned by the Eastern Communication Association for its Seventy-fifth anniversary (Benson, 1985). It came in Bochner and Eisenberg's (1985) essay contending that speech communication had so far failed to be recognized as a legitimate discipline. The authors argued that speech communication had gotten a slow start as an academic discipline. Graduate programs did not develop quickly, and even though speech communication was founded in 1914, there were only six doctoral programs in 1933, and there were limited journals where scholarship could be published. That slow start had sped up considerably. By 1985, there were 900 departments granting undergraduate degrees in speech communication, of which 250 offered graduate degrees, 50 of which conferred doctoral degrees.

Still, Bochner and Eisenberg contended that even though speech communication was theoretically "discipline material," it was facing elimination at several universities. This targeting was, in part, attributable to a difficulty in how the discipline was defined. Was it part of the humanities, part of the social sciences, or something else? Where were its defining constructs? What theories could it point to as having been developed by its scholars? Who, among its leading scholars, enjoyed an excellent reputation outside of the discipline?

Speech communication had always been a "big tent" area of study, welcoming faculty from Theatre, from Speech Pathology and Audiology. It also had defined itself as a "teaching discipline," one that borrowed concepts and theories from other disciplines but, unlike disciplines such as sociology, which was founded at a similar time, speech communication failed to make the concepts and theories it borrowed into a basis for concepts and theories associated with its discipline.

Bochner and Eisenberg also contended that speech communication lacked both coherence and cohesiveness, pointing to the example of psychology, which was a discipline of many different areas of study, but which also was a discipline where its members could all identify as "psychologists." There was no such term for communication scholars, though some were tried and rejected. Nor were department names consistent, the same for placement in larger units, such as colleges, within university structures. Communication at San Diego State University, for example, is in the College of Professional Studies and Fine Arts, rather than in the College of Arts and Letters. And, because mass communication had identified primarily with journalism, mass communication and speech communication had, for the most part, developed into separate academic departments.

While the authors did not surrender hope that speech communication would eventually be able to overcome these problems and create the "mystical sense of oneness" that characterize cohesive disciplines. They urged speech communication scholars to work in a concentrated way on strengthening the discipline's position and level of respect in the academy.

Five years later, another collection of essays (Phillips & Wood, 1990) sought to assess the state of speech communication on the occasion of the 75th anniversary of the Speech Communication Association. It fell to Dennis Gouran to provide the overview chapter (Gouran, 1990). Eschewing the opportunity to recount the history of speech communication, Gouran chose to focus instead on "the sorts of questions that have grown out of efforts to illuminate the processes in which human beings use speech and related forms of expression to relate themselves to others in different social situations" (p. 2).

There was little handwringing in Gouran's account. He did note that departmental names for the "discipline" (a term he used as if the issue were settled, though, he also used "field" as a synonym) were inconsistent, a problem, he noted, for clear perceptions of "who we are." In addition, SCA, in typical "big tent" fashion, had been expanding its organizational structure, making it difficult for an outsider to find central themes that unite varying aspects of the study of speech communication. Gouran listed six questions as being central to inquiry into the nature of communication:

1. What factors affect the selection and production of the symbols that comprise communicative acts?
2. How do the properties of symbols and their arrangement in communicative acts contribute to the ways in which they are understood, interpreted, and acted upon?
3. How do the characteristics of message producers affect the perception and interpretation of symbolic behavior?
4. How do characteristics of message recipients influence responses to symbolic behavior?
5. What roles do media play in the process of symbolic exchange?
6. In what ways do the social contexts in which symbolic exchanges occur contribute to the production and reception of communicative acts? (p. 5)

Gouran also posed a series of questions regarding methodological issues associated with the study of communication, and he elaborated on those questions as well as the substantive ones, listed above. He acknowledged that,

> the study of communication will continue to face the substantive, philosophical, and methodological problems discussed throughout this chapter and the others to follow. Indifference to those difficulties will retard inquiry and limit claims about communication that scholars can credibly and confidently advance. On such matters, not as much progress as some would like has been made. The fact that those in the scholarly community concerned with communication recognize the problems and are willing to debate them, however, is a positive sign and cause for optimism. (p. 27)

Five years later, another volume appeared (Wood & Gregg, 1995). This volume resulted from a project initiated by Michael Osborne when he was President of SCA. Groups of scholars gathered with the purpose of identifying areas that were ripe for study by communication scholars. The group identified four such areas: (1) Technology and Communication; (2) Definitions of Communication; (3) Diversity and Communication; and (4) Communication, Power, and Order. Essays were commissioned for each of the areas. Dennis Gouran (1995) was, once again, given the task of synthesizing the findings and offering suggestions for their effects on the discipline and its scholars.

Gouran commented that his task had been a frustrating one, because the issues addressed in the volume were so varied that they resisted synthesis. Nevertheless, Gouran proceeded to discuss two "emergent themes." The first, he titled "Restrictedness in the Choice and Conceptualization of Variables." By this, Gouran intended to highlight that the topics discussed represented emergent directions for theorizing and research, including directions that had been overlooked previously. In particular, he noted how communication scholars had "left us with distorted understandings of communication as a predominantly middle class, Euro-American, heterosexual, and male phenomenon" (p. 221). Gouran also noted that speech communication scholars had given short shrift to media other than face-to-face interaction, a restriction that Gouran argued needed to be rectified going forward.

Gouran's second theme was "Restrictedness in Social Contexts and Views of Them." In particular, he noted that the focus of speech communication scholarship on public discourse did injustice to the study of private interaction. He noted that the "contexts" typically in use (e.g., interpersonal, group, organizational, mass, and intercultural) were "artificial."

Gouran's third theme was "Restrictedness in Epistemological Perspective," by which he meant the process by which communication scholars decided they understood how they did what they did. He concluded:

Whether the future of our discipline will evolve along the lines identified by the contributors remains to be determined. What they are suggesting, however, is consistent with larger social trends and developments in other disciplines, especially ones in the humanities and social sciences. Diversity, inclusion, and power, in particular, are matters of increasing social importance that also have found their way into organizational, institutional, and political life. The compatibility of the agenda suggested by the contributors with these external developments, then, is certainly conducive to creation of the future they envision and of which they invite us to be a part. (p. 226)

The last assessment of the discipline appeared in the volume that the by-now National Communication Association commissioned from disciplinary historians Pat Gehrke and William Keith for the 100th anniversary of the association's founding (Gehrke & Keith, 2015). Many of the essays were historical in nature, and the one that critically "called out" the discipline was written by Joshua Gunn and Frank Dance. Gunn and Dance had each independently written about how central "speech" is to the discipline, and in this essay, they contended that the "death" of "speech" in the 1990s was detrimental to the discipline as a whole.

Gunn and Dance (2015) recounted in detail how "speech" came to be the agreed-upon term to describe the discipline, how the addition of "communication" made "speech" a weaker cousin, essentially, following Burgoon's (1989) use of "Dame" in his essay calling for a "divorce" effectively "feminized" the term, while at the same time putting forth "communication" as the masculine successor. Gunn and Dance also noted that the SCA membership was concerned with the issue of legitimizing the discipline and that dropping "speech" would be helpful in that regard, as too often it connoted "performance" and "skills development" over scholarship.

The authors concluded their lament by observing a resurgence of interest in "voice" and "speech"

as an object, both among communication studies scholars and in the wider humanities. In part, this is because scholars are starting to realize that the silencing of speech, either by the critique of phonocentrism or with the shift to "the text" or number, "foreclosed" a number of intriguing questions about the sound or acoustic character of speech. Both of us have advocated, in print and in person, for a revival of the study of speech as an object, not only because it is foundational to human communication—we cry before we write—but also precisely because there is an element of the human voice that is at once bodily, affective, and eludes the capture of language. As a field over the last century, we have responded to that elusive bodily character of speech as if it were histrionic and undisciplinable, a perception that has troubled our colleagues in performance

studies more than most. Somewhat in concert with Kendall R. Phillips, however, we wonder if the "general confusion concerning the term 'speech' among
those not in our field" is simply a failure of the field to embrace the body and its
affects, not necessarily a "failure of the term." (p. 76, italics from the authors)

Despite Gunn and Dance's concerns, this sampling of commentary indi-
cates that concerns about the disciplinary status of communication surfaced
in the early to mid-1980s and were taken seriously by those who wanted to
be in a discipline, not a field. Writing from the 1990s onward consistently
used the word "discipline" to describe speech communication and later
communication. The addition of "and Mass Communication" to the name
of the Association for Education in Journalism seemed to have settled any
issue that might have arisen among journalism professors. A 1990s rash of
attacks on academic departments with "speech" in their names may well have
hastened elimination of "speech" from most department names, in favor of
"Communication Studies" or another variant that did not include the term,
"speech." Nevertheless, those who observed that a lack of common department title may have contributed to a perception that communication was a
"weak" discipline made a well-taken point.

EXAMPLES OF CONTEMPORARY RESEARCH
FOR EACH OF THE FIVE "STRANDS" OF
SCHOLARSHIP IN COMMUNICATION

I have contended that the five strands of scholarship in communication
that I identified became prominent in the 1960s and 1970s continued to be
researched. In this section, I will provide an example of a study for each
strand, selected via a rudimentary search of the Communication Source
database.

Communication as Shaper of Individual and Public Opinion

Peter (2019) conducted a study of influences on public opinion in news
reports that quote ordinary citizens' opinions on the topic of the story will be
considered more credible than news reports that do not include the opinions
of ordinary citizens. The researchers also tested the influence of attitudes
toward populism on perceptions of the credibility of the stories.

In an online experiment, respondents read a news story that recounted
arguments about an issue. In one version of the story, the arguments were
attributed to an ordinary citizen. In the other version, the journalist presented
the arguments. A control group read a fact sheet on the issue that had the

same content as the material presented in the news stories. Respondents also completed a measure of their attitudes toward populism.

Contrary to expectations, the news story containing the arguments for the ordinary citizen was not any more persuasive than the story where the journalist presented the arguments. But, when attitudes toward populism were controlled for, the expected difference in the credibility of the story appeared.

Communication as Language Use

Yi and Samp (2019) studied the degree to which language use in remembered dialogues of same-sex couples was related to internalized homophobia and relationship satisfaction. Participants wrote dialogues they recalled from a prospective coming-out conversation that the participant had with a same-sex relationship partner. Participants also completed measures of internalized homophobia, relationship satisfaction, and length of relationship.

The dialogues that the participants wrote were scored for "clout" (a measure of confidence the dialogue writer displayed), "authenticity," or the degree of honesty displayed in the dialogue, and "emotional tone," or the degree to which emotions were expressed in the dialogue.

Relationship satisfaction was correlated in the predicted direction with all the variables measured except for authenticity, though authenticity mediated the relationship between internalized homophobia and relationship length. The authors concluded that open and honest talk may not always be best in stressful situations such as ones the participants recalled.

Communication as Information Transmission

Ganesan and Nimrod (2021) studied factors that might influence how health information might be recalled accurately after being transmitted. Participants read information about a fictitious patient who had one of four fictitious diseases. The diseases used in the study were either physiological or psychological, and they were caused by either genetics or the environment. Participants completed a multiple-choice questionnaire to measure what they recalled about the patient's disease. Participants also completed a measure of their preferred social distance from the patient, a measure of disgust for the patient's disease, and a measure of the participant's perception of that person's susceptibility to disease in general. They repeated the process for a second description of a patient with a disease.

There were three generations of transmission in the study. Prior to the second generation, the researchers replaced information in the disease descriptions with responses from the multiple-choice items in the first generation, some of which were accurate, some not. Second-generation participants received modified disease descriptions from the first generation. Third-generation participants received descriptions that were modified again after the second-generation participants responded.

As information transmission theory would predict, the first-generation participants were more accurate in their understanding of the information than were participants in either of the next two generations.

Results indicated that participants were more likely to be accurate in recalling a genetic disease that was psychological than one that was physiological. Participants wanted more social distance from patients who had psychological diseases, and they showed more disgust for patients who had diseases that were environmentally caused.

The authors concluded that steps may need to be taken to assist the public in processing disease information accurately, particularly information about diseases that may be physiological and genetically based, which showed the lowest accuracy of recall. Finding and mitigating potential sources of content bias may help to improve accurate transmission of health information.

Communication as Developer of Relationships

Workplaces have become prime dating sites, where the organizational culture doesn't expressly forbid it, and social media have become a primary way of "doing" workplace relationships. Cowan and Horan (2021) interviewed individuals who had experience with at least one workplace relationship, and they reported that information and communication technologies played a significant role in all stages of the relationship.

The authors identified three relationship stages from their interviews: initiation, maintenance, and termination, and they found that technology and social media use figured prominently in each stage. In the initiation stage, individuals used a device, usually a phone, to record contact information for the person in which they were interested. They used social networking sites to gather information about the other person covertly. They also used technology to hide their interest in the relationship from coworkers while continuing to gather information about the other person. And they used technology to keep the state of the relationship private while it was developing.

In the maintenance stage, technology such as phone calls was used to discuss how or if to disclose the relationship to mutual friends. Various technologies were also employed to maintain professionalism in the workplace, often helping the couple to navigate disagreements and other conflict. Cowan and Horan also reported that social media were often used to make the relationship public. Technology could also be used to maintain the relationship by giving the couple ways of keeping in touch throughout the day while attending to their work commitments.

In the termination stage—and the majority of people interviewed had ended at least one workplace relationship—changes in the patterns of technology use were indicators that the relationship might be on its way to ending. Oftentimes, technology or social media were the instrument of terminating the relationship, just as they had been used to make the relationship public.

Cowan and Horan wrote that workplace relationships can be a mixed bag for the organization. They can keep employees on the job, making sure that they are acting professionally, and promoting a culture that recognizes that work is typically an excellent place to meet dating partners. They can also create a culture of secrecy that serves to "poison the well" in some organizations. Clearly, though, workplace relationships are difficult to forbid, so effective ways for organizational members to manage them are key to handling them effectively.

Communication as Definer, Interpreter, and Critic of Culture

Taylor (2021) called attention to the intriguing phenomenon of "deepfake," a technology that allows users to create audio-visual products that have the capability of combining a variety of images to create media texts that look real but are not. These texts have often been created for fun, and sometimes take the form of parody, but the possibility exists that they could be used to create misleading media that could be used to disrupt politics or other societal functions. The possibilities of disruption are so strong that, in the United States, the government has moved to place security features on deepfake technology, something that Taylor labeled, "reflexive securitization" (p. 3).

According to Taylor, government authorities were responding to several concerns. First, the digital format allows exact copying and reproduction, facilitating the creation of texts that appear real but are not. Second, it is easy enough to create digital libraries whose images may be put to a variety of unauthorized uses. Third, standardization of digital formats allows for easy assemblage of material from multiple sources. Fourth, data compression technology makes it easy to collect and store images that violate individual rights to privacy. Fifth, the interactive nature of deepfakes makes it difficult to separate what's real from what's not. Sixth, the fact that deepfakes are easily spread across networks makes it easy for damaging information to be disseminated widely before it can be labeled as inaccurate. Seventh, the embedding of programming in deepfakes may facilitate the spread of harmful computer viruses. Eighth, deepfake potentially makes use of features of social media algorithms that can spread its media products quickly.

Taylor noted the potential problems with this technology, but he also warned that there were advantages to its use as well. He urged the development of ethical guidelines for deepfake use, and he suggested that satire, labeled as such, would allow deepfake to be used to critique society, rather than subvert it.

SOME REFLECTIONS ON THE FIVE HISTORICAL
STRANDS OF COMMUNICATION SCHOLARSHIP

As I have illustrated in the previous section, the five strands of communication scholarship that were prevalent in the 1960s through the early 1980s have continued to be viable labels for communication scholarship. The one that seemed a bit problematic as I researched it was "culture" strand, primarily because the term "culture" resists definition, and it was used in multiple ways within the strand. Yet, most research on communication and culture will focus on how people work through differences, or it will use a definition of culture as a lens to examine a phenomenon. Ethnographic studies in communication don't have a wholly comfortable fit within the five strands, though looking at the purpose of the study would potentially place in one of the five strands. Many ethnographies would fit into the culture strand.

I have asserted earlier that the five strands have differing definitions of communication. I should examine that assertion more thoroughly. Here is a table that lays out the definitional differences.

You'll notice that these definitions are similar only, in that they deal with success at something. What that "something" is depends on the emphasis of that strand of communication. The implication I draw from this exercise is that communication scholars need to take care in how they theorize about communication as they construct research projects. While the strands do have some degree of overlap, I believe that they represent five distinct ways of thinking about communication that are intuitively clear to anyone who has thought about communication for a while. They even seem to be clear to educated lay people to whom I've explained them. There's enough distinctiveness that I believe that theorizing would be improved if it were grounded in only one of the strands.

Now, the strands are not also all-inclusive of scholarship in communication. There are some wonderful journal articles that I couldn't categorize in one of the five strands. My favorite from the period I studied was Thomas W. Benson's "Another Shooting in Cowtown" (1981). The database terms for this article are "short story" and "fiction," which is true in a sense, but which also misses the point entirely.

"Cowtown" probably fits most closely in the "Definer, Interpreter, and Critic of Culture" strand of scholarship, though its tone is not especially critical. The story and how it is told has to sink in before one realizes how much Benson is exposing the hegemonic practices of creating media for a political

Table 9.1 Definitions of Communication and Effective Communication

Way of Understanding Communication	Effective Communication	Example of Effective Communication
Communication as shaper of individual and public opinion	Successful change of individual or public opinion	Personal feeling of connection to another
Communication as language use	Communicators interpret language used in similar ways	Experiencing a message as eloquent or uniquely interesting
Communication as information transmission	Certainty and uncertainty are balanced	Seeing greater good in an experience
Communication as developer of relationships	Common understanding of a relationship in the moment	Feeling of sense of bonding with another as the result of communication
Communication as definer, interpreter, and critic of culture.	Ability to analyze a cultural meaning of an event	Experiencing an unusual sense of insight from interacting with a person or place

campaign. The reason it has to sink in is because Benson doesn't come out and tell the reader that's what he's doing.

Because there are plenty of other scholarly works in communication that don't fit into one of the five strands of scholarship, it is reasonable to ask if other strands of scholarship have emerged. I had two candidates for additional strands in mind, but on further reflection, I'm not ready to declare either to be on the same level as the five I've already identified.

The first of the candidate strands I had tentatively labeled, "Communication as Developer of Individual Identity," and it makes sense to me that communication not only reflects who we wish to present ourselves as being but also is part of shaping continued refinement of individuals' self-concepts. There is even classic work to cite: Erving Goffman's (1959) *The Presentation of Self in Everyday Life*, a text that rather explicitly discusses the nature of interpersonal interactions.

In addition, "Developer of Individual Identity" can refer to identities that have been marginalized in a variety of ways. There is a wealth of feminist scholarship in all areas of communication study, reaching back into the 1964–1982 period, and women have advocated against marginalization across the communication scholarly societies. Perhaps the most effective advocacy has come in journalism, as there is a profession associated with that discipline, one that has historically in the United States been dominated by white males. There have also been efforts to study Black communication, though some of the early publications in this area would probably be regarded today as racist. Advocacy has continued in how Black Americans are represented in the discipline (the tag #COMMUNICATIONSOWHITE comes to mind: for a corrective, see Jackson and Brown Givens, 2006). And gay and lesbian individuals have led drives for increased visibility in the scholarly societies, as well as studying communication from a variety of viewpoints. There has been less effort to study communication for other ethnicities.

Does all this scholarship add up to a coherent strand built around the study of identity? I'm not ready to judge that it has, for two primary reasons. First, while clearly identity interacts with communication, I'm not certain that communication can be defined particularly by identity development, other than in the study of language development in children. Second, and perhaps more important, it seems to me that the study of identity overlaps significantly with the other candidate for a strand of scholarship.

That strand might be titled, "Communication as Performance," and the study of performance has a rich tradition, particularly in the speech discipline. One can go back to Woolbert's definition of the discipline of speech and see that it included oral reading as well as public speaking. Scholarship on what became known as "oral interpretation" has a history of appearing on Speech Association annual conventions from the early days, and certainly skills associated with oral interpretation overlap with skills associated with public speaking. There is an NCA journal in this area, titled, *Text and Performance Quarterly*. Here's where the overlap becomes clear: the description of the journal at the time of this writing was as follows:

> *TPQ* publishes original scholarship that explores and advances the study of performance as a social, critical, communicative practice; as a theoretical lens; as a critical method; as a technology of representation and expression; and as a hermeneutic. Scholarship in *TPQ* addresses performance and the performative from a wide range of perspectives and methodologies, and it investigates sites of performance from the classical stage to popular culture to the practices of everyday life.

The idea of performance seems to have moved away from an orientation about skills and toward a scholarly way to analyze how people perform in their everyday lives. I'd suggest that this move is an admirable one, but it is also one that creates some confusion about how a performance orientation to communication scholarship can be differentiated from scholarship that focuses on individual identity.

These are both areas of the communication discipline that have received considerable attention, and I'd think that there might be a way to organize this scholarship into a "strand" of the type that I've described here. For now, I'm not ready to declare that the ways I thought these strands might be labeled would be productive as "shortcuts" for thinking about these aspects of the discipline's scholarship.

By making such a declaration, I realize that I might be undermining my argument about communication as an academic discipline. Those who disagree with calling communication a discipline might resurrect the argument that its scholarship is too diffuse and doesn't lead to enough coherence to warrant labeling it an academic discipline. My response, as outlined in the chapters of this book, is that there were five "strands" of scholarship that emerged between 1964 and 1982, and these strands were exciting enough to speech and journalism faculties that they were motivated to make "communication" the central metaphor for their scholarly efforts. The scholarly societies picked up the cue: AEJ added a unit devoted to mass communication scholarship in 1964 and added "and Mass Communication" to its name in 1982. Speech resolved to study communication, convened a very influential conference on communication, and, in 1970, added "Communication" to its disciplinary name. Departments of Speech quickly moved to design curricula focused on communication, and by 1982, both speech and journalism were ready to embark on an academic journey that would see a surge in student enrollments, if not in prestige.

Prestige and acceptance would follow, including a somewhat-reluctant invitation for NCA to join the American Council of Learned Societies in 1997. Prestige would be driven in part by significant increases in monetary awards for scholarly research, as well as recognition of communication scholars with various sorts of career awards for research promise or accomplishment.

A discipline also increases its prestige through scholars who are familiar to the public through being interviewed on radio and television or being quoted in the press regularly. It is difficult to achieve status as someone who regularly appears in this role, though there are many communication scholars who share their work with the public and offer informed opinions on topics of public interest. Journalism and media scholars are often called upon by working journalists to comment, both on events of the day and on how journalism is covering such events. Historically, a prestigious position at a major university, often as a dean, draws interest in comments from media outlets. Publishing scholarly books on topics of public interest also qualifies, especially if the books are marketed outside of academe.

There are "stars" within disciplines as well, people whose appearances at major academic conferences always draw a crowd. Sometimes, disciplinary "stars" overlap with "stars" in the public domain, and there are many of the same reasons why public stars are also disciplinary stars.

Readers will note that I have not provided specific names as examples here—deliberately.

The key point to remember is that it has become commonplace for the American public to hear about communication professors or communication scholarship—and that's a mark that a discipline has achieved a certain amount of status in the academy.

In sum, I have argued that communication became an academic discipline, because its scholarly societies made some deliberate decisions to embrace the centrality of the term, "communication," even if they didn't agree on a definition, a set of primary concepts, methods of study, or whether communication was an art, a part of the humanities, or one of the social sciences. While I have not written the history of communication as an academic discipline, I hope that the historical evidence I offered to support my argument proves to be convincing.

The period between 1964 and 1982 saw the amount and diversity of published scholarship grow. Journalism scholars tended to settle on some key questions, develop theories to address those questions, and produce scholarship to advance those theories. Speech scholars had trouble agreeing what was important to study. They did, however, undertake scholarship in sufficient amounts and with sufficient depth that they were able to modify their curricula and begin to attract large numbers of students. Those students quickly became interested in the idea of communication, as well as its perceived value for post-degree employment.

COMMUNICATION BECAME A DISCIPLINE, BUT DID IT REMAIN ONE?

To this point, I have made an argument that communication had qualified as a discipline by 1982, when the Association for Education in Journalism added "and Mass Communication" to its name. As part of that argument, I have offered evidence that the five strands of scholarship I identified for both speech communication and mass communication are still being researched. As I reported in the chapter 8, however, the development of Cultural Studies in Communication signaled a significant shift, both in how communication was conceptualized and in how it was researched. I have also labeled communication as a somewhat fragile discipline; one whose members questioned its legitimacy and who wished to revisit its disciplinary status. Under these pressures, it would be easy for communication to lose whatever focus it had and become merely a label under which scholars conducted research on whatever tickled their fancy. It would be possible for communication to become some other form of academic enterprise, possibly interdisciplinary or what has been called "post-disciplinary."

I will consider first how media studies arguably emerged as an inter-disciplinary area of scholarship in communication, and then I will take up arguments that communication itself is actually either interdisciplinary or post-disciplinary.

The concept of media harkens to Marshall McLuhan (1964), whose *Understanding Media: The Extensions of Man*, shifted the focus of research from the nature of "mass" to the nature of "media." Mass communication continued to predominate, though as the dominant paradigm gave way to cultural studies, media became the symbol of popular culture that could be critically examined and dissected.

Sholle (1995) distinguished between mass communication and media studies scholarship by critiquing the disciplinary status of mass communication scholarship and by presenting media studies as a means of "disciplining" mass communication, calling media studies "radically interdisciplinary" and an example of how an area of study can be grounded in the public sphere, where knowledge is put into practice.

Parks and Wagman (2019) traced the development of media studies from 1984 to 2017. Their research used data from the National Center for Educational Statistics (NCES) to chronicle not only the growth of media studies but also how media studies were classified. Parks and Wagman found that mass communication was classified with journalism until 1992, then it received its own classification until 2002, when it was joined by media studies. Overall, the number of programs in mass communication (and later, mass communication and media studies) increased slowly over time, and the addition of media studies seemed to have an effect primarily on graduate programs, which increased significantly in the 1990s and 2000s.

In introducing the concept of media studies, Parks (2020) labeled it "a hybrid field growing out of communication, literary studies, sociology, art, critical theory, anthropology, psychology, philosophy, and cultural studies" (p. 643). The term, "hybrid," was also used to define business communication as an academic discipline (Shaw, 1993). In the case of business communication, Shaw argued that hybrid meant, "a field in which the traditional lines of thinking we derive from other disciplines account only indirectly for the shared characteristics of our curricula, pedagogy, and research efforts" (p. 302). In both cases, communication is assumed to be one of the disciplines contributing to the hybrid. For a comprehensive review of media studies as an interdisciplinary field of study see Briggle and Christians (2017). For the classification system these authors used in their analysis, see Klein (2017).

Communication also may have progressed to be interdisciplinary, however. To examine this issue, criteria for what might be considered "interdisciplinary" are needed. Julie Thompson Klein (1990), a leading advocate for interdisciplinarity, argued that while fields of study that combine to pursue specific problems may result in enduring disciplines (biochemistry and a variety of types of engineering come to mind), the social sciences have found that while an area of study may draw on the findings and theories of other disciplines, those findings and theories are typically incorporated into a disciplinary perspective. Klein noted that persistence of interdisciplinary academic units is often political in nature, and in a later book (Klein, 1996), she commented, "The only truly interdisciplinary theory possible . . . is a theory about the impossibility of creating a theory that is not implicated in disciplinary practice" (p. 50). Graff (2015) was more direct: after considering communication's claims to disciplinary and interdisciplinary status, he commented that communication had "failed" as an interdiscipline.

As I noted in chapter 1, the idea of "communication" has been pursued by interdisciplinary groups of scholars, the most famous of which occurred at the University of Chicago (Wahl-Jorgensen, 2004). Communication's history as an area of study, while attracting scholars who would become well known in their own disciplines, was animated by decisions of leaders of speech and journalism disciplinary societies to incorporate "communication" as integral part of what they did. Speech, as a result, transformed itself into communication, while journalism worked to keep mass communication—and later, media studies—within its boundaries. While it is undoubtedly a disciplinary weakness to have multiple titles for departments where the study of communication is a central focus, there is considerable unity when it comes to department names of universities offering doctoral programs. Of eighty-eight different university departments, schools and colleges listed in the National Communication Association's directory of doctoral programs, only one did not contain some form of "communication" in its title.

I conclude by returning to the work of Louis Menand (2001), on whose earlier work (Menand, 1997), I based my claim that academic disciplines such as communication were products of scholarly communities coming together in the form of national and international societies whose work organized the discipline and advanced common disciplinary interests. Menand's (2001) topic four years later was concerned about what had been termed "the collapse of the humanities" at a conference he attended. Menand provided an anecdote: the conference participants had been read a list of applicants for fellowships and were asked to guess the academic discipline of the author from the title. The only correct guess was a proposal on politics, which the participants guessed, must have come from an English department.

When disciplines are in trouble, Menand asserted, the usual course of action "has been to promote interdisciplinary teaching and scholarship" (p. 52). Menand further asserted, however, that "interdisciplinarity is not only completely consistent with disciplinarity . . . it actually depends on that concept" (p. 52). Instead, academia was experiencing what Menand called "postdisciplinarity," which he defined as "an escape from disciplines" (p. 52).

While Menand's analysis focused on English more than any other discipline, the trends he described seemed to apply more generally. Starting in the late 1970s, U.S. academy moved from being a predominantly white male institution to becoming significantly more diverse. Women began earning doctorates in far greater numbers than previously and sought academic careers, followed to a smaller degree by people of color. The student population changed much more quickly than the professoriate, and what Menand referred to as "culture wars" erupted over demands for revisions to the traditional curriculum. Student interest moved away from the liberal arts and toward majors that led directly to post-college employment. A large increase in Federal money for research led to research being valued over teaching and service. And the emphasis on research led to significant increases for research productivity to earn tenure. Even so, earned doctorates were the provinces of traditional disciplines, which were slow to adapt to new realities.

Interestingly, communication was forming as a discipline when all this clamor was going on. It went through a reconceptualization of "Speech" before many of the changes that drove the reconceptualization had taken place. "Speech" may have gone away reluctantly for some, but the revision was embraced by academic departments, afraid that students would be unwilling to study public speaking as a major. Speech communication faculty embraced new movements, and some welcomed the advent of "cultural studies" with open arms. Journalism, comfortable in its status as a professional discipline which relied on the liberal arts for curricular accreditation, was content to allow change to come slowly.

Some of this evolution is evident in the organizational structure of each of NCA, AEJMC, and ICA. A comparison of interest group structure showed NCA overlapping AEJMC by 58 percent. ICA overlapped AEJMC at 73 percent, and NCA overlapped ICA at 79 percent. NCA is the largest of the three associations, and with 49 divisions, NCA compares to the much larger American Psychological Association (54 divisions) and the somewhat larger American Sociological Association (53 sections). NCA has, perhaps, historically made it too easy to form divisions, and its number of divisions may be not only larger than its membership would warrant but also reflect NCA's "big tent" culture of supporting organizationally what its members wish to study.

To some degree, that's the point of the concept of post-discipline. As Silvio Waisbord (2019) put it in his analysis of communication as a post-discipline, "Post-disciplines eschew traditional ways of defining fields of study . . . They lack well-defined disciplinary canons . . . Post-disciplinarity assumes that disciplinary boundaries are fluid" (p. 127).

Susan Herbst (2008) celebrated the prospect of communication being considered a post-discipline. Following a review of efforts to establish communication as an academic discipline, she commented on the "tensions" within the discipline:

> On one hand, communication is a field born of other established disciplines. We cannot shed the borrowed notions from other fields because they are intellectually critical to us. And to prove to other fields that we matter, we have had to talk their talk to some extent. Yet, communication researchers have needed to downplay some of this heritage as well, to justify a new field. These conflicting dynamics, manifest in varying ways, have led to productivity and brilliant contributions but also to confusion, self-doubt, and even unfounded arrogance at times. We know who we are—sort of—but these forces are still not entirely aligned and may never be. (p. 605)

Herbst recommended that we acknowledge our interdisciplinary roots but not become caught up in justifying them. She contended that communication was, essentially, post-disciplinary before the term came into fashion. Communication, she argued, never developed a dominant paradigm, and we are better off for embracing eclecticism than becoming stuck in continually justifying a dominant paradigm when the model does not fit well. But we also need to be careful not to embrace eclecticism for its own sake, as doing so runs the danger of making anything appropriate fodder for communication scholarship.

Communication need not hide its light under a bushel. Herbst recommended publishing in journals outside of the discipline and writing public scholarship for magazines that appeal to educated audiences as ways of increasing our disciplinary stature. In fact, she ventured, the multi-disciplinary founders of communication would be pleased with our efforts.

Leave it to big data specialists to take up one of Herbst's challenges: to determine how fragmented is the communication discipline. Song, Eberl, and Eisele (2020) studied ten years of the full texts of publications in highly ranked communication journals. They looked for clusters of words and phrases that would demonstrate linkages among areas of communication scholarship. If there was severe fragmentation, the authors reasoned, they would not see many linkages emerge from examination of the texts of published research. If, on the other hand, there was an unidentified dominant paradigm in communication scholarship, that pattern would show itself as well.

The authors theorized that one of four networks of the communication discipline would emerge: (1) a traditional disciplinary core model; (2) a fragmented discipline model; (3) a "structural cohesion" model that mixed research specializations within the discipline about evenly, though without a theoretical core; and (4) what the authors called a "small-world network," which would show both increased specialization and broader integration. Each of these network patterns had been previously studied, both in theoretical terms and in studies of disciplines, such as sociology.

The research questions of the study focused on how various research topics cluster to form what the authors called "subdisciplines," as well as determining which of the four models described above would provide the best fit for this dataset. The data were taken from almost 9,000 articles published in communication journals between 2010 and 2019.

Results found seventeen subdisciplines for communication, including several that were related to methods of study. I won't reproduce the findings, because the labels of the subdisciplines seem to me to be somewhat idiosyncratic. In fitting the findings to the models, the researchers found first that the traditional disciplinary core model was the least likely fit, with the fragmented discipline model coming in a second least likely. The other two models exhibited some fit, but most importantly, the subdisciplines identified were no more fragmented than might be expected. The researchers observed that the data patterns exhibited some characteristics of the small-world network, with the structural cohesion model coming in second. Both models suggest that while the communication discipline's boundaries continue to be more open than closed, there is also some consensus among the discipline's scholars about how topics of study fit together. I was able to look through the topics that the data identified and find evidence for each of the five strands of scholarship that I contend have persisted through the process of identifying ourselves with the concept of communication. While these five strands may not constitute a "core," they are persistent enough that they can be found, even in contemporary scholarship.

It may be that communication fits Waisbrod's description of the "post-discipline" model in that Song, Eberl, and Eisele's findings indicate that we lack agreed upon disciplinary canons, we allow areas of study to develop around interests of groups of scholars, and our boundaries are certainly fluid. On the other hand, I would argue that these data also suggest that we have a degree of camaraderie and a sense of community that is unusual for disciplinary faculty in the United States. Our discipline is certainly not in a state of collapse, and our scholars are not looking to escape it. It hasn't been that long since we formed the discipline, and we worked hard to do so. I'm betting that, like a lot of things in communication, we'll take the best of the post-discipline idea and fit it into our discipline's structure and practices.

After all, communication is an academic discipline because we made it so.

REFERENCES

Benson, T. W. (1981). Another shooting in Cowtown. *Quarterly Journal of Speech, 67,* 347–406. doi:10.1080/00335638109383581

Benson, T. W. (ed.) (1985). *Speech Communication in the Twentieth Century.* Carbondale: Southern Illinois University Press.

Bochner, A. P. & Eisenberg, E. M. (1985). Legitimizing speech communication: An examination of coherence and cohesion in the development of the discipline. In Benson, T. W. (ed.), *Speech Communication in the Twentieth Century* (pp. 299–321). Carbondale: Southern Illinois University Press.

Briggle, A. & Christians, C. G. (2017). Media and communication. In Frodeman, R., Klein, J. T. & Pacheco, R. C. S. (eds.), *The Oxford Handbook of Interdisciplinarity* (2nd edition, pp. 201–213). Oxford: Oxford University Press.

Burgoon, M. (1989). Instruction about communication: On divorcing Dame Speech. *Communication Education, 28,* 303–308. doi:10.1080/03634528909378768

Cowan, R. L. & Horan, S. M. (2021). Understanding information and communication technology use in workplace romance escalation and de-escalation. *International Journal of Business Communication, 58,* 55–78. doi:10.1177/2329488417731860

Ellis, D. G. (1982, March). The shame of speech communication. *Spectra, 18*(3), 1–2.

Ganesan, A. & Dar-Nimrod, I. (2021). Experimental examination of social transmission of health information using an online platform. *Health Communication, 36,* 392–400. doi:10.1080/10410236.2019.1693126

Gehrke, P. J. & Keith, W. M. (eds.) (2015). *A Century of Communication Studies: The Unfinished Conversation.* New York: Routledge.

Goffman, E. (1959). *The Presentation of Self in Everyday Life.* Garden City: Doubleday & Company.

Gouran, D. S. (1990). Introduction: Speech Communication after seventy-five years, issues and prospects. In Phillips, G. M. & Wood, J. T. (eds.), *Speech Communication: Essays to Commemorate the 75th Anniversary of The Speech Communication Association* (pp. 1–32). Carbondale: Southern Illinois University Press.

Gouran, D. S. (1995). Epilogue. In Wood, J. T. & Gregg, R. B. (eds.), *Toward the 21st Century: The Future of Speech Communication* (pp. 219–229). Cresskill, NJ: Hampton Press.

Graff, H. J. (2015). *Undisciplining Knowledge: Interdisciplinarity in the Twentieth Century.* Baltimore, MD: Johns Hopkins University Press.

Gunn, J. & Dance, F. E. X. (2015). The silencing of speech in the late twentieth century. In Gehrke, P. J. & Keith, W. M. (eds.), *A Century of Communication Studies: The Unfinished Conversation* (pp. 64–81). New York: Routledge.

Herbst, S. (2008). Disciplines, intersections, and the future of communication research. *Journal of Communication 58,* 603–614. doi:10.1111/j.1460-2466.2008.00402.x

Jackson, R. L. & Brown Givens, S. M. (2006). *Black pioneers in communication research.* Thousand Oaks, CA: Sage Publications.

Klein, J. T. (1996). *Crossing Boundaries: Knowledge, Disciplinarities, and Interdisciplinarities.* Charlottesville, VA: University Press of Virginia.

Klein, J. T. (1990). *Interdisciplinarity: History, Theory and Practice.* Detroit: Wayne State University Press.

Klein, J. T. (2017). Typologies of interdisciplinarity: The boundary work of definition. In Frodeman, R., Klein, J. T. & Pacheco, R. C. S. (eds.), *The Oxford Handbook of Interdisciplinarity* (2nd edition, pp. 21–34). Oxford: Oxford University Press.

Li, Y. & Samp, J. A. (2019). Internalized homophobia, language use, and relationship quality in same-sex romantic relationships. *Communication Reports*, *32*, 15–28. do i:10.1080/08934215.2018.1545859

McLuhan, M. (1964). *Understanding Media: The Extensions of Man*. New York: McGraw-Hill.

Menand, L. (1997). The demise of disciplinary authority. In A. Kernan (ed.), *What's Happened to the Humanities?* (pp. 201–219). Princeton: Princeton University Press.

Menand, L. (2001, Autumn). Undisciplined. *The Wilson Quarterly, 25(4)*, 51–59.

Parks, L. (2020) Field mapping: What is the "media" of Media Studies? *Television & New Media, 21*, 642–649. doi:10.1177/1527476420919701

Parks, L. & Wagman, K. (2019, November 25). Charting the growth of Media Studies in US Higher Education: An analysis of Federal data from 1984-2017. Global Media Technologies and Cultures Lab. http://globalmedia.mit.edu/2019/11/25/ch arting-the-growth-of-media-studies-in-us-higher-education-1984-2017/

Peter, C. (2019). The people's voice—The people's choice? How vox pop exemplars shape audience judgments as a function of populist attitudes. *Journalism & Mass Communication Quarterly, 96*, 1004–1024. doi:10.1177/1077699019852323

Phillips, G. M. & Wood, J. T. (eds.) (1990). *Speech Communication: Essays to Commemorate the 75th Anniversary of The Speech Communication Association*. Carbondale: Southern Illinois University Press.

Shaw, G. (1993). The shape of our field: Business communication as a hybrid discipline. *Journal of Business Communication, 30*, 297–313. doi:10.1177/002194369303000304

Sholle, D. (1995). "No respect! Disciplinarity and media studies in communication": Resisting disciplines: Repositioning Media Studies in the university. *Communication Theory, 5*, 130–143. doi:10.1111/j.1468-2885.1995.tb00102.x

Song, H., Eberl, J.-M. & Eisele, O. (2020). Less fragmented than we thought? Toward clarification of a subdisciplinary linkage in communication science, 2010–2019. *Journal of Communication 70*, 310–334. doi:10.1093/joc/jqaa009

Taylor, B. C. (2021). Defending the state from digital deceit: The reflexive securitization of Deepfake. *Critical Studies in Media Communication, 38*, 1–17. doi:10.108 0/15295036.2020.1833058

Wahl-Jorgensen, K. (2004). How not to found a field: New evidence on the origins of mass communication research. *Journal of Communication, 54*, 547–564. doi:10.1111/j.1460-2466.2004.tb02644.x

Waisbord, S. (2019). *Communication: A Post-Discipline*. Malden, MA: Policy Press.

Wood, J. T. & Gregg, R. B. (eds.) (1995). *Toward the 21st Century: The Future of Speech Communication*. Cresskill, NJ: Hampton Press.

Bibliography

Adler, K. (1978). On the falsification of rules theories. *Quarterly Journal of Speech, 64*, 427–438. doi:10.1080/00335637809383448

Altman, I., & Taylor, D. A. (1973). *Social Penetration: The Development of Interpersonal Relationships.* New York: Holt, Rinehart and Winston.

Arnold, W. E., & McCroskey, J. C. (1967). The credibility of reluctant testimony. *The Central States Speech Journal, 18*, 97–103. doi:10.1080/10510976709362870

Asante, M. K. (2006). A discourse on black studies: Liberating the study of African people in the western academy. *Journal of Black Studies, 36*, 646–662. doi:10.1177/0021934705285937

Asante, M. K., Newmark, E., & Blake, C. A. (eds.) (1979). *Handbook of Intercultural Communication.* Thousand Oaks, CA: Sage Publications.

Association for Education in Journalism and Mass Communication (2010, June 25). AEJMC history. Retrieved from https://www.aejmc.org/home/about/aejmc-history.

Atkin, C. K. (1972). Anticipated communication and mass media information-seeking. *Public Opinion Quarterly, 36*, 188–199. doi:10.1086/267991

Austin, J. L. (1961). *Philosophical Papers.* Oxford: Clarendon Press.

Ball-Rokeach, S. J., & DeFleur, M. L. (1976). A dependency model of mass-media effects. *Communication Research, 3*, 3–21. doi:10.1177/009365027600300101

Bateson, G. (1958). *Naven* (2nd edition). Stanford, CA: Stanford University Press.

Becher, T., & Trowler, P. (2001). *Academic Tribes and Territories: Intellectual Enquiry and the Cultures of Disciplines* (2nd edition). Buckingham, UK: Open University Press/SRHE.

Becker, S. L. (1969). Directions for inter-cultural communication research. *Communication Studies, 20*, 3–13. doi:10.1080/10510976909362945

Benjamin, J. (1976). The viability of general semantics. *Speech Education, 4*, 155–160.

Benson, T. W. (1981). Another shooting in Cowtown. *Quarterly Journal of Speech, 67*, 347–406. doi:10.1080/00335638109383581

Benson, T. W. (ed.) (1985). *Speech Communication in the Twentieth Century.* Carbondale: Southern Illinois University Press.

Berelson, B. (1959). The state of communication research. *Public Opinion Quarterly, 23,* 1–17. doi:10.1086/266840

Berger, C. R. (1977). Interpersonal communication theory and research: An overview. In Rubin, B. D. (ed.), *Communication Yearbook 1* (pp. 217–228). New Brunswick, NJ: Transaction Books.

Berger, C. R. (1979). Beyond initial interaction: Uncertainty, understanding, and the development of interpersonal relationships. In Giles, H., & St Clair, R. N. (eds.), *Language and Social Psychology* (pp. 122–144). Baltimore, MD: University Park Press.

Berger, C. R., & Calabrese, R. J. (1975). Some explorations in initial interaction and beyond: Toward a theory of interpersonal communication. *Human Communication Research, 1,* 199–112. doi:0.1111/j.1468-2958.1975.tb00258.x

Berger, C. R., Gardner, R. R., Parks, M. R., Schulman, L., & Miller, G. R. (1976). Interpersonal epistemology and interpersonal communication. In Miller, G. R. (ed.), *Explorations in Interpersonal Communication* (pp. 149–171). Thousand Oaks, CA: Sage Publications.

Berlo, D. K. (1960). *The Process of Communication.* New York: Holt, Rinehart and Winston.

Berlyne, D. (1960). *Conflict, Arousal, and Curiosity.* New York: McGraw-Hill.

Berryman, C. L., & Wilcox, J. R. (1980). Attitudes toward male and female speech: Experiments on the effects of sex-typical language. *Western Journal of Speech Communication, 44,* 50–59. doi:10.1080/10570318009373985

Bertalanffy, L. (1969). *General System Theory: Foundations, Development, Applications* (International library of systems theory and philosophy). New York: George Braziller.

Beth, E. F. (1965). Official minutes of the 1964 convention, Association for Education in Journalism. *Journalism Quarterly, 42,* 149–160. doi:10.1177/107769906504200122

Bitzer, L. F., & Black, E. (eds.) (1971). *The Prospect of Rhetoric: Report of the National Developmental Project, Sponsored by Speech Communication Association.* Englewood Cliffs, NJ: Prentice-Hall.

Bitzer, L. F. (1968). The rhetorical situation. *Philosophy & Rhetoric, 1,* 1–14.

Blankenship, J. (2004). Marie Hochmuth Nichols (1908-1978): A retrospective. *Review of Communication, 4(1/2),* 75–85. doi:10.1080/1535859042000250295

Blumer, H. (1969). *Symbolic Interactionism: Perspective and Method.* Englewood Cliffs, NJ: Prentice-Hall.

Blumler, J. G. (1978). Purposes of mass communications research: A transatlantic perspective. *Journalism Quarterly, 55,* 219–230. doi:10.1177/107769907805500201

Bochner, A. P. (1977). Whither communication theory and research? *Quarterly Journal of Speech, 63,* 324–332. doi:10.1080/00335637709383392

Bochner, A. P., & Eisenberg, E. M. (1985). Legitimizing speech communication: An examination of coherence and cohesion in the development of the discipline. In Benson, T. W. (ed.), *Speech Communication in the Twentieth Century* (pp. 299–321). Carbondale: Southern Illinois University Press.

Booth, W. C. (1974). *Modern Dogma and the Rhetoric of Assent*. Notre Dame: University of Notre Dame Press.

Bostrom, R. M., & Kemp, A. P. (1969). Type of speech, sex of speaker, and sex of subject as factors influencing persuasion. *Central States Speech Journal, 20*, 245–251. doi:10.1080/10510976909362975

Bowers, T. A. (1977, August). A history of the Division of Communication Theory and Methodology of the Association for Education in Journalism. Presented at the annual meeting of the Association for Education in Journalism, Madison, Wisconsin.

Briggle, A., & Christians, C. G. (2017). Media and communication. In Frodeman, R., Klein, J. T., & Pacheco, R. C. S. (eds.), *The Oxford Handbook of Interdisciplinarity* (2nd edition, pp. 201–213). Oxford: Oxford University Press.

Burgoon, M. (1989). Instruction about communication: On divorcing dame speech. *Communication Education, 28,* 303–308. doi:10.1080/03634528909378768

Burke, K. (1950). *A Rhetoric of Motives*. Berkeley, CA: University of California Press.

Cassirer, E., & Yale University. Louis Stern Memorial Fund. (1944). *An Essay on Man: An Introduction to a Philosophy of Human Culture* (Yale paperbound). New Haven: London: Yale University Press; H. Milford, Oxford University Press.

Chaffee, S. H., & Rogers, E. M. (eds.) (1997). *The Beginnings of Communication Study in America: A Personal Memoir*, by Wilbur Schramm. Thousand Oaks, CA: Sage Publications.

Cissna, K. N., Eadie, W. F., & Hickson, III, M. (2009). The development of applied communication research. In Frey, L. R. & Cissna, K. N. (eds.), *Routledge Handbook of Applied Communication Research* (pp. 3–25). New York: Routledge.

Cohen, B. (1963). *The Press and Foreign Policy*. Princeton, NJ: Princeton University Press.

Cohen, H. (1994). *The History of Speech Communication: The Emergence of a Discipline, 1914-1945*. Annandale, VA: Speech Communication Association.

Corcoran, F. (1981). Towards a semiotic of screen media: Problems in the use of linguistic models. *Western Journal of Speech Communication, 45*, 182–193. doi:10.1080/10570318109374040

Cowan, R. L., & Horan, S. M. (2021). Understanding information and communication technology use in workplace romance escalation and de-escalation. *International Journal of Business Communication, 58*, 55–78. doi:10.1177/2329488417731860

Craig, R. T. (1999). Communication theory as a field. *Communication Theory, 9*, 117–161. doi:10.1111/j.1468-2885.1999.tb00355.x

Crockett, W. H. (1965). Cognitive complexity and impression formation. *Progress in Experimental Personality Research, 2*, 47–90.

Cronkite, G. (1984). Perception and meaning. In Arnold, C. C., & Bowers, J. W. (eds.), *Handbook of Rhetorical and Communication Theory* (pp. 51–229). Boston, MA: Allyn and Bacon.

Cushman, D. P., & Pearce, W. B. (1977). Generality and necessity in three types of human communication theory—Special attention to rules theory. In Ruben, B. D.

(ed.), *Communication Yearbook 1* (pp.173–182). New Brunswick, NJ: Transaction Books.

Czitrom, D. (1982). *Media and the American mind: From Morse to McLuhan*. Chapel Hill, NC: University of North Carolina Press.

Dance, F. E. X., & Larson, C. E. (1976). *The Functions of Human Communication: A Theoretical Approach*. New York: Holt, Rinehart and Winston.

Dance, F. X. (2006). Frank E. X. Dance, 1982 President, National Communication Association. *Review of Communication, 6*, 221–227. doi:10.1080/1535859 0600918714

Daniel, J. L. (1995). *Changing the Players and the Game: A Personal Account of the Speech Communication Association Black Caucus origins*. Annandale, VA: Speech Communication Association.

Delia J. G. (1987). Communication research: A history. In Berger, C. R., & Chaffee, S. H. (eds.), *Handbook of Communication Science* (pp. 20–98). Thousand Oaks, CA: Sage Publications.

Delia, J. G. (1974). Attitude toward the disclosure of self-attributions and the complexity of interpersonal constructs. *Speech Monographs, 41*, 119–126. doi:10.1080/03637757409375827

Delia, J. G., Clark, R. A., & Switzer, D. E. (1974). Cognitive complexity and impression formation in informal social interaction. *Speech Monographs, 41*, 299–308.doi :10.1080/03637757409375854

Delia, J. G., Crockett, W. H., Press, A. N., & O'Keefe, D. J. (1975). The dependency of interpersonal evaluations on context-relevant beliefs about the other. *Speech Monographs, 42*, 10–19. doi:10.1080/03637757509375872

Dietrich, J. E. (1968). Conference background and procedures. In Kibler, R. J., & Barker, L. L. (eds.), *Conceptual Frontiers in Speech-Communication* (pp. 3–15). New York: Speech Association of America.

Ehninger, D., & Brockriede, W. (1963). *Decision by Debate*. New York: Dodd, Mead.

Ellingsworth, H. W. (1977). Conceptualizing intercultural communication. In Ruben, B. D. (ed.), *Communication Yearbook 1* (pp. 99–106). New Brunswick, NJ: Transaction Books.

Ellis, D. G. (1982, March). The shame of speech communication. *Spectra, 18*(3), 1–2.

Emery, E., & McKerns, J. P. (1987, November). AEJMC: 75 years in the making: A history of organizing for journalism and mass communication education in the United States. *Journalism Monographs, 104*.

Farrell, T. B., & Aune, J. A. (1979). Critical theory and communication: A selective literature review. *Quarterly Journal of Speech, 65*, 93–120. doi:10.1080 /00335637909383461

Fishbein, M. (1967). A behavior theory approach to the relations between beliefs about an object and the attitude toward the object. In Fishbein, M. (ed.), *Readings in Attitude Theory and Measurement* (pp. 257–265). New York: Wiley.

Fishbein, M., & Ajzen, I. (1975). *Belief, Attitude, Intention and Behavior: An Introduction to Theory and Research*. Reading, MA: Addison-Wesley.

Fisher, B. A. (1978). Information systems theory and research: An overview. In Ruben, B. D. (ed.), *Communication Yearbook 2* (pp. 81–124). New Brunswick, NJ: Transaction Books.

Fisher, W. R. (1978). Toward a logic of good reasons. *Quarterly Journal of Speech, 64*, 376–384. doi:10.1080/00335637809383443

Folkerts, J. (2014). History of journalism education. *Journalism and Communication Monographs, 16*, 227–299. doi:10.1 177/1522637914541379

Funkhouser, G. R. (1973). The issues of the sixties: An exploratory study in the dynamics of public opinion. *Public Opinion Quarterly, 37*, 62–75. doi:10.1086/268060

Ganesan, A., & Dar-Nimrod, I. (2021). Experimental examination of social transmission of health information using an online platform. *Health Communication, 36*, 392–400. doi:10.1080/10410236.2019.1693126

Gehrke, P. J., & Keith, W. M. (eds.) (2015). *A Century of Communication Studies: The Unfinished Conversation.* New York: Routledge.

Gerbner, G. (1969). Toward 'Cultural Indicators': The analysis of mass mediated message systems. *AV Communication Review, 17*(2), 137–148.

Gerbner, G., & Gross, L. (1976). Living with television: The violence profile. *Journal of Communication, 26*(2), 172–199. doi:10.1111/j.1460-2466.1976.tb01397.x

Gerbner, G., Gross, L., Morgan, M., & Signorielli, N. (1980). The "mainstreaming" of America: violence profile no. 11. *Journal of Communication, 30*(3), 10–29. doi:10.1111/j.1460-2466.1980.tb01987.x

Gerbner, G., Gross, L., Morgan, M., & Signorielli, N. (1981, May/June). Scientists on the TV screen. *Society, 18*(4), 41–44. doi:10.1007/BF02701349

Gerbner, G., Gross, L., Morgan, M., & Signorielli, N. (1981, October 8). Health and medicine on television. *New England Journal of Medicine 305*(15), 901–904. doi:10.1056/NEJM198110083051530

Gerbner, G., Gross, L., Morgan, M., & Signorielli, N. (1982). Charting the mainstream: Televisions contributions to political orientations. *Journal of Communication, 32*(2), 100–127. doi:10.1111/j.1460-2466.1982.tb00500.x

Gerbner, G., Gross, L., Signorielli, N., & Morgan, M. (1980). Aging with television: Images on television drama and conceptions of social reality. *Journal of Communication, 30*(1), 37–47. doi:10.1111/j.1460-2466.1980.tb01766.x

Gerbner, G., Gross, L., Signorielli, N., Morgan, M., & Jackson-Beeck, M. (1979). The demonstration of power: Violence profile No. 10. *Journal of Communication, 29*(3), 177–196. doi:10.1111/j.1460-2466.1979.tb01731.x

Goffman, E. (1959). *The Presentation of Self in Everyday Life.* Garden City: Doubleday & Company.

Goldberg, A. (1965). The effects of a laboratory course in General Semantics. *ETC: A Review of General Semantics, 22*, 19–24. Retrieved September 5, 2020, from http://www.jstor.org/stable/42574076

Gorman, M. (1967). A critique of general semantics. *Western Speech, 31*, 44–50.

Gouran, D. S. (1990). Introduction: Speech Communication after seventy-five years, issues and prospects. In Phillips, G. M., & Wood, J. T. (eds.), *Speech Communication: Essays to Commemorate the 75th Anniversary of the Speech Communication Association* (pp. 1–32). Carbondale: Southern Illinois University Press.

Gouran, D. S. (1995). Epilogue. In Wood, J. T., & Gregg, R. B. (eds.), *Toward the 21st Century: The Future of Speech Communication* (pp. 219–229). Cresskill, NJ: Hampton Press.

Graff, H. J. (2015). *Undisciplining Knowledge: Interdisciplinarity in the Twentieth Century.* Baltimore, MD: Johns Hopkins University Press.

Gudykunst, W. B. (1983). *Intercultural Communication Theory: Current Perspectives.* Thousand Oaks, CA: Sage.

Gunn, J., & Dance, F. E. X. (2015). The silencing of speech in the late Twentieth Century. In Gehrke, P. J., & Keith, W. M. (eds.), *A Century of Communication Studies: The Unfinished Conversation* (pp. 64–81). New York: Routledge.

Hall, E. T. (1959). *The Silent Language.* Garden City: Doubleday.

Hall, E. T. (1966). *The Hidden Dimension.* Garden City: Doubleday.

Hall, S. (2016). *Cultural studies 1983*, edited and with an introduction by Jennifer Daryl Slack and Lawrence Grossberg. Durham, NC: Duke University Press.

Hample, D. (1977). Testing a model of value argument and evidence. *Communication Monographs, 44,* 106–120. doi:10.1080/03637757709390121

Hample, D. (1978). Predicting immediate belief change and adherence to argument claims. *Communication Monographs, 45,* 219–228. doi:10.1080/03637757809375967

Hample, D. (1979). Predicting belief and belief change using a cognitive theory of argument and evidence. *Communication Monographs, 46,* 142–146. doi:10.1080/03637757909376000

Hample, D. (1981). The cognitive context of argument. *Western Journal of Speech Communication: WJSC, 45,* 148–158. doi:10.1080/10570318109374037

Hample, D. J. (1980). A cognitive view of argument. *Journal of the American Forensic Association, 16,* 151–158. doi:10.1080/00028533.1980.11951168

Hart, R. P., & Burks, D. M. (1972). Rhetorical sensitivity and social interaction. *Speech Monographs, 39,* 75–91. doi:10.1080/03637757209375742

Hastorf, A., Schneider, D., & Polefka, J. (1970). *Person Perception (Topics in Social Psychology).* Reading, MA: Addison-Wesley.

Hawes, L. C. (1971). Information overload and the organization of 1984. *Western Speech, 35,* 191–198. doi:10.1080/10570317109373703

Hawes, L. C. (1975). *Pragmatics of Analoguing: Theory and Model Construction in Communication.* Reading, MA: Addison-Wesley.

Hawkins, R. P., & Pingree, S. (1982). Uniform content and habitual viewing: Unnecessary assumptions in social reality effects. *Human Communication Research, 7,* 291–301. doi:10.1111/j.1468-2958.1981.tb00576.x

Hayakawa, S. I. (1944). *Language in Thought and Action.* New York: Harcourt, Brace.

Hefferline, R. F. (1955). Communication theory: I. Integrator of the arts and sciences. *Quarterly Journal of Speech, 41,* 223–233. doi:10.1080/00335635509382071

Held, D. (1982). Critical theory and political transformation. *Media, Culture and Society, 4,* 153–160. doi:10.1177/016344378200400205

Herbst, S. (2008). Disciplines, intersections, and the future of communication research. *Journal of Communication 58,* 603–614. doi:10.1111/j.1460-2466.2008.00402.x

Hewes, D. E. Finite stochastic modeling of communication processes: An introduction and some basic reading. *Human Communication Research, 1,* 271–283. doi:10.1111/j.1468-2958.1975.tb00274.x

Holbrook, A., & Hsiao-Tung Lu. (1969). A study of intelligibility in whispered Chinese. *Speech Monographs, 36*, 464–466. doi:10.1080/03637756909375641

Howell, W. S. (1972, February). Presidential address – 1971. *Spectra, 8*(2), 2–7.

Hsu, H. (2017, July 17). Stuart Hall and the Rise of Cultural Studies. *The New Yorker.* Retrieved from https://www.newyorker.com/books/page-turner/stuart-hall-and-the -rise-of-cultural-studies.

Hughes, M. (1980). The fruits of cultivation analysis. A re-examination of the effects of television watching on fear of victimization, alienation, and the approval of violence. *Public Opinion Quarterly, 44*, 287–302. doi:10.1086/268597

International Communication Association (2020, March 27) *History.* https://www .icahdq.org/page/History

Jackob, N. G. E. (2010). No alternatives? The relationship between perceived media dependency, use of alternative information sources, and general trust in mass media. *International Journal of Communication (19328036), 4*, 589–606.

Jackson, R. L. & Brown Givens, S. M. (2006). *Black pioneers in communication research*. Thousand Oaks, CA: Sage Publications.

Jamieson, K. (1976). The rhetorical manifestations of *Weltanschauung. Central States Speech Journal, 27*, 4–14. doi:10.1080/10510977609367860

Johnson, W. (1946). *People in Quandaries: The Semantics of Personal Adjustment.* New York: Harper & Row.

Katz, E., Blumler, J. G., & Gurevitch, M. (1973). Uses and gratifications research. *Public Opinion Quarterly, 37*, 509–523. doi:10.1086/268109

Katz, E., Lazarsfeld, P. F., & Roper, E. (1955). *Personal Influence: The Part Played by People in the Flow of Mass Communications.* New York: Routledge.

Kelly, G. A. (1955). *The Psychology of Personal Constructs.* New York: Norton.

Kibler, R. J., & Barker, L. L. (1968). *Conceptual Frontiers in Speech Communication: Report on the New Orleans Conference on Research and Instructional Development.* Annandale, VA: Speech Association of America.

Kibler, R. J., Barker, L. L., & Cegala, D. J. (1970). Effect of sex on comprehension and retention. *Speech Monographs, 37*, 287–293. doi:10.1080/03637757009375680

Klapper, J. T. (1960). *The Effects of Mass Communication.* New York: Free Press.

Klein, J. T. (1990). *Interdisciplinarity: History, Theory and Practice.* Detroit: Wayne State University Press.

Klein, J. T. (1996). *Crossing Boundaries: Knowledge, Disciplinarities, and Interdisciplinarities.* Charlottesville, VA: University Press of Virginia.

Klein, J. T. (2017). Typologies of interdisciplinarity: The boundary work of definition. In Frodeman, R., Klein, J. T., & Pacheco, R. C. S. (eds.), *The Oxford Handbook of Interdisciplinarity* (2nd edition, pp. 21–34). Oxford: Oxford University Press.

Knapp, M. L. (1978). *Social Intercourse: From Greeting to Goodbye.* Boston, MA: Allyn and Bacon.

Knapp, M. L., Hart, R. P., & Dennis, H. S. (1974). An exploration of deception as a communication construct. *Human Communication Research, 1*, 15–29. doi:10.1111/j.1468-2958.1974.tb00250.x

Knapp, M. L., Hart, R. P., Friedrich, G. W., & Shulman, G. M. (1973). The rhetoric of goodbye: Verbal and nonverbal correlates of human leave-taking. *Speech Monographs, 40*, 182–198. doi:10.1080/03637757309375796

Korn, C. J., Morreale, S. P., & Boileau, D. M. (2000). Defining the field: Revisiting the ACA 1995 definition of communication studies. *Journal of the Association for Communication Administration 29*, 40–52.

Korzybski, A. (1948). *Science and Sanity: An Introduction to Non-Aristotelian Systems and General Semantics* (3rd edition). Lakeville, CT: International Non-Aristotelian Library Pub. Co.

Kramer, C. (1974). Women's speech: Separate but unequal? *Quarterly Journal of Speech, 60*, 14–24. doi:10.1080/00335637409383203

Krippendorff, K. (1975). Information theory. In Hannenman, G. J., S., & McEwen, W. J. (eds.), *Communication and Behavior* (pp. 351–389). Reading, MA: Addison-Wesley.

Krippendorff, K. (1977). Information systems theory and research: An overview. In Ruben, B. D. (ed.), *Communication Yearbook 1* (pp. 149–171). New Brunswick, NJ: Transaction Books.

Kuhn, T. S. (1962). *The Structure of Scientific Revolutions*. Chicago, IL: University of Chicago Press.

Lakoff, R. (1975). *Language and Woman's Place*. New York: Harper and Row.

Langer, S. K. (1951). *Philosophy in a New Key: A Study in the Symbolism of Reason, Rite and Art*. Cambridge: Harvard University Press.

Langer, S. K. (1960). The origins of speech and its communicative function. *Quarterly Journal of Speech, 46*, 121–135. doi:10.1080/00335636009382402

Lasswell, H. D. (1927). *Propaganda Technique in the World War*. New York: A. A. Knopf.

Lasswell, H. D. (1948). The structure and function of communication in society. In Bryson, L. (ed.), *The Communication of Ideas: A Series of Addresses* (pp. 203–243). New York: Institute for Religious and Social Studies.

Lasswell, H. D. (1948). *Power and Personality*. New York: Norton.

Lazarsfeld, P. F., Berleson, B., & Gaudet, H. (1944). *The People's Choice: How the Voter Makes Up His Mind in a Presidential Campaign*. New York: Columbia University Press.

Lederer, W., & Burdick, E. (1958). *The Ugly American*. New York: Norton.

Lee, I. J. (1941). *Language Habits in Human Affairs: An Introduction to General Semantics*. New York: Harper & Brothers.

Leeds-Hurwitz, W. (1990). Notes in the history of intercultural communication: The Foreign Service Institute and the mandate for intercultural training. *The Quarterly Journal of Speech, 76*, 262–281. doi:10.1080/00335639009383919

Levine, T. R., & Park, H. S. (2017). The research of James C. McCroskey: A personal and professional remembrance. *Communication Research Reports, 34*, 376–380. doi:10.1080/08824096.2017.1368474

Li, Y., & Samp, J. A. (2019). Internalized homophobia, language use, and relationship quality in same-sex romantic relationships. *Communication Reports, 32*, 15–28. doi:10.1080/08934215.2018.1545859

Lippmann, W. (1922). *Public Opinion*. New York: Macmillan, 1922.

Liska, J., Mechling, E. W., & Stathas, S. (1981). Differences in subjects' perceptions of gender and believability between users of deferential and nondeferential language. *Communication Quarterly, 29*, 40–48. doi:10.1080/01463378109369388

Littlejohn, S. W., & Jabusch, D. M. (1982). Communication competence: Model and application. *Journal of Applied Communication Research, 10*, 29–37. doi:10.1080/00909888209365210

Martin, H. R. (1981). The prosodic components of speech melody. *Quarterly Journal of Speech, 67*, 81–92. doi:10.1080/00335638109383553

Marwell, G., & Schmitt, D. R. (1967). Dimensions of compliance-gaining behavior: An empirical analysis. *Sociometry, 30*, 350–364. doi:10.2307/2786181

Matson, F., & Montagu, A. (1967). *The Human Dialogue: Perspectives on Communication*. New York: The Free Press.

McCombs, M. E., & Shaw, D. L. (1972). The agenda-setting function of mass media. *Public Opinion Quarterly, 36*, 176–187. doi:10.1086/267990

McCroskey, J. C. (1966). Scales for the measurement of ethos. *Speech Monographs, 33*, 65–72. doi:10.1080/03637756609375482

McCroskey, J. C. (1969). A summary of experimental research on the effects of evidence in persuasive communication. *The Quarterly Journal of Speech, 55*, 169–176. doi:10.1080/00335636909382942

McGuire, W. J. (1960). A syllogistic analysis of cognitive relationships. In Rosenberg, M. J., [and others], *Attitude Organization and Change: An Analysis of Consistency Among Attitude Components* (pp. 65–111). New Haven, CT: Yale University Press.

McLuhan, M. (1964). *Understanding Media: The Extensions of Man*. New York: McGraw-Hill.

Mead, G. H. (1934). *Mind, Self & Society from the Standpoint of a Social Behaviorist*, edited by Charles W. Morris. Chicago, IL: University of Chicago Press.

Menand, L. (1997). The demise of disciplinary authority. In A. Kernan (ed.), *What's Happened to the Humanities?* (pp. 201–219). Princeton, NJ: Princeton University Press.

Menand, L. (2001, Autumn). Undisciplined. *The Wilson Quarterly, 25*(4), 51–59.

Millar, F. E., & Rogers, L. E. (1976). A relational approach to interpersonal communication. In Miller, G. R. (ed.), *Explorations in Interpersonal Communication* (pp. 87–103). Thousand Oaks, CA: Sage Publications.

Miller, G. R. (1968). Communication and persuasion research: Current problems and prospects. *Quarterly Journal of Speech, 54*, 268–276. doi:10.1080/00335636809382900

Miller, G. R. (1969). Some factors influencing judgments of the logical validity of arguments: A research review. *Quarterly Journal of Speech, 55*, 276–286. doi:10.1080/00335636909382954

Miller, G. R. (1971). Readings in communication theory: Suggestions and an occasional caveat. *Today's Speech, 19*, 5–10. doi:10.1080/01463377109368958

Miller, G. R., & Burgoon, M. (1978). Persuasion research: Review and commentary. In Ruben, B. (ed.), *Communication Yearbook 2* (pp. 29–47). New Brunswick, NJ: Transaction Books.

Miller, G. R., & Steinberg, M. (1975). *Between People: A New Analysis of Interpersonal Communication*. Chicago, IL: Science Research Associates.

Morgan, M. (1982). Symbolic victimization and real world fear. *Human Communication Research, 9*, 146–157. doi:10.1111/j.1468-2958.1983.tb00689.x

National Center for Education Statistics (2010). Detail for CIP Code 09. Retrieved from http://nces.ed.gov/ipeds/cipcode/cipdetail.aspx?y=55&cipid=88043.

Nichols, M. H. (1970). The tyranny of relevance. *Spectra, 6*(1), 1, 10.

Nofsinger, R. E., Jr. (1976). On answering questions indirectly: Some rules in the grammar of doing conversation. *Human Communication Research, 2*, 172–181. doi:10.1111/j.1468-2958.1976.tb00709.x

Nofsinger Jr., R. E. (1977). A peek at conversational analysis. *Communication Quarterly, 25*(3), 12–20. doi:10.1080/01463377709369259

Norton, R. W. (1978). Foundation of a communicator style construct. *Human Communication Research, 4*, 99–112. doi:10.1111/j.1468-2958.1978.tb00600.x

O'Hair, H. D. (2006, November). *The promise of communication*. Presidential address delivered at the annual convention of the National Communication Association, San Antonio, Texas.

O'Neill, J. M. (1928). After thirteen years. *Quarterly Journal of Speech, 13*, 242–253. doi:10.1080/00335632809379741

Ogden, C. K., & Richards, I. A. (1946). *The Meaning of Meaning: A Study of the Influence of Language Upon Thought and of the Science of Symbolism*. New York: Harcourt, Brace.

Oliver, R. T. (1967). Communication—community—communion. *Today's Speech, 15*(4), 7–9. doi:10.1080/01463376709368847

Osgood, C. E. (1953). *Method and Theory in Experimental Psychology*. New York: Oxford University Press.

Ott, B. L., & Domenico, M. (2015). Conceptualizing meaning in communication studies. In Gehrke, P. J., & Keith, W. M. (eds.), *A Century of Communication Studies: The Unfinished Conversation* (pp. 224–260). New York: Routledge.

Palmgreen, P., & Clarke, P. (1977). Agenda-setting with local and national issues. *Communication Research, 4*, 435–452. doi:10.1177/009365027700400404

Park, D., & Pooley, J. (2008). *The History of Media and Communication Research: Contested Memories*. New York: Peter Lang.

Parks, L. (2020). Field mapping: What is the "media" of media studies? *Television & New Media, 21*, 642–649. doi:10.1177/1527476420919701

Parks, L., & Wagman, K. (2019, November 25). Charting the growth of Media Studies in US Higher Education: An analysis of Federal data from 1984-2017. Global Media Technologies and Cultures Lab. http://globalmedia.mit.edu/2019/11/25/charting-the-growth-of-media-studies-in-us-higher-education-1984-2017/

Parks, M. R. (1977). Relational communication: Theory and research. *Human Communication Research, 3*, 372–381. doi:10.1111/j.1468-2958.1977.tb00541.x

Pearce, W. B. (1976). The coordinated management of meaning: A rules based theory of interpersonal communication. In Miller, G. R. (ed.), *Explorations in Interpersonal Communication* (pp. 17–35). Thousand Oaks, CA: Sage Publications.

Pearce, W. B., & Cronen, V. E. (1980). *Communication, Action, and Meaning: The Creation of Social Realities*. New York: Praeger.

Peter, C. (2019). The people's voice—The people's choice? How vox pop exemplars shape audience judgments as a function of populist attitudes. *Journalism & Mass Communication Quarterly, 96*, 1004–1024. doi:10.1177/1077699019852323

Peters, J. D. (1999). *Speaking into the Air: A History of the Idea of Communication.* Chicago, IL: University of Chicago Press.

Petrie Jr., C. R., & Carrel, S. D. (1976). The relationship of motivation, listening capability, initial information, and verbal organizational ability to lecture comprehension and retention. *Communication Monographs, 43*, 187–194. doi:10.1080/03637757609375931

Philipsen, G. (1975). Speaking "Like a Man" in Teamsterville: Culture patterns of role enactment in an urban neighborhood. *Quarterly Journal of Speech, 61*, 13–22. doi:10.1080/00335637509383264

Phillips, G. M., & Wood, J. T. (eds.) (1990). *Speech Communication: Essays to Commemorate the 75th Anniversary of the Speech Communication Association.* Carbondale: Southern Illinois University Press.

Richards, I. A. (1936). *The Philosophy of Rhetoric.* New York: Oxford University Press.

Roever, J. E. (1974). New Orleans, Wingspread, and Pheasant Run briefly revisited. *Western Speech, 38*(1), 7–12. doi:10.1080/10570317409373803

Rogers, C. (1961). *On Becoming a Person: A Therapist's View of Psychotherapy.* Boston, MA: Houghton Mifflin Company.

Rogers, E. M. (1994). *A History of Communication Study: A Biographical Approach.* New York: The Free Press.

Saral, T. B. (1977). Intercultural communication theory and research: An overview. In Ruben, B. D. (ed.), *Communication Yearbook 1* (pp. 389–396). New Brunswick, NJ: Transaction Books.

Saussure, F. de. (1959). *Writings in General Linguistics.* Translated by Wade Baskin. New York: Columbia University Press.

Scott, R. L. (1967). On viewing rhetoric as epistemic. *Central States Speech Journal, 18*, 9–17. doi:10.1080/10510976709362856

Seibold, D. R. (1975). Communication research and the attitude-verbal report-overt behavior relationship: A critique and theoretical reformulation. *Human Communication Research, 2*, 3–32. doi:10.1111/j.1468-2958.1975.tb00466.x

Shannon, C. E. (1949). *The Mathematical Theory of Communication.* Urbana, IL: University of Illinois Press.

Shannon, C. E., & Weaver, W. (1963). *The Mathematical Theory of Communication.* Chicago, IL: University of Illinois Press.

Shaw, G. (1993). The shape of our field: Business communication as a hybrid discipline. *Journal of Business Communication, 30*, 297–313. doi:10.1177/002194369303000304

Sholle, D. (1995). "No respect! Disciplinarity and media studies in communication": Resisting disciplines: Repositioning media studies in the university. *Communication Theory, 5*, 130–143. doi:10.1111/j.1468-2885.1995.tb00102.x

Signorielli, N. (1982). Marital status in TV drama: A case of reduced options. *Journal of Broadcasting, 26,* 585–597. doi:10.1080/08838158209364027

Smith, A. G. (ed.) (1966). *Communication and Culture: Readings in the Codes of Human Interaction.* New York: Holt, Rinehart and Winston.

Smith, D. H. (1972). Communication research and the idea of process, *Speech Monographs, 39,* 174–182. doi:10.1080/03637757209375755

Smith, D. R. (1971). From id to information: A Biblogical (*sic*) view of communication. *Today's Speech, 19,* 11–16. doi:10.1080/01463377109368959

Song, H., Eberl, J.-M, & Eisele, O. (2020). Less fragmented than we thought? Toward clarification of a subdisciplinary linkage in communication science, 2010–2019. *Journal of Communication 70,* 310–334. doi:10.1093/joc/jqaa009

Stewart, J. (1972). An interpersonal approach to the basic course. *Speech Teacher, 21,* 7–14. doi:10.1080/03634527209377916

Stewart, J. (1972). Concepts of language and meaning: A comparative study. *Quarterly Journal of Speech, 58,* 123–133. doi:10.1080/00335637209383108

Taylor, B. C. (2021). Defending the state from digital deceit: The reflexive securitization of Deepfake. *Critical Studies in Media Communication, 38,* 1–17. doi:10.1080/15295036.2020.1833058

Thonssen, L., & Baird, A. C. (1948). *Speech Criticism: The Development of Standards for Rhetorical Appraisal.* New York: Ronald Press Company.

Toulmin, S. (1958). *The Uses of Argument.* Cambridge [England]: University Press.

Towers, W. M. (1977). Lazarsfeld and Adorno in the United States: A case study in theoretical orientations. In, Ruben, B. D. (ed.), *Communication Yearbook 1* (pp. 133–145). New Brunswick, NJ: Transaction Books.

Wahl-Jorgensen, K. (2004). How not to found a field: New evidence on the origins of mass communication research, *Journal of Communication, 54,* 547–564. doi:10.1111/j.1460-2466.2004.tb02644.x

Waisbord, S. (2019). *Communication: A Post-Discipline.* Malden, MA: Policy Press.

Wallace, K. R. (1963). The substance of rhetoric: Good reasons. *Quarterly Journal of Speech, 49,* 239–249. doi:10.1080/00335636309382611

Watzlawick, P., Beavin, J. H., & Jackson, D. D. (1967). *Pragmatics of Human Communication: A Study of Interactional Patterns, Pathologies, and Paradoxes.* New York: W. W. Norton & Company.

Weaver, C. H. (1973). History of the International Communication: The first twenty-three years. Unpublished Manuscript, Ohio University. Currently held by the International Communication Association, 1500 21st Street, NW, Washington, DC 20036 USA.

Weaver, C. H. (1977). A history of the International Communication Association. In Ruben, B. D. (ed.), *Communication Yearbook I* (pp. 607–618). New Brunswick, NJ: Transaction Books.

Weick, K. E. (1969). *The Social Psychology of Organizing.* Reading, MA: Addison-Wesley Publishing Company.

Weick, K. E. (1979). *The Social Psychology of Organizing* (2nd edition). Reading, MA: Addison-Wesley.

White, R. A. (1983). Mass communication and culture: Transition to a new paradigm. *Journal of Communication*, *33*, 279–301. doi:10.1111/j.1460-2466.1983.tb02429.x

Wiener, N. (1948). *Cybernetics, or, Control and Communication in the Animal and the Machine*. New York: John Wiley and Sons.

Wilder, C. (1979). The Palo Alto Group: Difficulties and directions of the interactional view for human communication research. *Human Communication Research*, *5*, 171–186. doi:10.1111/j.1468-2958.1979.tb00632.x

Winans, J. A. (1915). The need for research. *Quarterly Journal of Speech Education*, *1*, 17–23. doi:10.1080/00335631509360453

Winter, J. P., & Eyal, C. H. (1981). Agenda-setting for the civil rights issue. *Public Opinion Quarterly, 45,* 376–383. doi:10.1086/268671

Wood, J. T., & Gregg, R. B. (eds.) (1995). *Toward the 21st Century: The Future of Speech Communication*. Cresskill, NJ: Hampton Press.

Woolbert, C. H. (1923). The teaching of speech as an academic discipline. *Quarterly Journal of Speech Education, 9,* 1–18. doi:10.1080/00335632309379407

Work, W., & Jeffrey, R. C. (1989). Historical notes: The Speech Communication Association, 1965-1989. In Work, W., & Jeffrey, R. C. (eds.), *The Past is Prologue: The 75th Anniversary Publication of the Speech Communication Association* (pp. 39–67). Annandale, VA: Speech Communication Association.

Wyer, R. (1974). *Cognitive Organization and Change: An Information Processing Approach*. Potomac, Md.: L. Erlbaum Associates.

Zelizer, B. (2011). Journalism in the service of communication. *Journal of Communication, 61*, 1–21. doi:10.1111/j.1460-2466.2010.01524.x

Index of Names

Adler, Keith, 97
Ajzen, Icek, 64
Allen, Harold, 36
Altman, Irwin, 115, 118
Arnold, Carroll, 42
Arnold, William, 56–58
Asante, Molefi, 21, 38, 131
Atkin, Charles, 100, 101
Auer, J. Jeffery, 35
Aune, James, 133, 134
Austin, John, 74

Baird, A. Craig, 18, 43, 128
Ball-Rokeach, Sandra, 119
Barker, Larry, 1, 6, 20, 38, 78
Bateson, Gregory, 110, 111, 127
Beavin, Janet, 10, 110, 111
Becher, Tony, 3, 19
Becker, Samuel, 35, 44, 127
Benjamin, James, 78
Benjamin, Walter, 133
Benson, Thomas, 43, 140, 148, 149
Berelson, Bernard, 9, 23, 29, 30
Berger, Charles, 10, 108, 114–18
Berlo, David, 30–32, 56, 62, 97
Berlyne, Daniel, 62
Bernstein, Basil, 36
Berryman, Cynthia, 78
Bertalanffy, Ludwig, 93

Bitzer, Lloyd, 8, 41, 42
Black, Edwin, 8, 42
Blake, Cecil, 131
Blankenship, Jane, 7, 8, 39
Blumer, Herbert, 76
Blumler, Jay, 9, 94, 100, 132
Bochner, Arthur, 97, 140
Boileau, Don, 1
Booth, Wayne, 80
Bostrom, Robert, 78
Bowers, Thomas, 33–35
Briggle, Adam, 153
Brockriede, Wayne, 62
Brown, Irving, 35
Burdick, William, 125
Burgoon, Michael, 62–64, 143
Burke, Kenneth, 74
Burks, Don, 6, 87

Calabrese, Richard, 10, 108, 114–16
Carrel, Susan, 99
Cassirer, Ernst, 75, 76
Chaffee, Steven, 23, 24
Christians, Clifford, 153
Cissna, Kenneth, 45
Clark, Kenneth, 40
Clark, Ruth Anne, 109
Clarke, Peter, 35, 54
Clevenger, Theodore, 35

Cohen, Bernard, 53
Cohen, Herman, 14
Corcoran, Farrell, 85, 86
Cowan, Renee, 146, 147
Craig, Robert, 1, 52
Crockett, Walter, 109
Cronkite, Gary, 72
Cushman, Donald, 97
Czitrom, Daniel, 19

Dance, Frank, 37, 46, 52, 143, 144
Daniel, Jack, 38
Dar-Nimrod, Ilan, 145
DeFleur, Melvin, 119
Delia, Jesse, 14, 108, 109
Dennis, Harry, 108
Deutsch, Morton, 36
Dietrich, John, 35, 39
Domenico, Mary, 69, 72–76

Eadie, William, 45
Eberl, Jakob-Moritz, 156, 157
Ehninger, Douglas, 39, 79
Eisele, Olga, 156, 157
Eisenberg, Eric, 140
Ellingsworth, Huber, 128–30
Ellis, Donald, 139, 140
Emery, Edwin, 13, 19
Eyal, Chaim, 54

Farrell, Thomas, 133, 134
Fishbein, Martin, 59, 64
Fisher, B. Aubrey, 96–98
Fisher, Walter, 80, 81
Folkerts, Jean, 19
Friedrich, Gustav, 118
Funkhouser, Ray, 54

Ganesan, Asha, 145
Gardner, Royce, 117
Gaudet, Hazel, 9, 23
Gehrke, Pat, 69, 143
Gerbner, George, 1, 9, 45, 48, 54, 55, 135
Goffman, Erving, 149

Goldberg, Alvin, 77, 78
Gorman, Margaret, 78
Gouran, Dennis, 141, 142
Graff, Harvey, 154
Gross, Larry, 9, 54, 55
Gudykunst, William, 131, 132
Gunn, Joshua, 143, 144
Gurevitch, Michael, 9, 94, 100

Hall, Edward, 125, 126, 129, 130
Hall, Robert, 32, 33, 35
Hall, Stuart, 132, 134, 135
Hample, Dale, 56, 58–62
Hart, Roderick, 6, 87, 108, 118, 139
Hastorf, Albert, 108
Hawes, Leonard, 110, 133, 138
Hawkins, Robert, 56
Hayakawa, S. I., 70
Hefferline, Ralph, 97
Held, David, 133
Herbst, Susan, 156
Hewes, Dean, 108
Hickson, Mark, 45, 46
Holbrook, Anthony, 126
Horan, Sean, 146, 147
Howell, William, 126, 135
Hsu, Hue, 135
Hughes, Michael, 56

Jackob, Nicholas, 107
Jackson, Don, 10, 110, 111
Jackson, Ronald, 150
Jamieson, Kathleen, 126
Jeffrey, Robert, 35, 39
Johnson, F. Craig, 35
Johnson, Wendell, 43, 116

Katz, Elihu, 9, 23, 94, 100
Keith, William, 69, 143
Kelly, George, 109
Kemp, Alan, 78
Kibler, Robert, 1, 6, 38, 78
Klapper, Joseph, 53, 54
Klein, Julie, 153, 154
Knapp, Mark, 108, 114, 117–19

Korn, Charles, 1
Korzybski, Alfred, 70, 73
Krippendorff, Klaus, 94–96
Kuhn, Thomas, 2

Lakoff, Robin, 78
Langer, Suzanne, 70, 75, 76
Larson, Carl, 52
Lasswell, Harold, 7, 22, 30, 94
Lazarsfeld, Paul, 9, 22, 23, 29, 53, 132, 133
Lederer, William, 125
Lee, Irving, 70
Levine, Timothy, 56
Lippmann, Walter, 22, 52
Liska, Jo, 78
Littlejohn, Stephen, 108
Lu, Hsiao-Tung 126

MacLean, Malcolm, 36
Martin, Howard, 126
Marwell, Gerald, 64
Matson, Floyd, 70
McCombs, Malcom, 9, 35, 53, 54
McCroskey James, 56–58
McGuire, William, 59, 60
McLuhan, Marshall, 41, 153
Mead, George, 22, 23, 76, 87
Mechling, Elizabeth, 78
Menand, Louis, 2, 3, 154, 155
Menzel, Herbert, 36
Millar, Frank, 111, 112
Miller, Gerald, 8, 42, 56, 62–64, 108, 110, 117
Montagu, Ashley, 70
Morgan, Michael, 55
Morreale, Sherwyn, 1

Newmark, Eileen, 131
Nichols, Marie Hochmuth, 7, 8, 39
Nofsinger, Robert, 9, 86, 87
Norton, Robert, 108

O'Hair, Dan, 1
O'Keefe, Daniel, 38

Ogden, Charles, 70, 74
Oliver, Robert, 127
Osgood, Charles, 71
Ott, Brian, 69, 72–76

Palmgreen, Philip, 54
Park, David, 14, 75
Park, Hee Sun, 56
Park, Robert, 22, 52
Parks, Lisa, 153
Parks, Malcolm, 108, 112–14, 117
Pearce, W. Barnett, 97, 108, 131
Peter, Christina, 144
Peters, John, 1, 2
Petrie, Charles, 99
Philipsen, Gerry, 9, 81–85
Phillips, Gerald, 141, 144
Pingree, Suzanne, 56
Polefka, Judith, 108
Pooley, Jefferson, 14

Richards, I. A., 70, 74
Roever, James, 42, 43
Rogers, Carl, 108
Rogers, Everett, 13, 23, 24
Rogers, L. Edna, 111, 112

Samp, Jennifer, 145
Saral, Tulsi, 128, 130
de Saussure, Ferdinand, 74, 75
Schmitt, David, 64
Schneider, David, 108
Schulman, Linda, 117
Scott, Robert, 8, 41, 79
Seibold, David, 108
Shannon, Claude, 24, 31, 95
Shaw, Donald, 9, 53, 54
Shaw, Gary, 153
Shaw, George Bernard, 15
Sholle, David, 153
Shulman, Gary, 118
Signorielli, Nancy, 55
Smith, Alfred, 125
Smith, David, 32
Smith, Dennis, 110

Song, Hyunjin, 156, 157
Steinberg, Mark, 108
Stewart, John, 69–71, 73–76, 110
Switzer, David, 109

Taylor, Brian, 147
Taylor, Dalmas, 115, 118
Thompson, George, 36
Thonssen, Lester, 41, 43
Toulmin, Stephen, 79
Towers, Wayne, 132, 133
Trowler, Paul, 3

Wahl-Jorgensen, Karin, 9, 22, 154
Waisbord, Silvio, 155
Wallace, Karl, 80
Washburn, Wilcomb, 36

Watzlawick, Paul, 10, 110, 111
Weaver, Carl, 28, 40, 41, 45
Weaver, Warren, 24, 31
Weick, Karl, 10, 94, 102–4
White, Robert, 134
Wiener, Norbert, 24
Wilcox, James, 78
Wilder, Carol, 110
Winans, James, 16–18
Winter, James, 54
Wood, Julia, 141, 142
Woolbert, Charles, 6, 17, 37
Work, William, 32, 35, 42
Wyer, Robert, 59–61

Zelizer, Barbie, 10

Index of Topics

academic departments, 3, 4, 18, 141, 144, 155

accreditation, 20, 155

Accrediting Council for Education in Journalism and Mass Communication (ACEJMC), 20

advertising, 5, 21, 27, 30, 34, 38, 139

agenda-setting, 9, 53–55, 120

American Association of Teachers of Journalism, 19, 33

American Association of University Professors, 3

American Council of Learned Societies, 151

American Historical Association, 3

American Mathematical Society, 3

American Physical Society, 3

American Political Science Association, 3

American Sociological Association, 3, 155

American Speech and Hearing Association, 18

argument, 5, 17, 30, 37, 47, 51, 59–61, 71, 79, 89, 110, 151, 152

Association for Education in Journalism (AEJ), 5, 28, 32–35, 44, 47, 151

Association for Education in Journalism and Mass Communication (AEJMC), 5, 13, 14, 21, 28, 47, 51, 136, 144, 152, 155

attitude change, 10, 24, 32, 56, 58, 59, 64

audiences, 16, 17, 52, 54, 58, 62, 64, 89, 107, 119–21, 127, 134, 156

axioms, 10, 110, 111, 113, 115

belief change, 59, 60

big tent, 17, 18, 47, 140, 141, 155

biographical disciplinary history, 13

Birmingham School, 9, 125, 132, 134

boundaries, 89, 129, 130, 154, 155, 157

British cultural studies, 89, 132, 134

claims (as a concept), 57, 59, 61, 80, 142, 154

Classification of Instructional Programs (CIP), 1

cognitive, 10, 58, 60–63, 72, 73, 79, 83, 89, 93, 100, 108, 109, 117, 120, 121

Committee on Social Relevance, 38

Communication Education, 8, 44

Communication Monographs, 8, 44, 65, 99

Communication Quarterly, 45

communication studies, 45, 143, 144

Communication Yearbook, 40, 45, 63, 65, 94, 96, 107, 128, 130

179

communicator style, 108
content analysis, 21, 54, 69, 94
context, 28, 55, 60, 74, 76, 95, 98, 105,
    107, 108, 111, 129, 130
conversation, 6, 9, 10, 17, 31, 76, 80,
    83, 84, 86, 87, 89, 109, 112, 114,
    118, 129, 145
cooperation, 108, 127
Council on Communications Research,
    33
credibility, 10, 49, 56–58, 63, 144, 145
Critical Theory, 125, 132–35, 153
cultivation, 9, 54–56
cultural studies, 9, 89, 132, 134, 135,
    152, 153, 155
culture, 2, 47, 81–83, 89, 125–33, 135,
    146–48, 150, 153, 155

deepfake, 147, 148
definition, 1, 2, 6, 7, 32, 52, 70, 79, 104,
    111, 130, 148, 150, 152
dialogue, 1, 145
digital and analogic language, 111
disciplinary societies, 6, 14, 154
discipline, academic, 1–7, 9–11, 13–15,
    17, 18, 22, 24, 27, 30, 32, 33, 35, 37,
    41, 44, 47, 49, 51, 52, 74, 88, 89, 93,
    94, 110, 121, 136, 139–44, 149–57
discourse, 9, 10, 72, 86, 142
doctoral, 6, 16, 20, 24, 27, 58, 82, 111,
    127, 140, 154
double interact, 102–4

Eastern Communication Association,
    140
Eastern Public Speaking Conference, 15
Educational Theatre Association, 18
elocution, 15
enactment, 81, 103, 104
episodes, 55, 84, 88, 89, 111, 127
equifinality, 97, 98
equivocation, 95, 103, 104
ethnographic, 10, 45, 81, 83, 85, 89, 148
evidence, 5, 21, 29, 56, 58–61, 63, 64,
    120, 152, 157

field (of study), 1, 18, 25, 30, 34, 37, 43,
    45, 48, 111, 128, 130, 134, 135, 141,
    143, 144, 153, 156
first amendment, 21, 27, 44
fragmented, 110, 156, 157
Frankfurt School, 9, 23, 125, 132, 133,
    135

general semantics, 70, 73, 77, 78
General Systems Theory, 24, 93

hegemony, 54, 134
higher education, 1, 2, 16, 25, 42
Human Communication Research, 8, 45,
    62, 65, 112

identity, 3–5, 29, 40, 83, 84, 112, 118,
    130, 149, 150
information systems, 41, 93–96, 102,
    128
information transmission, 10, 24, 49, 52,
    93, 94, 145, 146, 149
initial interactions, 114–16
inquiry, 3, 4, 34, 79, 96, 97, 141, 142
Institute for Communications Research,
    24
intellectual disciplinary history, 2, 13,
    14
intercultural communication, 126–32,
    135
interdisciplinary, 9, 23, 25, 28, 33, 35,
    36, 42, 48, 51, 152–54, 156
International Communication
    Association (ICA), 8, 14, 28, 40, 41,
    45, 46, 48, 62, 63, 65, 94, 107, 108,
    155
*International Communication Research
    Journal*, 44
interpersonal communication, 7, 10, 41,
    64, 105, 107–9, 114, 117, 128
interpersonal relationships, 87–89, 115
Iowa Writers' Workshop, 23

journalism, 1, 4–6, 9, 10, 13, 14, 19–21,
    24, 27, 28, 32–36, 44, 47–49, 51, 52,

69, 74, 77, 125, 132, 135, 136, 140,
141, 144, 149, 151–55
*Journalism and Mass Communication
Quarterly*, 9, 44, 65
Journalism History, 44
Journalism Monographs, 44
*Journal of Applied Communication
Research*, 45, 46
Journal of Communication, 8, 9, 28, 29,
31, 45, 48, 65, 135
Journal of Critical Inquiry, 44
journals, 3, 4, 8, 11, 15, 44–47, 49, 77,
78, 105, 110, 132, 140, 156, 157

language use, 7, 10, 11, 21, 31, 49, 69,
71, 72, 74, 76, 77, 79, 86, 88, 89,
145, 149
liberal arts, 2, 3, 15, 20, 155
listening, 98–100

mass communication, 6, 8–10, 23,
24, 30, 34–36, 41, 47, 48, 51–55,
65, 89, 93, 94, 98, 100, 104, 105,
107, 128, 135, 136, 140, 141, 144,
151–54
mass media, 22, 53, 119, 131, 133, 134
meaning (as a concept), 1, 6, 31, 32, 55,
69–76, 86, 87, 103, 108, 131, 149
media dependency, 120
media effects, 8–10, 53, 54, 119, 121
media studies, 9, 47, 89, 132, 135, 136,
153, 154
message(s), 1, 7, 10, 31, 39, 55–64, 80,
83, 86, 94–96, 98, 112–14, 119
Modern Language Association, 3, 38
Morrill Act, 3, 15
National Association of Teachers of
Speech, 16, 17

National Communication Association
(NCA), 8, 14, 16, 51, 69, 73, 143,
150, 151, 154, 155
National Council of Teachers of
English, 15

National Developmental Project on
Rhetoric, 41, 42
National Society for the Study of
Communication (NSSC), 18, 28, 29,
32, 40, 41, 47, 48
New Orleans conference, 1, 6, 7, 37–39,
41–44, 48, 70
Newspaper Research Journal, 44
nonverbal communication, 108, 111,
115, 116, 125, 126

ordinary language, 69–71, 74, 81
organizational communication, 6, 41,
46, 102, 128, 139
organizing (as a concept), 94, 102–5

Palo Alto group, 10, 110
paradigm, 2, 5, 14, 131, 153, 156
performance (as a concept), 6, 14, 17,
27, 58, 83, 143, 150
persuasion, 10, 14, 17, 53, 56–58,
61–65, 74, 108
phase model, 114, 117
Pheasant Run, 42–44, 48
Philosophy and Rhetoric, 41
political disciplinary history, 14
post-discipline, 152, 153, 156, 157
process (as a concept), 1, 2, 7, 10,
30–32, 35, 52, 53, 56, 61, 64, 65, 76,
79, 82, 83, 87, 88, 93–95, 100–105,
108, 110, 116, 127, 130, 134, 141,
142, 145, 157
propaganda, 22, 53
public opinion, 9, 10, 22, 49, 51, 52, 54,
55, 100, 144, 149
Public Opinion Quarterly, 29
public relations, 5, 21, 27, 34, 139
public speaking, 6, 7, 14–16, 64, 107,
121, 150, 155

Quarterly Journal of Speech, 8, 16, 39,
44, 58, 69, 70, 81, 126, 133

receiver, 31, 56, 57, 61, 62, 93–95

relational communication, 105, 107–9, 111, 112, 119, 133
Research Board, 35–37, 41, 139
retention (as a concept), 98, 99, 103, 104
rhetoric, 6–8, 17, 21, 36, 41–44, 61, 69, 71, 72, 74, 76, 79, 80, 82, 87, 88, 134, 140
rhetorical scholars, 6, 8, 43, 85
rhetorical sensitivity, 6, 87, 88
rules, 75, 76, 86, 87, 96, 97, 103, 104, 108, 118, 131

schemata, 61, 73, 79
selection (as a concept), 103, 104, 141
semiotics, 74, 75, 85, 86, 89
sender, 31, 93, 95
signs, 70, 75, 89
social media, 146, 147
Source, Message, Channel Receiver (SMCR), 31, 32, 62
Southern Communication Journal, 45
Spectra, 33, 46, 139
speech (as a concept), 5–10, 14–19, 21, 27, 28, 32, 33, 35–38, 40, 41, 43–45, 47–49, 51, 56, 62, 65, 69–71, 74, 78, 81, 83–86, 97, 107, 121, 125, 128, 135, 141, 143, 144, 150, 154, 155
speech acts, 74, 88, 89
Speech Association of America (SAA), 7, 8, 18, 28, 29, 32, 33, 35–41, 47, 48, 127
speech communication, 5, 9, 14, 35–38, 42–44, 49, 58, 65, 69–73, 77, 88, 89, 104, 132, 133, 139–42, 144, 152, 155
Speech Communication Association (SCA), 6–8, 39, 41–46, 48, 65, 126, 131, 135, 139, 141–43
speech correction/pathology, 14, 27, 48, 140

speech professors, 5, 7, 16, 28, 29, 38, 40
spoken symbolic interaction, 1, 6, 37, 70
strands (of communication scholarship), 10, 11, 49, 51, 52, 89, 93, 136, 139, 144, 148–52, 157
symbolic interactionism, 76, 87
symbols (as a concept), 31, 70, 71, 76, 86, 112, 141
symmetry and complementarity, 111–13
systems approaches, 94, 96, 97

Teamsterville, 81, 83–85
technology, 15, 16, 96, 98, 129, 142, 146, 147, 150
Text and Performance Quarterly, 45, 150
Theory and Methodology Division, 35
traditional disciplines, 16, 155
two-step flow, 9, 53, 65

uncertainty, 10, 11, 38, 79, 95, 102, 114–17, 129, 149
University of Chicago, 9, 22, 52, 154
uses and gratifications, 9, 94, 100
U.S. Office of Education, 7, 33, 35

values, 3, 42, 43, 61, 80, 81, 114, 118, 120

warrants, 59, 61, 80
Western Journal of Communication, 45
Western Speech Communication Association, 46
Wingspread, 8, 35, 42
Women's Studies in Communication, 46

Yale Program in Communication, 24, 29, 32, 56, 65

About the Author

William F. Eadie is professor emeritus of journalism and media studies at San Diego State University, where he also served as director of the School of Communication. He became interested in communication as an academic discipline during his time as associate director of the National Communication Association.